"Rhoads is particularly adept at finding deeper meanings in what she sees, and the questions she puts to the reader about the places she visits can gently guide us in our own search for meaning in the places we encounter. If you've struggled to explain your love of burial grounds to others, this may be a great way to help them understand." — The Association for Gravestone Studies

"Loren Rhoads started visiting cemeteries by accident. It was the start of a love affair with cemeteries that continues to this day. In *Wish You Were Here*, Rhoads blends history with storytelling. Her photos accompany each essay." — *American Cemetery* magazine

"*Wish You Were Here* captures well why many of us find cemeteries fascinating: because of the history and stories of so many interesting people buried there!" — *Waterhouse Symbolism Newsletter*

"Lovingly researched and lushly described, Loren's essays transport you to the graveyard, where she is quite a tour guide. Curiosity and compassion burn at the heart of these essays." — Paula Guran, editor of *Dark Echo* magazine

"Loren describes each deathly visit with true feeling. She discovers, through visiting places of death, more about life and the living." — *Gothic Beauty*

"With her dead-on honesty and her fascination for the dark side of life in all its complexity, Loren's writing never fails to make me think." — Thomas Roche, author of *The Panama Laugh*

" 'It's good to be a card-carrying member of the Association for Gravestone Studies,' Loren writes. I agree. After half a lifetime of guided and self-guided tours, Loren observes, 'What I've learned from cemeteries is that limestone melts, marble breaks, slate slivers, and sandstone cracks.' That is what draws some of us to graveyards." — *Quigley's Cabinet*

"Cemeteries the world over are unique places, showcasing the diverse history, art, and culture of the areas they represent. Loren Rhoads explores these fabulous graveyards, then writes vividly about them, providing a unique travelogue." — Karen Kruse, author of *A Chicago Firehouse: Stories of Wrigleyville's Engine 78*

Paperback ISBN: 978-0-9636794-6-8

ebook ISBN: 978-0-9636794-7-5

Automatism Press
PO Box 12308
San Francisco, California 94112-0308
http://automatismpress.com

WISH YOU WERE HERE:

ADVENTURES IN CEMETERY TRAVEL

LOREN RHOADS

AUTOMATISM PRESS

SAN FRANCISCO

WITH THANKS

MANY PEOPLE HAVE AIDED my explorations of graveyards. Foremost among them is my husband Mason, whom you will meet many times in these essays. Mason reads the maps, arranges the transportation, and never grows impatient when I want to visit "just one more" grave. This book, and my life, would be impossible without him.

Another co-conspirator is Kathleen Rhoads, my mother. Mom has explored graveyards with me from Maui to Michigan. Mom introduced me to my first cemetery as a child and continues to seek out more that will interest me. She even visits cemeteries in my name, in order to photograph them for me when I can't be there myself. This book is dedicated to her, with love and gratitude.

Thanks to everyone who pointed me toward graveyards in their hometowns. Thanks to the people who opened cemeteries for me, who gave me private tours, and who graciously shared their knowledge and fascinations with me. Thanks to the members (especially Andrea) of the Association for Gravestone Studies, who offered a community of like-minded souls. Thanks to Michael Svanevik, for being my role model, and to Cypress Lawn Memorial Park, for their series of monthly lectures in their lovely cemetery.

Thank you, in no particular order, to those who joined me on my excursions or otherwise supported my obsession with graveyards over the years: my dad Roy, my brother Allen, friends Brian, Samuel, Jeff, Tim & Wendy, Tim & Alison, Christine, Paul, Hiroshi & Mayuko, Nanjo, and all the rest who've come along, but whose stories I couldn't cram into this book.

Finally, thank you to Judi Culbertson and Tom Randall (who informed many of my wanderings), Ivory and Venus at the Red Room Writers Society (where many of these essays were drafted), and the Round Robins at the Writing Salon (where I practiced introducing the book and its cemeteries to strangers). Extra special thanks to Thomas Roche, who agreed to let me write a column on visiting cemeteries for Gothic.Net—and to Darren Mckeeman, who published it monthly for all those years. Thanks to Aerin, Allegra, and Mehitobel, who read those early essays very carefully. Thank you to the editors who published and republished these essays and to the Paramental Appreciation Society, who helped me make them better.

Last, but *so* not least: thanks to John Palisano and Western Legends Press, who gave the first edition of this collection a home. It was an honor to work with you.

This book has been a labor of love. I have been lucky to have so much guidance—and such good company—along the way.

WISH YOU WERE HERE

Kennedy gravesite, Arlington National Cemetery, Washington, DC

VACATIONING IN THE LAND OF THE DEAD

I GREW UP ON A FARM DOWN THE ROAD from a graveyard. My family drove past the cemetery all the time, without ever stopping in to visit. Eventually, when my mom needed a way to entertain my younger brother and me the summer I turned twelve, we rode our bikes to Bendle Cemetery. Tucked in the basket of her bike, Mom brought butcher's paper and a box of Crayolas. Taping the paper tightly against the headstones, she showed us how to make gravestone rubbings. That was my introduction to tombstone typography, iconography, and epitaphs.

Bendle Cemetery is called after its first caretaker. I recognized names on the gravestones: Nichols, Carpenter, and Calkins were roads around the mile. I was an adult before I realized the roads had been named for tracks that originally led to the first farms in the area, settled by families that cleared the land and built red-painted barns that continued to stand.

The Lyons family, whose descendants still live a mile away on Nichols Road, donated an acre of land to the fledgling community to serve as a burial ground. Around 1838, Bendle Cemetery's first occupant was one of Seth Hathaway's children. That monument, if ever there was one, vanished. The oldest surviving tombstone remembers Albert Ottaway, less than a year old when he died in 1844.

That initial acre fascinated me. There I saw my first lamb on a child's grave. Lambs signify innocence. One of the Nichols graves said only "Infant Son," dead so young he wasn't given a name. Among the oldest monuments stood a limbless six-foot limestone tree trunk dedicated to the Youell family. Later I read that the height of the tree stump can indicate the age of the deceased. Having its limbs lopped off means that the family left no heirs. Nearby stood a "white bronze" obelisk for the Carpenters. What was called white bronze is actually made of zinc. Those monuments could be ordered as interchangeable components through a catalog. The company made nameplates to order. They had a branch office in Detroit.

In that little graveyard lay my grandfather and a cousin, both of whom died before I knew them. My grandmother's birth date had already been engraved on her headstone, which I found endlessly creepy. When she'd bought the stone after my grandfather's death, the funeral home persuaded her that it would be cheaper to carve her name and birth year onto the monument at the 1961 price. Only her death year would need to be carved after the stone was set in place. That procedure was more expensive, since the engraver needs to travel to the cemetery to do the job. My grandmother had lived through the Depression and knew the value of a dollar. Therefore, throughout my childhood, the ground beside my grandfather's coffin waited to swallow my grandmother. She joined him in 1999.

In all of Bendle Cemetery, the grave that mesmerized me most belonged to my cousin Karen. She lived less than a year, killed in a car accident that also sentenced my dad's youngest sister to a coma. A little bird with upraised wings adorned Karen's gray granite headstone. Her epitaph said, "Think of her still as the same, and say she is not dead, she is just away." The phrase haunted me. It's one of the reasons I became enamored of cemeteries.

That and, of course, I read too many Edgar Allan Poe stories at an impressionable age. Thanks to Poe, I don't want to be embalmed, closed in, covered over. Burn me to ashes. In an 1800-degree flame, the pain should be brief.

The travel component of my study of cemeteries began early in life. At age four, I got lost inside Arlington National Cemetery. Just outside Washington, DC, the Arlington necropolis is huge: 624 acres of headstones in military formation commemorate the dead of every American "conflict" since the Revolutionary War. More than three million people visit Arlington every year. Buried among the famous dead are two presidents, as well as Dashiell Hammett, Audie Murphy, explorers Richard Byrd and Robert Peary, Supreme Court Justices Oliver Wendell Holmes Jr., Thurgood Marshall and Harry Blackmun, and more than 400,000 others.

When I was four, I wandered off while my parents paid their respects at John F. Kennedy's eternal flame. Even though I was too young to realize my mother had any name other than Mom, I don't remember being frightened. A nice lady fed me peppermints from her purse by the tour bus parking lot until my parents returned. Graveyards bring out the best in most people. Maybe the recognition of our own mortality gives us an urge to do good while we can.

My family often visited incidental graves when we traveled. Mom had family in Richmond, Virginia, so from there it was a day trip to see Mount Vernon, the plantation George Washington had called home. Near the Potomac edge of his property, he lies in a white marble sarcophagus inside a tomb made of red bricks. Washington had been given a Masonic funeral—and my dad was a Master Mason, so the tomb was a point of family interest.

We continued on to Monticello, gracious home of Thomas Jefferson. In the days when townsfolk chose the churchyard and farmers set aside an acre of land, Jefferson owned a family graveyard a quarter mile from his house. The third president lies modestly under a white obelisk that remembers him as the author of the Declaration of Independence and architect of the University of Virginia. That it doesn't mention his presidency hints at his modesty. The graveyard of his slaves lies elsewhere on the property.

You could say that I was trained from an early age. It's not so much that I seek out cemeteries everywhere I go—although I *have* been known to do that. It's more like every time I turn around, there's a cemetery. People have died all over the place. They had to be put somewhere.

It's been my experience that almost every tourist destination has a graveyard. For instance: You go to Yosemite National Park: there's the pioneer graveyard. You go to Maui: there's the Seaman's Cemetery. Saint Peter is buried in the crypt at the Vatican. Gettysburg is arguably a National Park *because* it has a graveyard. The whole archaeological site at Pompeii *was* a graveyard. The *Arizona* Memorial in Pearl Harbor and the Hiroshima Peace Memorial Park: both graveyards. There's a national cemetery in San Francisco with a view of the Golden Gate Bridge. The #1 tourist destination in Michigan has three cemeteries. America's best-preserved Gold Rush ghost town has five. Some graveyards are even tourist destinations in themselves: the Old Jewish Cemetery of Prague, the Revolution-era burial grounds of Boston, and the Municipal Ossuary in Paris, among others.

Every place that people have lived, they've had to bury their dead, whether it's on an island (Venice), a megalopolis (Tokyo), or a mine so abandoned that no other vestige of its ghost towns remains (Black Diamond Mines Regional Park).

I like to visit cemeteries when I travel. I like to see what people in different cultures do to commemorate the lives of those they've lost. I've learned a lot from graveyards: about what people value, about what's important. Do headstones note familial connections: beloved husband, devoted wife, cherished son? Do they carry symbols of fraternal organizations: a Masonic square and compass, the International Order of Odd Fellows' three links of chain, the Eastern Star? Do they note religious affiliation with a Star of David or the Buddhist wheel? Do they count the deceased's life to the day? Do they mention cause of death? Do they express survivors' grief or hope of reunion?

Part of what I find appealing about grave markers is their attempt at permanence. By definition, they outlive the people whose names they bear. Cold, hard, unfeeling stone strives for immortality by its presence. In truth, what I've learned from cemeteries is that limestone melts, marble breaks, slate slivers, and sandstone cracks. White bronze can become brittle. The materials of permanence are not so permanent after all.

I considered enclosing a glossary at the end of this book to help you read gravestones, but there are several good ones available like Douglas Keister's *Stories in Stone* or Minda Powers-Douglas's *Translating Tombstones*. Anyway, I discovered as I tried to gather definitions from as many sources as possible that any list will, of necessity, be incomplete. The meaning of symbols changes over time and from place to place, culture to culture, even person to person. Like interpreting a dream, a book on a gravestone isn't always just a book: it could be a Bible, the Book of Life in which the names of the blessed are inscribed, or perhaps the deceased was an author or a librarian. A tombstone glossary would need to be a book in itself.

To me, the best graveyards are public sculpture gardens. My favorite outdoor artwork resides in Père Lachaise Cemetery in Paris. Larger than life, Prometheus is shackled to a boulder. The vulture thrusts its cruel beak into the Titan's side, but Prometheus still has the strength to raise his fist against the gods. I know nothing at all about the life celebrated by the stone, but the courage implied by this monument, railing against fate, speaks to me across the gulf of time.

My favorite graveyard, in all its glorious decay, is London's

Highgate Cemetery. Practically abandoned after World War II, Highgate was overrun in the early 1970s by self-proclaimed vampire hunters. In reaction to the desecration, the Friends of Highgate Cemetery took over the management and upkeep of the cemetery. They walk a fine line between maintaining picturesque disarray and preventing the monuments from falling completely to ruin. It's spectacular.

In the course of my studies of graveyards, I learned that cemeteries, as we think of them, are a fairly recent phenomenon. This surprised me, since people have been burying their dead for eons. However, before Père Lachaise Cemetery was established in 1804, bodies in most Western countries were interred in churchyards.

Mozart's anonymous mass grave was more common than I realized. Typically, the pious were wrapped in shrouds, laid side by sideUS, sprinkled with lime, and covered with a thin layer of earth. The next layer of dead were laid atop them, and the next... Finally, the whole seething mass was covered over. New construction keeps uncovering these forgotten burial grounds.

In fact, I was shocked when I discovered the "final" resting places of millions throughout the US and around the world are rarely final. In Manhattan alone, nearly 90 cemeteries have been exhumed and shifted—or merely built over. In the 1990s in my hometown of San Francisco, forgotten graveyards have been rediscovered during the expansion of the Palace of the Legion of Honor and in the Civic Center, where the old public library became the new Asian Art Museum, as well as behind the old Veterans Administration hospital, on Russian Hill, and South of Market. The dead can literally lie forgotten beneath our feet.

Where gravestones have not been shifted to clear land for real estate, they have been vulnerable to vandalism from high school pranks to the Nazi demolition of graveyards in Eastern Europe to the intentional looting of Tiffany windows for the antique trade. Once a graveyard is neglected and brutalized, it is often cheaper to dismantle it than to replace what has been lost.

The way to protect these treasures is to return them to being part of the community they inhabit, to emphasize what is restful about them, rather than what is morbid. Some cemeteries have gone so far as to encourage visitors by listing themselves on registers of historic places and conducting scheduled tours.

In fact, a tour may be the best way to begin to explore graveyards, until you've got a fair amount of cultural knowledge: an understanding of the cemetery's home community, a familiarity with local history, and a grasp of graveyard iconography. The best time to look around for tours, at least in California, is in October, when people's thoughts turn toward the macabre. If you don't turn anything up, contact the cemetery office and ask. Some of them offer annual tours or can put you in touch with local guides. Some, if they discover there's an audience, will find you a tour guide, even if it's merely someone on their staff. Some cemeteries have "Friends" that offer tours and raise money for restoration. Local historical organizations are also a good place to look for tours. These groups can be passionate resources.

There's been a welcome trend toward guidebooks and histories of specific cemeteries. Images of America is the chief source for these, as is the bookstore Dark Delicacies in Burbank, California, home of the largest collection of cemetery books for sale that I've seen in one place. Sue can advise you.

Other than Scott Stanton's *Tombstone Tourist: Musicians*, cemetery guidebooks are notoriously poor at giving directions inside cemeteries. (The present book included, unfortunately. Graveyard directions are *hard*.) Find A Grave (*www.findagrave.com*), a crowdsourced encyclopedia of gravesites, often has GPS coordinates, but if that fails you, stop by the cemetery office and ask for a map. If they aren't too busy—and you don't look disreputable—office staffs nearly always seem eager to help you find what you're looking for.

Which makes this a good place to talk about being respectful. I always carry my camera in a cemetery, but I don't photograph live people without permission. I steer clear of mourners. I don't touch or rearrange offerings, even to make a better picture. If I find something broken that looks as though it could be carried off, I let the cemetery staff know.

In this book, I date my visit to each graveyard, because cemeteries are landscapes in flux. All it takes is one night of vandalism or a windstorm or a levy breaking to alter them significantly. Hopefully, any damage I've seen may have already been repaired. Cemeteries can be rescued, as several of the following stories attest.

The idea of cemetery tourism may seem new and shocking, but

actually cemeteries have been sites of pilgrimage from the beginning.

In the West, there is a long tradition of making visits to the graves of the venerated. That's basically what the pilgrimages of the Middle Ages were about: traveling to pray at the sepulcher of Saint James in Compostela, hiking to Canterbury to kneel at the tomb of Thomas Becket ("that had helped them when they were sick"), or walking to Cologne to visit the bones of the Three Wise Men. People believed that it was better to ask favors near the remnants of a holy body, that mortal remains had the power to transmit a prayer directly to their owners, who would relay messages to God. Anneli Rufus, in her book *Magnificent Corpses*, said, "A journey to see the relic of Saint Thomas or Saint James offered the only valid excuse for leaving home."

Pilgrimages generated revenue. To get in on that, soon every cathedral had to have a saint's finger bone or virgin's skull. The presence of holy bones sanctified the building. People wanted to be buried near these holy relics, hoping that proximity would increase their chances of going to heaven. Some churches, like London's Westminster Abbey, are so full of dead people that it's difficult to move around.

In a way, the Crusades might have been the longest (and bloodiest) cemetery visit of them all. One could argue the medieval wars to "regain" the Holy Land were initiated because the ground was literally blessed with God's blood. The Church of the Holy Sepulcher in Jerusalem contains a rock tomb where worshippers believe the body of Jesus lay for three days before he reinhabited it. The site has drawn countless millions of visitors since Constantine built a church on the spot in 326.

Before the advent of Christianity, the tomb of Mausolus was considered one of the Seven Wonders of the Ancient World. Built on a hill overlooking the sea in what is now Turkey, the grand building gave us the word *mausoleum*. In ancient Greece, a man wasn't considered truly learned until he'd seen all Seven Wonders, so a visit to Mausolus's tomb was a step on the road to wisdom.

Of course, the only surviving Ancient Wonder is the Great Pyramid of Giza, a tomb long ago looted of its inhabitants, but no less marvelous despite that.

Today, the Taj Mahal is one of the wonders of the modern world. The exquisite white marble building was constructed by Shah Jehan as a tomb for his favorite wife. When tourists visit for the architecture, they keep alive the memory of a grief so powerful that it erected a monument to stand through the ages.

Which seems a more noble cause than the reasons behind Lenin's mausoleum on Red Square in Moscow. For decades, a team of scientists has been employed to hold decay at bay while millions of people came to pay their respects—or to make certain the Great Leader was really, most sincerely dead.

See, it's not just me poking around in cemeteries. School field trips and scouting groups visit the graves of patriots in Boston and Philadelphia. History buffs visit the boot hills of the California Gold Country. Horticulturists study the arboretums at Green-Wood and Mount Auburn. Even bird watchers prowl graveyards in springtime, seeking to add to their life lists.

Perhaps the most popular gravesite for modern pilgrimage is Jim Morrison's grave at Père Lachaise Cemetery in Paris. When Morrison's lease on the space was due to run out in 2001, it seemed Père Lachaise might evict him. In the end, they decided to welcome the 1.5 million tourists who buy their tourist maps to commune with him each year.

Hollywood Forever, formerly known as Hollywood Memorial Park, offered Morrison a "final" resting place. That cemetery is used to fans on pilgrimages, from the Ladies in Black visiting Rudolf Valentino's grave to punk rockers who leave guitar picks at the grave of Johnny Ramone. Morrison would have fit right in.

Other gravesites also continue to be places of pilgrimage. Wach year, 600,000 people visit Elvis's grave at Graceland. Roses continue to appear on Marilyn Monroe's grave. People still stand before JFK's eternal flame. They still smoke pot with Jimi Hendrix and drink whiskey with Errol Flynn. They pray at the tomb of Saint Sebastian or compose poetry at the grave of Shelley or drop orchids into the water above the wreck of the *Arizona*.

For cemeteries to flourish in the 21st century, they must make themselves useful parts of their communities. For decades they rested, content to allow people to come to them. That's no longer good enough. There are too many final options now, beyond a plot in the boneyard down the road. If cemeteries will survive, they need to reach out.

Many have. Some graveyards are looking for ways to draw the living in, in order to keep themselves viable. You can see films projected on the wall of the Cathedral Mausoleum at Hollywood Forever, hear a concert in the Green-Wood, get married or graduate from high school at Forest Lawn. You can speak with costumed re-enactors on Mackinac Island or watch birds at Mount Auburn or volunteer to place flags on veterans' graves at any national cemetery.

People take care of things they love. If they have fond memories of a place, they'll watch out for it and donate time or money to keep it restored.

Cemeteries want you to care for them. I want you to care for them. I'd be thrilled if you're inspired to join the groups or individuals who struggle to halt time and save these fragile relics of the past.

So where did this book come from? In 1994, my husband Mason and I visited Highgate Cemetery completely by accident. Five years later, I felt as if I'd visited enough cemeteries that it might be fun to write about them. I pitched a graveyard travel column to Gothic.Net. For the next 45 months, I wrote about cemeteries both important and forgotten, urban and rural, tourist graveyards and family burial grounds. At some point along the journey, I started to think about collecting my travel tales into a book.

For the purpose of that column and now this book, I define a cemetery as anywhere that bodies (or ashes or parts of bodies) are or have been buried. In addition to what is traditionally thought of as a burial ground, that definition allowed me to poke into ossuaries, columbaria, cathedrals, synagogues, and no end of historical parks. Seeing cemeteries provides purpose and a goal to my travels.

In the beginning, I explored graveyards when I stumbled across them. As I continued my column for Gothic.Net, I discovered there were gaps in my cemetery education that I needed to fill. In the spring of 2002, Mason and I built a whole vacation around burial grounds. We visited eighteen graveyards in ten days. Many of those adventures round out this book.

Still, this book is not complete by any means. In order to keep it a reasonable length, there were essays I couldn't include. There are places I would like to visit and haven't been able to: the American South and the Southwest, Mexico, Montreal, Moscow... Exploring cemeteries is a project that will occupy me for the rest of my life.

A friend of mine keeps a tattered US map in her bag. It's held together with tape and scrawled with ballpoint. No one else could make any sense of it, but to her, it's a treasure map. It's her list of cemeteries people have recommended she visit.

I think every now and then about making myself such a map. For now, I keep it in my head, backed up with my box of antique postcards.

Which brings us to the title of this book: I started buying cemetery postcards twenty years ago. At first I was fascinated by the things people chose to commemorate. There seemed to be no end to the images of Grant's Tomb or the oven vaults in New Orleans' Saint Louis Cemetery #1. Sometimes the postcards showed cemeteries all gussied up for Decoration Day or All Souls' Day. Sometimes the cards recorded an especially lovely view across an ornamental lake or between a row of monumental angels. Sometimes they showed a famous person's grave: Buffalo Bill's stone under a lonely leafless tree or Benjamin Franklin's slab against the fence in Philadelphia or Robert Louis Stevenson's grave in Samoa. I understand the star power in those images.

Other times, though, there was nothing special about the view or the headstones or the cemetery itself. Often antique cards simply showed people picnicking amongst the graves or posed beside their Model Ts or with their arms draped around a tombstone like it was part of the family. These cards were made to advertise graveyards, like business cards. While I could understand the thinking behind the creation of the cards, less clear to me was the motivation of the people who saved them. Was looking at them merely a form of armchair travel? Were they treasured mementos? Memento mori?

Some, though not all, of my vintage postcards were sent through the mail. The posted ones are my favorites, since they hint at the people who wrote or collected these cards. One phrase I was surprised to see on them—one that appeared over and over—was the ubiquitous vacation tag line, "Wish you were here."

I like that the phrase has a double meaning when written on a picture postcard of a cemetery. I assume that the senders meant they wished the recipient could have come along for the trip. However, it could also be read to mean, "I wish you were buried in this lovely place." I find that dichotomy amusing. It seemed to sum up this collection of essays perfectly.

In the end, I'm not obsessed with death so much as obsessed with life. I hate to let a sunny day pass because it means one more I will never see again. I love blue sky and green grass and the songs of birds and the scents of flowers. Graveyards, I've found, combine all those things.

More than that, cemeteries blend family with history, two more elements of my obsession with life. I love to puzzle out what's important to people, how they express affection and grief. In their way, gravestones are as covered with hieroglyphs as any Egyptian fresco. If you can comprehend the symbolism, more of the story unfolds—and yet, because the story is shrouded in time, important elements must remain a riddle.

I think that what I like best about cemeteries is the mystery of them. I don't know where people go when they die. There are a lot of things I don't yet understand about graveyard rituals and iconography, despite my reading: things I might never understand. There are stories below my feet that I will never know in full. I find all of that ineffably beautiful.

I'm sure there are errors in this book and I apologize. I've researched to the best of my ability, but there are undoubtedly lapses in my interpretations and wild leaps beyond accepted knowledge into speculation. The one thing I am certain of is that I will always be a student of graveyards. There is just too much to learn. I find that beautiful, too.

Thank you for accompanying me on my journeys.

— Loren Rhoads
San Francisco, California

Highgate Cemetery, London

WHERE DOES ONE START?

Highgate Cemetery, London: January 22, 1991

MICHIGAN'S CLAYTON TOWNSHIP, WHERE I GREW UP, had been farming country, but by the 1970s, it was hard to make a living with a family farm. Most of the farm boys I grew up with looked forward to working on the assembly line in Flint, building Buicks or Chevrolet trucks.

My dad was a farm boy who combined growing corn and wheat with a desk job at Buick. Growing up near the Motor City, my parents didn't think anything of throwing my brother and me into the truck camper and going for a drive. We drove from Michigan to Yellowstone one year. Another summer we drove to the Rocky Mountains. Once I married Mason, he and I would drive six hours to Chicago or Toronto, just for the weekend. Road trips are in my blood.

After Mason and I moved to San Francisco, Survival Research Laboratories—a performance group with whom Mason volunteered—arranged a show in Barcelona. They asked if Mason wanted to come do sound for them in Spain. SRL did apocalyptic large-scale robot performances, which sounded like a good excuse to leave the country, even if no one in either of our immediate families had ever been to Europe. Mason and I decided we'd have a real adventure. SRL couldn't help with our traveling expenses, but luckily, airfares in January were cheap.

We decided to start our trip with a week in Barcelona, then go to Paris. I began to research our trip of a lifetime.

The adventure grew from the moment we arrived at SFO. Airport security was extremely tight as Congress moved toward approving the First Gulf War. Our flight to JFK got delayed so long that, by the time we finally arrived in New York, we'd missed our connection to Spain.

The airline refused to put us up anywhere, because national security had caused the delay. They wouldn't budge. We declined to spend twenty-four hours without our luggage until their next flight left for Barcelona. After we did some pleading, they decided to reroute us through London, but we'd have to run through the terminal at JFK to catch the plane. When we arrived, breathless, the only seats left on the plane were in business class. Like magic, we got upgraded. Things seemed to be looking up.

Then that flight—also delayed—missed our second connection to Spain. As we crossed the Atlantic Ocean, Mason asked one of the flight attendants what we should do when we arrived at Heathrow. The business class flight attendants were amused by us because we were actually grateful to receive service like we'd never had before. She confided in him that America had begun bombing Baghdad.

So Mason and I landed in London without British money, guidebooks, or a place to stay. Despite all that, we were freaked out enough that we chose to remain in a country where we spoke the language, at least for a day or two, until we could contact Survival Research Laboratories and make certain the show would go on.

The decision turned out to be wise. These were the days before cell phones, so actually reaching someone from SRL proved challenging. Then we found out that one of the trucks loading SRL's equipment into the performance area had toppled a wall and killed someone. SRL arranged a second site near Barcelona's docks, but as Spain geared up to join the Gulf War, the Spanish Army commandeered the area. The show did eventually go on, but with things so confused—and having to pay our own way to travel— Mason and I elected to remain in London, hoping to keep clear of SRL's bad luck.

I'd always wanted to go to England, anyway. All my life I'd read books set in London, so I jotted down a rough list of things to do. We bought ourselves a *London A-Z* book map: because, we discovered, London is such a maze, you need a book of maps to navigate it. We also had the *Let's Go: Europe* we'd intended to rely on in Paris. We figured those two things could keep us entertained for a week. We did pretty well. We toured the British Museum, Westminster Abbey, the Museum of the City of London, Saint Paul's Cathedral, saw the Tenniel illustrations for *Alice in Wonderland* at the Barbican, and walked miles down Baker Street and the Thames Embankment. It was a wonderful, relaxing trip.

Toward the end of the week, we started to run low on things to see. London was proving to be expensive and, ahead of us, we still had a week in Paris for which to budget. We needed something less costly to amuse us for a day.

I'd purchased a beautiful book of cemetery photos called *Highgate Cemetery: Victorian Valhalla* from the tourist bureau at Victoria Station. In our tiny hotel room, Mason and I pored over John Gay's luminous black-and-white images. Highgate Cemetery—once a showpiece of the Victorian death cult—appeared to be toppling to ruin, lushly overgrown with ivy and Queen Anne's Lace: the epitome of romance, decadence, and death.

"I think we should go," Mason said.

"Really?" It honestly hadn't occurred to me; the January wind had been bitter while we'd explored our unintended destination.

"It looks beautiful. I'd rather see Highgate Cemetery than the Tower of London." He pulled out the *London A-Z* and found Highgate Station on the tube map.

The village of Highgate stands on a tall hill overlooking the city of London, which sprawls across the river plain below. Highgate's name describes its former function: it served as point of entry for farm goods coming from the countryside to feed and clothe the metropolis. In the early days, the only sinister thing about the area was Hampstead Heath. Highwaymen flourished there, men like Dick Turpin, whose ghost reportedly still loiters 'round The Spaniard's Inn, a pub once owned by his father.

Following the nondenominational fashion set by Père Lachaise Cemetery in Paris, the London Cemetery Company founded Highgate Cemetery in 1839. They envisioned the "garden cemetery" as a place of beauty where Londoners could escape the smoke and dirt of their city. The graveyard offered controlled nature—serene, park-like, safe—beside the wilderness of Hampstead Heath.

The cemetery made the Highgate area fashionable. While it was no Kensal Green—final home of a Prince of England, as well as William Makepeace Thackeray, Wilkie Collins, Lady Byron, and friends of Shelley's—Highgate Cemetery managed to land the mortal remains of various balloonists, menagerists, scientists, and philosophers like Karl Marx, as well as authors Christina Rossetti, George Eliot, Radclyffe Hall, and the family of Charles Dickens (who had been entombed in Westminster Abbey against his wishes).

Among the artistic souls buried in the western half of the graveyard lies Elizabeth Siddal, muse, mistress, and eventually wife to Pre-Raphaelite painter Dante Gabriel Rossetti. A hat maker's assistant, beautiful Lizzie had been wooed by the dashing Italian immigrant, who refused to settle down after he'd won her heart. Increasingly depressed after a stillborn child, Lizzie took her own life with an overdose of laudanum in 1862. At the graveside service, the distraught Rossetti placed a handwritten volume of poems on her pillow just before the undertaker sealed her coffin.

Rossetti's fortunes faltered after his muse removed herself from the mortal plane. He became convinced that he was going blind and losing his skill as a painter, that he was destined to be remembered as a poet rather than as an artist. His questionably scrupulous agent persuaded Rossetti that he could cement his literary reputation if only he'd publish the poems consigned to Lizzie's grave. In October 1869, the Home Secretary granted permission to exhume the coffin, as long as it was done by night and did not upset the neighbors or patrons of the cemetery. By flickering torchlight, workmen peeled back the damp rich earth of England.

When the gravediggers forced Lizzie's coffin open, the only remnant of her beauty was the mass of her auburn mane. The grave robbers brushed tendrils of hair from the silk-bound manuscript and returned Lizzie's sad remains to the cold autumn ground. After the poet had his manuscript fumigated, he submitted it to his publisher.

The story leaked, possibly via one of the horrified torchbearers, to *Lloyd's Weekly Newspaper*. Elizabeth Miller, in her book *Dracula: Sense and Nonsense*, theorizes that Bram Stoker read the news while working on *Dracula*, because that issue of the paper also reviewed the Lyceum's production of *King Lear*, overseen by Stoker. If Stoker *did* read the story, Lizzie Siddal served in death as another man's muse, transmuted into Lucy Westenra and given life beyond the grave.

In the middle of the 19th century, people flocked to Highgate Cemetery. They brought picnics and strolled the lanes, marveling over the wealth of statuary and beautiful greenery. Inspired by the birdsong, they courted here. With thirty funerals a day, there was a constant flow of people in and out.

The 20th century dawned. England endured World War I, in which one of every three soldiers perished. At the war's end, the influenza pandemic swept the country, killing thousands. The young and vigorous, plucked in their prime, glutted the nation's graveyards.

World War II finished the job, wiping out most of a generation of men. By the 1950s, whole families had ceased to exist. No one survived to tend the graves; no money came from new burials in family plots. Without income to pay the army of gardeners, Highgate was abandoned to nature. And nature ran rampant.

By the end of the 1960s, Highgate Cemetery was choked with weeds, shadowed by a dense forest of ornamental trees, and colonized by wildlife from Hampstead Heath that included foxes, hedgehogs, rabbits, songbirds, and hundreds of insect varieties.

In 1968, the cemetery featured in *Taste the Blood of Dracula*, one of Hammer Studio's costume thrillers starring Christopher Lee as the immortal count. Perhaps that led to the outbreak of vampire hunting that mutilated Highgate Cemetery in the 1970s. Both the British Occult Society, helmed by Sean Manchester, and the British Psychic and Occult Society, headed by David Farrant, investigated the cemetery, poking into open graves.

The British Psychic and Occult Society officially closed its examination in 1973, due, Farrant writes, to the "concern of the cemetery authorities and the police who saw the Society investigation as being responsible for a marked increase in damage and desecration at the cemetery." He appeared in court in June 1974. The prosecution contended that "Farrant *was* the vampire of Highgate," according to Rosemary Ellen Guiley in her book *Vampires Among Us*. Farrant was charged with maliciously damaging a memorial to the dead, interfering with a dead body, tampering with witnesses by sending them poppets (the British version of voodoo dolls), and possession of a firearm. The final charge earned him several years in prison.

Unfortunately, by getting off at Archway station to change money, Mason and I out-clevered ourselves. Rather than taking the tube to the next station and climbing down Highgate Hill, we had to hike up it. In the 1800s, the hill took a full day for heavily laden horse carts to traverse. I was gasping when we found Swains Lane, the street that bisects Highgate Cemetery.

To our left hunched a large ornate chapel built around a courtyard. The wrought iron gates of Highgate West opened only at noon, two o'clock, and three, and then only to groups chaperoned by a guide provided by the Friends of Highgate Cemetery. Mason and I arrived just after ten a.m.

The Friends of Highgate Cemetery (FOHC) formed in 1975, after the cemetery's owner went bankrupt and padlocked the western half of the cemetery. FOHC volunteers worked on Saturday afternoons to clear brambles, fell invasive trees, and reopen access to grave sites. Eventually, the Friends bought the entire cemetery. They now sell guidebooks and offer tours to fund their work.

We gawked through the fence at the yellow brick chapel. It had arched windows, a crenellated roofline, and an arched carriage entry beneath a peak so sharp an angel could lose an eye. Felix Barker's introduction to *Highgate Cemetery: Victorian Valhalla* said the chapel had inspired the "undertakers' gothic" fashion in cemetery architecture. *Mortal Remains* reported, "From the 1840s onwards, Gothic became the universal style for cemetery buildings." This, because middle-class Victorians felt a need to demonstrate Christian belief. Gothic was deemed the most Christian of architectural styles.

We turned reluctantly toward the newer eastern section of the cemetery, the less overgrown and therefore less atmospheric side.

John Gay's pictures in *Victorian Valhalla* showed cemetery monuments that had crumbled and shifted as trees muscled them over. Ivy shrouded everything. It looked very romantic, but one of the book's captions said that some of the pictures would be impossible to duplicate since the upkeep began. Mason hoped the FOHC hadn't completely destroyed the ambiance.

A white-bearded gnome with eyes as green as his bright rubber boots met us. His white beard formed a bushy bib on his chest. He told us it cost a pound each to enter. For an additional pound, a camera permit would allow us to photograph both halves of the cemetery.

The caretaker asked what we would like to see, but we really didn't know. A map of the cemetery cost 25 pence. He didn't encourage us to buy one, but let us look over his. The main looping path would take us around the cemetery, but he cautioned us to take care on the smaller paths. And he wasn't saying we'd be interested in seeing it, but if we were, Karl Marx's grave lay straight ahead. That made me smile.

He also told us we were the only people in the cemetery so far on this chilly gray day.

The eastern side of Highgate Cemetery turned out to be *glorious* in its decay. Graves tucked into every conceivable area. Gravestones leaned drunkenly against each other. Some stones glowed pale green with lichen. Several broken crosses had been propped at the foot of their headstones. A dove flying downward capped one broken stone. It must've been beautiful before the stone toppled, before the dove's head disappeared. In fact, it seemed that everything small enough to carry away had vanished from the graveyard.

All of the back paths—where there were paths—lay inches deep in muck. I wondered if it ever dried out. The damp seemed perfect for the ivy, but daffodils glowed brightly in the gloom beneath skeletal trees. I didn't realize anything bloomed in England in January.

When we returned to the gently curving main path, Marx's monument was impossible to miss. A huge bronze bust stood on a granite pedestal that exhorted—in gilded letters—"Workers of All Lands Unite." We didn't photograph it, which I regretted later. I decided to come back to Highgate Cemetery some summer's day. I wanted to see the Egyptian Avenue, the Circle of Lebanon, the cemetery at its wildest. I wondered how I could afford the trip.

While Marx wasn't the only celebrity in Highgate East, he was apparently the most visited. The graves of actor Sir Ralph Richardson, social reformer George Jacob Holyoake (the last man arrested for atheism in Great Britain), William Friese-Green (inventor of "kinematography"), and Carl Mayer (co-author of the screenplay for *The Cabinet of Dr. Caligari*) are worthy of social calls, even if they don't inspire pilgrimages on their own. (Since my first visit, Douglas Adams, author of *The Hitchhiker's Guide to the Galaxy*, has joined the other notables.)

Coming from the Midwest, where cemeteries tend to be full of sedate granite monuments, the detail of the statuary in Highgate East amazed me. What impressed me most were all the angels. They appeared everywhere: clutching lilies, standing on a dragon's back, clinging to crosses, lifting a woman from the foliage overgrowing her tomb.

Ivy wreathed the face of one angel. Its glossy green leaves formed a gown, which revealed only her slim white arms. The epitaph on her plinth said she would hold her post "Until the day break and the shadows flee away." I discovered later the quote came from the Song

23

of Solomon. It appears on Victorian-era graves all over the English-speaking world.

Another angel hung suspended in midair against a simple cross. She wore a toga—perhaps her shroud?—draped over one shoulder and beneath the opposite arm. Its hem trailed down below her bare feet. I'd assumed that angels wore sandals in Heaven, but I guess there's no reason why they should. The golden streets are undoubtedly spotless. The epitaph beneath her read, "In Loving Memory of Our Devoted Mother." Was the angel meant to represent Mummy as she ascended after death?

A third angel knelt with her forehead pillowed on her long flowing hair as she grieved against a low stone wall. The stone drapery she wore caressed her every curve. Two stone lilies sprouted from the stone wall towering over her. For the first time I came across the epitaph, "A light is from our household gone, a voice we loved is stilled; a place is vacant in our home, which never can be filled."

As I thought about it, I realized I didn't see these cemetery angels as sinister Christian figures at all. In my mind, the excessively feminine winged guardians had more in common with the faery godmothers of my childhood than with the stern warriors of the Bible. Something about their angelic serenity, their total devotion, seemed too intensely focused to survive the real world. Silhouetted against the white January sky, standing their posts come rain or snow, the angels inspired me with the desire to see and photograph as many of their earthly forms as I could. I would have to visit more graveyards. My mission in life revealed itself.

On the far side of the looped path, I heard something like a creaky gate. A mewing black and white kitten trotted after us, all roly-poly body and stubby legs. I carried it to a sarcophagus. The kitten purred as I stroked it. Its irregularly shaped irises were pale blue, surrounded by pale green. Unlike a true cat, it held my gaze, mesmerizing me with its unusual eyes. Mason snapped our portrait before I broke the trance and we continued on. As we neared the cemetery entrance, something distracted the kitten. It vanished into the undergrowth.

Unfortunately, the day was too dark and the wind too icy to wait an hour for the western half of the cemetery to open. Mason and I walked back to the Archway tube station, holding hands inside my coat pocket.

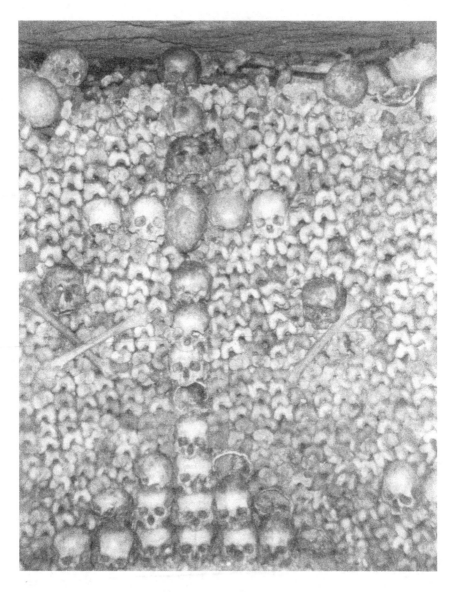

Municipal Ossuary, Paris

THE EMPIRE OF DEATH

Paris Municipal Ossuary: January 27, 1991

"Un monstre sans raison aussi bien que sans yeux est la Divinité que l'on adore dans ces lieux on l'appele la mort et son cruel empire s'étend également sur tout qui respire."

"A monster without reason and without eyes is the God one worships in those places where one recognizes death and his cruel empire extends equally over all who breathe."

OSSUARY, FROM THE LATIN FOR BONES, means a container or vault for the remains of the dead. A friend who'd lived in Paris placed the Municipal Ossuary at the top of our "must-see" list. I wasn't entirely convinced. As much as I loved the busy, funereal jumble of Highgate Cemetery, the Paris Catacombs would be an encounter with death of a more...embodied nature. I'd never seen a real de-fleshed human skull before, never confronted the harsh reality of our interior architecture. Death had come and gone from Highgate; in the catacombs, death lingered. Despite my curiosity, I was in no hurry to look the grave in the eye—or such eyes as it had.

However, Paris during the First Gulf War was bitter cold and increasingly menacing. While Mason and I had heard from Survival Research Labs about the anti-American protests in Barcelona, the propriety of the *International Herald Tribune* had shielded us from the War's reality. Several days into our week in Paris, we stepped out of the medieval splendor of the Musée de Cluny to find police cars and paddy wagons lining Boulevard Saint-Michel. The sidewalks stretched away, ominously vacant. Turning a corner to escape, I stopped short in front of the dripping muzzle of a water cannon. The police had tested it in anticipation of a protest march.

Mason and I decided to avoid the Left Bank for a while. Our solution was to go underground.

"Heureux celui qui a toujours devant les yeux l'heure de sa mort et qui

se dispose tous les jours à mourir."

"Happy are they who have always before their eyes the hour of their death and who prepare all their days to die."

For centuries, Christian philosophy taught that the soul was fundamental and the body mere dross, to be discarded. Simultaneously, the Church preached bodily resurrection. When the trumpet sounded on the final day, the dead would rise out of their graves to be judged. Bodiless spirits would not rise. Therefore, bones could not be cremated or otherwise destroyed. They had to be buried, preferably in hallowed ground. Of course, such an interment required a donation to the church. Aristocrats and wealthy merchants might purchase coveted space inside the sanctuaries, but everyone else squeezed into the churchyards. The clergy were not eager to part with a guaranteed source of income by condoning burial just any old place.

Unfortunately, the dead piled up faster than churches could be built.

Beginning in the Middle Ages, the Cimetière des Innocents (near where the mall Les Halles now stands) served as Paris's chief graveyard. For over 500 years, corpses were laid shoulder to shoulder in thirty-foot pits, then blanketed thinly with earth. Cadavers were stacked layer upon layer, until they filled the graves. An estimated 2,000 bodies were interred there *each year.* Five hundred times two thousand: my mind boggled.

The Cemetery of the Holy Innocents, glutted with corpses, inspired a theme in medieval art that found its highest expression in the woodcuts of Hans Holbein the Younger. The first known *Danse Macabre* was painted as a mural on walls surrounding the Holy Innocents in 1424. The *Danse Macabre,* or Dance of Death, depicted the equality of all humanity before Death. Rank, wealth, and privilege offered no protection. Death—personified as a gaunt, anonymous corpse—*always* led his chosen victim away. In one of the earliest illustrated Parisian books, woodcuts thought to have been based on the Holy Innocents' murals show Death emasculated and naked, his abdomen yawning open upon shadows.

"Insensé que vous êtes, vous promettez-vous de vivre longtemps, vous qui ne pouvez compter sur un seul jour."

"Fool that you are, you promise yourself you'll live a long time, you
who can't count on a single day."

Linguists suggest the word catacomb comes from the Greek *kata
kumbas*, which means "near the low place." It's unclear why this
Greek phrase became attached to a district in Rome where, in the
second century AD, Christians buried their dead. Now the word is
applied to any mazelike burial place.

The catacombs of Paris originally had nothing to do with death.
They began as a network of underground quarries, providing gypsum
to build the city above. After they'd been mined, the tunnels stood
empty.

Concurrent with the reconstruction of Paris in the 1780s, a
movement gained momentum to clean out the old churchyards. The
Revolution had loosened the grip of the Catholic Church in France.
With Reason as the new philosophy, people questioned the Church's
system of mass graves.

Accounts of the period speak of pestilential hellholes, jammed
with liquefying cadavers. One report said that the notorious
Cimetière des Innocents broke through an adjoining wall to spill
corpses into an apartment building. Fearing epidemics, the city
fathers voted to excavate the Parisian graveyards.

Beginning at dusk, workmen emptied charnel pits around Paris by
bonfire light. It was impossible even to consider individualizing the
remains. Once the bones were loaded onto carts, priests chanting the
funeral service followed them to the underground quarry.

In 1786, after the ossuary was filled, the Archbishop of Paris
consecrated the residue of approximately six million people. Among
the now-anonymous dead lay Lavoisier, father of modern chemistry;
Madame de Pompadour, Louis XV's girlfriend; alchemist, spy, and
reputed immortal Saint-Germain; the philosopher of the
Enlightenment, Montessqieu; Mirabeau, who advocated
constitutional monarchy and whose corpse had been ejected from the
Panthéon; Danton, who participated in storming the Bastille only to
be guillotined during the Reign of Terror; Robespierre, who
engineered the Reign of Terror, then became its prey; and
numberless other victims of the Revolution.

In 1874, the Municipal Ossuary opened to viewers, including
Bismarck and Napoleon III.

"Venez, gens du monde, venez dans ces demeures silencieuses, et votre âme alors tranquille sera frappée de la voix qui s'éleve de leur intérieur: 'C'est ici le plus grandes des maîtres, la Tombeau.'"

"Come, people of the world, come into the silent resting places and your tranquil soul will be struck by the voice that rises inside you: 'Here is the greatest of masters: the tomb.'"

"Come, people of the world!" I imagined a barker calling. "Step right up. Here is the Greatest of Masters!" Who wouldn't be tempted to pay the admission and take a look? The more I considered the exploration before me, the more my curiosity increased. What could possibly be down there?

A spiral staircase of stone wound down and down and down until it reached a path paved with dressed stone and edged with pebbles. From the arching ceiling, bare light bulbs warmed the buttery yellow stone. I couldn't touch the sides of the tunnel when I stretched out my hands, but I didn't reach up to measure the short distance overhead. A sign said we were twenty meters below the streets of Paris, deeper than the Métro. Thank goodness Paris isn't prone to earthquakes.

Access Paris recommended keeping close to a tour group, as the tunnels "stretch for miles." It related a cautionary tale about a Parisian who went downstairs to check his wine cellar and took a wrong turn. Seven years later, he was discovered, mummified.

Permanent Parisians: An Illustrated Guide to the Cemeteries of Paris reported that there were no catacomb tours and you were on your own. It suggested you take a flashlight. I wondered if a ball of string might be in order, too.

As we discussed the discrepancy in the guidebooks, Mason turned a corner to find a large tour group blocking the tunnel ahead of us. The guide talked interminably in French about the composition of the rock, the excavation of the tunnels, the "quarriers" themselves. While the quarry is historically significant, in terms of the architecture of modern Paris, it wasn't nearly so interesting as death.

A child of eight, bored by the lecture, started crawling up the side of the "cavern" where the group clustered. The soft rock crumbled and shifted under his feet. My sleeping claustrophobia roused. If he caused a cave-in, I thought, I'd drag my broken body through the rubble and... The boy's father persuaded him to stop fooling around, averting multiple catastrophes.

Some Germans pushed forward through the crowd. The guide blathered on without stopping them, so Mason and I followed.

We found a pair of niches carved with miniature cityscapes. *Permanent Parisians* said that the stonemason who sculpted them had been a prisoner in the city they represented. After he finished the carving, he tried to cut steps down from the street so the public could view his masterpiece. The stairway excavation caused a cave-in. The story, surely romanticized, said that he died with his chisel in hand.

Next we came upon steps down to a well of perfectly clear water. Though the stone stairs looked sturdy enough, an iron gate blocked them off. A plaque said that the quarrymen used to drink the water. They called the well Samaritaine, after the woman Jesus met at the well. I wondered if this well had any connection to the shopping center. We could only look down into the shimmering water from what seemed like a balcony.

Eventually Mason and I reached a doorway, the first since we'd come underground. Wooden panels, painted white and black, flanked yawning darkness. Above the lintel, a sign warned, "*Arrêtez. C'est ici l'empire de la mort.*" Stop. Here is the Kingdom of Death.

The warning frightened away the Nazis, who never discovered the French Resistance fighters hiding in the catacombs after August 1944. Right beneath the Parisian streets, the Resistance had concealed a radio capable of reaching London. They worked in the tunnels until the liberators came. How terrifying could Death's Kingdom be?

We paused outside the doorway, while I gathered my courage. Taking Mason's hand, I stepped through the portal, into the empire of Death.

"*Pensez le matin que vous n'irez peut-être pas jusqu'au soir et au soir que vous n'irez peut-être pas jusque'au matin.*"

"Think in the morning that perhaps you might not last until evening and in the evening that you might not last until morning."

Inside, the brown knobs of fibulas and femurs stacked higher than our heads. Skulls formed contrasting lines among the leg bones: a decorative motif. The domed craniums looked naked and sad. Empty eye sockets gazed patiently at us.

Bone upon bone upon bone. The sheer number of these anonymous memento mori staggered me. I had trouble grasping the concept of six million skulls, twelve million shinbones, seventy-two million ribs.... If a human body has 206 bones, there must be over a billion bones stacked in the catacomb tunnels: assuming, that is, that the gravediggers moved everything. I imagined some bourgeoise matron trying to gather herself together after the Trump of Doom sounded. The hipbone's connected to the backbone.... *Which of these backbones are mine?*

Now that I thought of it, I wondered where the remainder of the skeletons lay. I expected to stroll past towers of hipbones and stacks of shoulder blades. Instead, we saw nothing but skulls and long bones. Everything else must have been tucked away somewhere else.

I stopped in a passage so narrow my elbows could have touched skulls on either side. The caverns must have been enormous before these mortal remains filled them.

Mason and I photographed everything that struck a chord in us: the walls and pillars and columns of bones, the piles that had collapsed and spilled their melancholy relics onto the stone floor, the arrangements of skulls and crossbones. I worried that the gloom might be too much for my little 126 camera, even with the flash. Shadows lurked beyond the occasional round fluorescent light fixtures.

Beautiful inscriptions graced plaques set amongst the remains. Here and there a yellow spotlight cast a narrow beam, but overall our flashlight turned out to be a blessing. Other visitors burned their fingers by lighting matches to read the inspirational words. One plaque spoke of shadows among shadows, another about the empty eyes of skulls and the full eyes of God. All men fall, several said.

Why, I wondered, is Death female in French?

"Où est-elle, la Mort? Toujours futur ou passé. A peine est-elle présente,
que déjà elle n'est plus."

"Where is Death? Always in the future or past. As soon as it is present,
it is already gone."

After more than two centuries and at least two burials, some of the bones were beginning to decompose. White fuzz grew on one wall of shinbones. Elsewhere, two skulls had turned quite green. Some crania sported round holes. I imagined someone grasping a skull, only to have it crunch like an eggshell in his fingertips.

I discovered that I'm funny about human bones. I find something especially creepy about the geometry of a skull, inside which someone once lived and loved and dreamed. A skull, more than any other relic, seems too personal to be examined by a stranger. All those skulls, all those empty eyes, unnerved me.

Throughout the catacombs, everything was well within reach. Although a sign had cautioned us not to touch, nothing prevented us. We could have easily taken a souvenir. As an intellectual exercise, we speculated on how one might sneak human remains through US Customs.

In reality, I had no desire to touch the bones or to allow them to touch me. Little matter that they could not possibly be contagious after so many years postmortem. I did not want to feel the brittle evidence of death beneath my fingers. If looking into the void means the void looked back, I expected that touching the dead meant that Death returned the gesture. You see where fondling Yorick's skull got Hamlet. I kept my hands jammed resolutely inside my coat pockets.

"Si vous avez vu quelquefois mourir un homme, considérez toujours que le même sort vous attend."

"If you have ever seen a man die, always consider that the same fate awaits you."

One of the guidebooks warned us to take sweaters but, compared to the January winds outside, the tunnels were comfortably warm. It might have been cozy, if it hadn't been so damp.

Tiny nubbins—future stalactites—hung from the ceiling. Water dripped incessantly, puddling on the floor. I didn't want any of that water falling into my face. When the two of us stood alone amidst the dead, it sounded like slowly falling tears. The atmosphere definitely affected me.

The catacombs provided a perfect cathedral in which to meditate on the folly of human aspirations, to think about the war in the Persian Gulf. Death was so universal, so inescapable, why seek to hasten it? There were so many things I had yet to do before I could surrender to death. Did those American boys in the foreign sand feel the same? Did the Iraqi boys?

Wars should always be considered among *memento mori* like these. Perhaps life would seem more precious to the politicians who wage them.

We rounded a bend in the tunnels in time to see a man stumble. His friends snatched him back before he could topple into the stacked bones. What a nightmare that would be: falling into the arms of death, hearing them snap beneath you. Once you stopped falling, bones would tumble down over your face. I shivered in empathy at his near escape.

Mason was glad when we encountered the family with the small boy again. "Imagine," he said, "the dreams you would have if your parents had brought you here as a child." Instead I imagined the dreams I would have that night. This might be a good night to drink red wine before bed.

The ossuary seemed to go on and on. I wondered if we'd gotten lost, since we'd separated from the tour, but locked gates clearly delineated the direction we could go. When at last we climbed the tall steps of the spiral staircase to the exit, we found ourselves on an unfamiliar street. The pedometer said we had gone only a mile underground.

White powder edged our shoes, dried residue of the moisture on the path. The chilly January wind felt fresh on my face and in my lungs. I thanked goodness to find myself alive and in Paris.

I linked arms with Mason. "If we aren't going to last until evening," I said, "we'd better find a pâtisserie." I had a burning desire for *une tarte aux pommes*.

Père Lachaise Cemetery, Paris

ORNAMENTAL CEMETERIES

Cimetière du Père Lachaise, Paris: January 25, 1991
Cimetière du Montparnasse, Paris: October 22, 1991

WE PLANNED TO STOP AT THE GUARDHOUSE as we came in, to get a map. I even practiced my schoolgirl French on the subway so I wouldn't embarrass myself. Unfortunately, the guard hadn't hung around in the January cold. It didn't really matter. We wandered at random, letting my camera be our guide.

Père Lachaise (pronounced pear la shez) Cemetery was amazing, of course, even with the cold. The weak winter sunlight wore itself out forcing its way through the white sky. Bare branches poked into the air like arthritic fingers. We had the huge graveyard almost completely to ourselves.

Named for Father François d'Aix de La Chaise, the confessor to Louis XIV who once owned the land, Père Lachaise Cemetery spans 110 acres, much more than Mason and I could comfortably explore in January.

Unlike London's Highgate Cemetery, we found few angels in Père Lachaise. Various shrouded figures of bright green bronze mourned here and there, but since cloaks shadowed their faces, they seemed fairly interchangeable. The only one that excited me was the Widow Raspail, a hefty matron shrouded from head to foot in bronze. She stood at the back of her husband's tomb, hand stretched above her head to clutch the window's bars. The band Dead Can Dance used a photo of the statue as the cover for *Within the Realm of a Dying Sun*. Raspail had been imprisoned twice during the French Revolution. I don't know what became of his wife.

Avenue Circulaire rounded the edge of the graveyard, leading us to memorials for the French victims of the Nazi extermination camps. The first monument we came upon remembered the inmates of Mauthausen. An emaciated man in a loincloth shouldered a rock, his body twisted beneath its weight. He climbed an almost vertical stairway with steps too narrow for his bony feet. Mason thought he looked like Sisyphus. At Mauthausen, prisoners had been forced to carry stones out of the quarry until they collapsed. If they weren't worked to death, they were shot.

Beside that stood a monument to those swallowed by Neuengamme. A despairing woman clutched a huge granite block against her torso. I don't know the story of the Neuengamme camp, but the inscription translated to, "Under this stone rests a little of the cinders of the 13,500 French martyrs who were assassinated by the Nazis. They died so we could live in freedom."

Next, a pair of huge white marble hands seemed to burst up out of the ground. A tourniquet of stone bound them at the wrist. This remembered the victims of Ravensbruck, a camp for women.

A black granite pillar recalled the men, women, and children who died at Auschwitz. A figure—its featureless head too large for its spindle of neck—had struggled half free of the column.

Two skeletal bronze figures, almost too thin to support themselves, clutched a dead comrade between them. That put the suffering into perspective, reminding me that not all of the victims of Buchenwald perished. Elie Wiesel had survived that camp.

For me, the most inspiring was the monument to the victims of Orainenburg and Sachsenhausen. A skeletal man rose on a sweeping column of flame; his arms flung behind him like wings. His toes pointed down toward the fire as he soared upward, free.

By the time we'd examined the row of monuments, I'd gotten shaky. Mason had grown up Jewish, put through a Bar Mitzvah by a grandmother who subsequently disowned him for marrying me. We didn't speak as we found our way out of the graveyard. I didn't have words for the things I wanted to say.

One of the benefits of traveling during the Gulf War had been that the airlines wanted to reward our bravery. They gave us enough miles for two free tickets back to Europe. The catch was that they had to be used before the end of 1991.

We didn't want to brave the summer crowds (Rick Steves's *Europe Through the Back Door* warned that even Père Lachaise could be packed in summer), but autumn seemed like a friendly time to visit. We made plans to use the windfall miles in October, to celebrate my birthday.

Our friend Samuel hadn't been to Europe before and decided to join us. We'd known Samuel a couple of years, ever since he and

Mason met at Mason's first job in California. Samuel seemed like a kindred soul. We planned to fly separately to Paris, meet up to take the train to Amsterdam for a couple of days, then spend the remainder of our trip together in the City of Light. It might have been a flawless plan, except that we discovered the things Samuel liked to do while traveling didn't necessarily correspond to what we wanted to do. He expected to hang out in Amsterdam's Brown Cafés. We wanted to see Rembrandts and Van Goghs. It made for some awkward moments. By the time we returned to Paris, we mutually agreed to find separate places to sleep.

Still, the reason for the trip was my birthday. I regard my birthday as a holy day, a yearly celebration that death hasn't caught up with me yet. Every year I try to stage a worthy festivity. After breakfast on October 22, Samuel joined us and we began my day with an exploration of Montparnasse Cemetery, where we discovered one of my favorite pieces of mortuary art in the world.

Several years earlier, our mutual friend Christine had stumbled across a life-sized four-poster bed in the middle of the Cimetière du Montparnasse. On the bed lay a man and a woman sculpted in bronze. She slept beneath the covers, fully dressed in Victorian finery, complete with a veil. Half out of bed, he wore a coat and tie, boots, and clutched a book in one hand. Christine laughingly titled the monument, "As the Husband Found Them."

After a long and enjoyable ramble through Montparnasse Cemetery, we discovered the Pigeon family bed. The monument was as amusing as I'd been told. I stepped back to take a picture.

Ron suddenly freaked out. He didn't mind spending the day with the dead, but he drew the line at being photographed with them. I thought he would tear the film from my camera. I feared my mistake would end a treasured friendship. Worse, I didn't understand the boundary I'd transgressed.

I apologized again and again. It hadn't occurred to me that people might still think of photographs as magical objects, capturing your soul or foretelling the future. Mason had been photographing me in graveyards since we first set foot in Highgate. I promised to compose my photos more carefully, leaving Samuel out.

Since we'd drained all the enjoyment from Montparnasse, Mason and I escorted Samuel to the Paris Catacombs in an effort to salvage the day. Everyone needs to experience the Municipal Ossuary at least once, preferably on her birthday. It was as spooky as the first time we'd visited.

The day culminated at La Cimetière du Père Lachaise.

Before Mason and I visited Paris, a friend recommended *Permanent Parisians: An Illustrated Guide to the Cemeteries of Paris*. It was one of a series written by Judi Culbertson and Tom Randall, guidebooks that pointed out the number of famous people who'd stopped for good, whether by luck or design, in tourist destinations. If John Gay's *Highgate Cemetery: Victorian Valhalla* demonstrated why a person might visit a graveyard in search of beauty, *Permanent Parisians* explored the more sensational pleasures of sightseeing in cemeteries. Amongst the juicy gossip, the guidebook gave a sense of the history recorded in the lands of the dead.

Although we didn't know on our first visit, Père Lachaise is the most important cemetery in the modern history of the Western dead. Prior to its creation, the bulk of defunct Europeans were jammed into anonymous mass graves in churchyards or jumbled together in ossuaries like the Catacombs. As the Industrial Revolution concentrated the living into larger and ever denser cities throughout the Western world, city churchyards grew equally overcrowded, devolving into noxious charnel pits where cholera and other diseases festered. Paris arrived at a solution first.

In June 1804, Napoleon banned burial within or just outside churches, synagogues, and temples. With his blessing, Père Lachaise opened on December 2nd: the week he was declared emperor. Founded on French Enlightenment ideals, some of Père Lachaise Cemetery's innovations seem obvious now: the cemetery as park, with trees and benches; bodies lying side by side, rather than atop each other; burial space purchased in perpetuity; survivors allowed to erect monuments to their dead.

Tom Weil points out in *The Cemetery Book* that this "represents less a turning point than a returning point...a reversion to the time of antiquity when the pyramids in Egypt, the Kerameikos Cemetery in Athens, the Etruscan burial grounds in Italy, and other necropolises around the Mediterranean Basin served as sites or even cities of the dead, with identifiable graves and, in some cases, individual markers."

Innovation or not, the opening of Père Lachaise ran counter to fifteen hundred years of ecclesiastical history. From the first, Père Lachaise—though named for a churchman—was conceived as a secular burial ground where all faiths could be interred together. It set aside no unconsecrated ground for suicides, actors, or others held in low esteem by the Church. In fact, the Church's domination of death was specifically rejected.

However, the graveyard needed more than high ideals to attract clientele; it needed a gimmick. Nicolas Frochot, a lawyer who later served as executor of Napoleon's will, recognized that, for centuries, people clamored to be buried near the remnants of saints. To attract the paying customers in Empire-era France, one needed secular saints.

First to be reburied in Père Lachaise were Héloïse and Abélard, medieval lovers punished for their passion: Héloïse by confinement to a convent, Abélard by castration. In Père Lachaise, the two were reunited beneath a monument echoing the medieval graves of royalty. Statues depict them lying on their backs beneath a sharply pointed Gothic canopy, hands clasped in prayer.

Soon to follow in the new cemetery was a corpse advertised as Molière's. When the famous playwright collapsed in 1673 during a performance of *The Imaginary Invalid*, he died without repudiating his profession and, consequently, received no last rites. Initially forbidden burial in a Catholic cemetery, Molière's interment was allowed in Paris's Saint Joseph Churchyard only by special permission of Louis XIV—and only if it was done at night without ceremony. According to *After the Funeral: the Posthumous Adventures of Famous Corpses*, rumors of the time said that the Church immediately exhumed Molière from his private grave and "cast [him] into the mass grave set aside for unbaptized persons." In 1792, a skeleton was removed from the plot of the unbaptized, stored for a while in a guardhouse, then put on display at Alexandre Lenoir's Museum of French Monuments. For eighteen years, the bones of this alleged Molière drew pilgrims. That notoriety induced the proprietors of Père Lachaise to purchase the purported bones of the playwright in order to add cachet to their new cemetery.

Other celebrities with better provenance followed: writers (Balzac, Colette, Alfred de Musset, Proust); painters (Corot, Daumier, David, Delacroix, Max Ernst, Modigliani, Pisarro, and Seurat); photographers (Nadar); composers (Bizet, Poulenc); and entertainers (Sarah Bernhardt, Georges Mélies, Edith Piaf, and Isadora Duncan), to mention a few. *Access Paris* calls Père Lachaise "a museum of

French history, but far more lively than either a cemetery or a museum."

Nine years after his death, an anonymous benefactor (believed to be Robert Ross, a former lover) retrieved Oscar Wilde's body from his pauper's grave in Bagneaux Cemetery and reburied him in Père Lachaise beneath a winged art deco sphinx commissioned from Sir Jacob Epstein. As originally designed, the sphinx was generously endowed, which scandalized one visitor enough to take a rock to its privates. According to *Permanent Parisians*, the severed appendage resided in the conservateur's office for many years, where it served as a paperweight. In 2000, the angel's genitalia were recast in silver and reattached by artist Leon Johnson for a video called *Re(Membering) Wilde*. Now a glass barrier protects Wilde's angel from the lipstick kisses of exuberant fans.

Chopin's body rests in Père Lachaise, although his heart lies buried in Warsaw. According to *Access Paris*, modern-day lovers use his tomb for posting "billets-doux" (love notes). I've never availed myself of the pleasure of reading them, but the temptation remains.

Gertrude Stein and Alice Toklas lie together beneath a simple granite block. Unfortunately, typos in Stein's hometown and date of death mar their monument. The couple still gets no respect.

Soprano Maria Callas rested in Père Lachaise after her cremation—at least, she rested until her ashes were stolen. One (disputed) source claims the thief was her cuckolded ex-husband, whom she left for Aristotle Onassis. After her remains were recovered, the Greek minister of culture scattered them in the Aegean Sea.

With all those famous names, be sure that the cemetery has its share of gossip and impropriety. In fact, Père Lachaise could be a miniature Paris. Its "lanes" are called "rues" just like Parisian streets. Family sepulchers line them like houses, complete with doorknockers. For the most part, the tombs reminded me of British call boxes. They were deeper, of course, but similar in width. They ranged from simple unadorned marble to "miniature Notre Dames," as Mason put it. The cathedral-like ones had ornate Gothic spires and sharply peaked roofs. Some even sported gargoyles.

Visible through their iron cutwork doors, many of the mausoleums were lit by stained glass windows. Some windows had a simple white cross fleury (the kind with the flares like fleur-de-lys at each terminal). Others had windows of rainbows or geometric stars like kaleidoscope patterns. The grandest windows might have come from churches: Christ with a lamb over his shoulders, the Virgin with palms stretched down, a blond woman with her arms around the foot of the crucifix like the Rock of Ages. The windows lent light and beauty and personality to what were otherwise grim little tombs.

In its way, Père Lachaise created the Victorian-era attitudes toward death. Death ceased to be hidden. Mourning could be flaunted. It required accouterments, even fashions. The cemetery became an appropriate place for a family cultural outing, an afternoon stroll, or courtship. *Going Out in Style: The Architecture of Eternity* reports that Père Lachaise had become a tourist attraction by 1830. A guidebook titled *Véritable Conducteur aux Cimetières aux Père Lachaise, Montmartre, Montparnasse, et Vaugirard* was published as early as 1836. It might have been the first cemetery guidebook, but it certainly wasn't the last.

After his ignominious death in a Paris bathtub, Jim Morrison was buried secretly by his girlfriend in Père Lachaise. Even though the grave lacked a marker, it became the site of pilgrimages, impromptu concerts, and purported satanic rituals. When "fans" attempted to steal Morrison's skeleton, his estate placed a granite slab over the gravesite. It's weighted down by a simple granite cube with a bronze plaque that says merely, "James Douglas Morrison 1943-1971" and bears an inscription in Greek that translates to "True to his own spirit."

Off and on for decades, there were movements to evict the most disruptive celebrity from Paris's most exclusive resting-place. After the grave's lease was set to expire in 2001, the debate intensified. Eventually, the Morrison estate arranged for Jim to stay in perpetuity. The decades he's lain in Père Lachaise have surpassed the years he walked around aboveground. He's become part of the landscape now, a legitimate tourist attraction in the City of Light. A spokesman for Père Lachaise estimated that a three and a half million visitors come to the cemetery each year. Most of them want to see Jim.

Finding Morrison's grave in January had been easy. Mason and I followed the legend "Jim" and arrows chalked on graves throughout the lower part of the cemetery. Ten months later, the cemetery had been cleaned up. We wandered around, consulting the less than helpful map in *Permanent Parisians* and arguing about how to find him. Mostly, I think, Samuel wanted to get high with some like-minded souls. I didn't care if we found Morrison's grave again or not. I'd seen it.

The October afternoon grew old. Ominous slate blue clouds massed overhead, but the golden leaves underfoot glowed, oddly luminous. I tried to ignore the men I loved sniping at each other as we wandered around lost. I tried to cling to the joy of celebrating my birthday in three of the world's finest burial grounds.

Finally we stumbled across a crowd of people huddled against the cold and growing darkness. Since our first visit in January, Morrison's bust had been stolen again. That hadn't been the original anyway, but a reproduction placed on the grave by Oliver Stone to film the ending of *The Doors*. Despite the cleanup of the rest of Père Lachaise, Morrison's grave and those around it were scrawled with graffiti on the order of "Break on Thru, Jim" and "No one here gets out alive." (In response to the vandalism, a security guard now monitors the grave.)

A knot of gaunt hairy men with swirling black eyes watched some innocent hippie children giggle as they photographed the grave. The accident about to happen was too much for me to watch. I wandered away, letting Samuel take his photos and smoke his hash.

I'd been so excited about my birthday and all the cemeteries, about the giddy sense of being alive in Paris when so many were not, that I'd been very selfish. In all of Père Lachaise, Samuel had wanted to see two things: Morrison's grave and the Holocaust Memorials. Unfortunately, we'd lost too much time in the other graveyards and the rain began to patter down before we got back to Division 97, where the memorials stand.

By the time we found our way out of the maze of tombs, night was closing in. This was the first time we worried about being trapped in a cemetery overnight, but it wouldn't be the last.

Ron excused himself and headed off into the city alone. Still willing to spoil me, Mason asked, "What do you want for your birthday dinner?"

"Let's go back to the Latin Quarter and see if that Chinese place is still there."

Mason gave me a birthday kiss that echoes in my body years later. Then we ran together through the rain to the Metro Station.

The Mizuko Jizo of the Hasedera Shrine, Kamakura, Japan

CURIOSITY AND THE CAT

Hasedera Shrine, Kamakura, Japan: April 13, 1994

UNLIKE MOST OF THE MUSICIANS who hosted us on Mason's first solo guitar tour of Japan, I considered Mayuko a friend, rather than a business acquaintance. I looked forward to staying in Yokohama as if she offered sanctuary rather than crash space. Mayuko spoke relatively fluent English; the difficulty of communicating in Japan—even with people I knew—hit me harder than expected. I obsessed about being an ignorant foreigner, blundering through a culture I could not comprehend. I worried about offending our hosts by accident. At Mayuko's, I thought I could relax.

When we arrived at Mayuko's tiny apartment, she immediately took me under her wing. She gauged the effects of culture shock and jet lag, then drew me a Japanese bath. All I needed was to sleep well, she said. Tomorrow would be my first day as a tourist in Japan: a day without business meetings, music clubs, or any reason to carry around Mason's guitar. Things would be better in the morning.

Mayuko wanted to show us a bit of "Old Japan," the Japan of samurai movies. She even convinced her boyfriend Hiroshi to take the day off from work to accompany us. After a breakfast of sliced green apples, yogurt, and huge croissants, Mayuko and Hiroshi took us by train to Kamakura. Kamakura had been the capital of Japan from 1185 AD until 1333. Now its Buddhist shrines draw pilgrims from around the world. Mayuko was surprised we hadn't heard of it.

Although Hiroshi had grown up in Kamakura, he'd avoided the shrines. Mayuko said he had been a "bad boy." With a smile, I wondered what that meant; Hiroshi was the most introspective Japanese I'd met. He rarely spoke, even in Japanese.

A short walk from the train station brought us to the Hasedera, the Hase Temple. The English-language tickets Mayuko bought for us explained that the "temple" was actually a collection of shrines. It had been established in 736 AD as a sacred place for the bodhisattva

Kannon. I knew from high school Comparative Religions class that a bodhisattva was an enlightened being who vowed not to enter Paradise until all other creatures reached enlightenment. Even though Buddhism defines life as suffering, bodhisattvas work to ease human misery. What a wonderful introduction to religion in Japan, I thought.

Just inside the temple gate, Mayuko demonstrated the ritual washing of hands. She dipped water out of a black stone basin with a bamboo ladle and trickled it first over one hand, then the other. Distracted by the water's chill, I didn't see how she dried her hands. I shook the water from my fingers, then wiped them on my jeans. So much for ritual purification. I felt every inch a *gaijin*.

A broad stone staircase led us up the hill. At the first landing clustered statues with no roof over their heads. "This shrine," Mayuko said, "belongs to Jizo." In answer to our puzzled expressions, she typed the name into her electronic translator. It defined him as the bald guardian of children and travelers.

In the shade of a flowering tree, a large bronze figure sat on a lotus throne. Verdigris had turned him a beautiful green. He clasped a slim staff in his right hand; a bronze orb rested in his left. The folds of his robe were as measured and graceful as a Greek statue's. Large earlobes hung to his shoulders, more Indian in my mind than Japanese. The statue's smooth chubby face seemed childlike. Someone had tied a scarlet bib under his chin and pulled a matching knit cap down over the dome of his round head. Rather than affronting the statue's dignity, the garb seemed lovingly offered. Jizo looked all the more serene for his indifference to the handmade gifts.

At the base of his throne thronged foot-high Jizos, each standing on its own lotus blossom. Many statuettes wore red cloth capes, some faded to pink by the elements. One wore a mantle of white fabric so unwrinkled it must have just been put on. Others had necklaces of flowers or beads. One Jizo had a little yellow ceramic dog at his feet. "These are *Mizuko Jizo*," Mayuko said, "the Thousand Jizo."

Struggling to put the concept into English, Mayuko said, "If I have a child—" she placed her hand on her belly "—and I kill my baby, I come here and name a statue. Then I come each year to pray. You understand?" I understood she meant having an abortion. It seemed right to have a ritual to commemorate the sacrifice, but I wasn't sure if a yearly pilgrimage seemed morbid. Did women return every year for the rest of their lives?

Hiroshi lit a candle and bowed briefly. I pondered the significance of that. Hiroshi and Mayuko weren't married. They lived in an apartment owned by his mother. Mayuko appeared to be somewhere in her late thirties; Hiroshi was younger. I had no idea how long they had been together. Was he honoring Jizo? Atoning for something? I didn't dare speculate.

As we continued up the hill, Hiroshi said shyly, "I pray for your safe journey."

"Thank you," Mason and I answered. Hiroshi bowed his head and smiled.

Farther up the hill, old-fashioned stucco and wood buildings gathered around a plaza. I'd never seen anything like them in my life. The buildings shrank as they ascended. Each story had its own sloping roof, tiled in gray slate. Small golden ornaments capped the eaves. Stern-faced guardians stared out from every corner.

A steady stream of people climbed the temple steps to pose for photographs. An American tour group chattered about the holy places they'd visited. Japanese children chased each other. The plaza had a picnic area with chairs and tables overlooking Yokohama Bay. Old women sat placidly, watching surfers bob in the distant waves. Yokohama lay out of sight beyond the rocky hills to the north. Mayuko plucked at my sleeve and led us into the shrine for which the temple complex was named.

The Hasedera Kannon is called eleven-faced. Above eyes half-lidded in meditation, Kannon wore a crown with ten additional faces. My guidebooks interpreted this differently: either the faces depicted the stages of enlightenment or—the story I prefer—Kannon watched in every direction so he could help people in need.

Yes, he. One of the mysteries of Kannon, the "Goddess of Mercy," is his gender. My entrance ticket used the masculine pronoun. The *Insight Guide to Japan* says, "He only looks feminine." Though his jeweled and gilded dress swells at the bosom, he is considered without gender. Is that the true state of enlightenment?

Kannon's statue towered above us, over nine meters tall. Drifting through the skylights, the soft natural light made the tarnished gold leaf on the statue's surface glow. Kannon held a slim wooden staff in his huge fleshy right hand and a golden vase of twining lotus flowers in his left. A rosary of tiger's eye beads had been looped around his left elbow, falling two meters to his knees.

I wondered if Kannon was related to Quan Yin, the Chinese Goddess of Compassion. I couldn't ask if the goddess was an import. The room felt cool and sacred, as if the atmosphere were differently composed than the steamy, bustling plaza outside. I'd gotten a similar feeling amidst the ruins at Delphi and in a kiva in New Mexico: something holy was present. I wondered if I'd ever felt that in a Christian church.

Both Hiroshi and Mayuko prayed before Kannon's altar. It never occurred to me that they might be religious. However, the seriousness with which they visited each shrine seemed more than respectful. If only I could frame one simple question that, when answered, would clarify everything they showed us. I wanted desperately to understand what this meant to them.

Mason, the most confirmed atheist I know, also put his hands together. I added my own plea for understanding.

Signs in English, the first I'd seen, said, "No Photo." Hiroshi explained, "The god is too powerful." I took that to mean Kannon's aura would overexpose the film. That would be something to see, I thought: photographic evidence of divinity. I wasn't tempted to break the taboo to experiment.

Mason whispered, "I bet there are postcards in the gift shop." To my delight, there were not. As much as I would have liked something to remember the beautiful goddess by, I was pleased that if the temple said "No Photo," they meant it.

Two silent women waited behind a glass case lined with prayer beads. The price tags of the crystal beads, flawless as dewdrops, listed a lot of zeroes. We quickly moved along.

Out in the plaza, I took snapshots of Mason, Mayuko, and Hiroshi on the temple steps. When the photos were developed, they came back with a strange overexposure above the temple roof. Maybe it was some weird reflection from the overcast sky—or perhaps the evidence of divinity I'd been seeking.

We left the crowded plaza. Behind the temple buildings, we found a little graveyard cut into the hillside. Mayuko and Hiroshi knew of my fascination with cemeteries. They knew I'd put together a book of graveyard photographs called *Death's Garden: Relationships with Cemeteries.* "Could I go in?" I asked.

Mayuko and Hiroshi exchanged a long glance. If they'd said no, I would have respected that. Instead, they shrugged. No one else entered the cemetery while we visited.

Buckets and ladles for washing the monuments lined a wooden shelf near the entrance. "Is grave-washing only done at ritual times, like the Bon festival?" I asked Mayuko, simply because her English came easier than Hiroshi's. She didn't know. I wondered if her father was alive. Did she have relatives for whom she performed the ritual cleansing? When she didn't offer the information, I restrained myself from prying.

The graves lay very close together. Only paving stones separated one from the next. The placement would truly have been cheek by jowl, except for the long Buddhist tradition of cremation. Since we didn't see stone urns, I guessed the ashes must have been placed under the blocks. Interment must be a major procedure.

"Are these the graves of monks?" I asked. "How does one arrange to be buried on temple grounds?" I merely voiced my questions, not expecting answers. Mostly, I was thinking aloud. I'd already learned in Japan that if I didn't address a question to someone by name, they didn't realize I was speaking to them. Questions not directed to a specific person went unanswered.

The simplest—probably the oldest—gravestones stood upright, engraved with kanji. Other monuments reminded me of family altars. These had several levels of base stones, usually a low riser, topped by a second riser double the height of the first. Above these rose two large blocks of darker stone. Each block was smaller in dimension than the one below, so that the monuments were roughly pyramid-shaped. At the very top stood an upright stone engraved with kanji or simple round medallions like the badges of samurai. Five stones, five levels. I considered the significance of the number five.

Because he had explained about not taking photos of Kannon, I asked Hiroshi if I could photograph the cemetery. He thought it would be okay.

Many graves had a pair of vases of either brown earthenware or stainless steel. These held bouquets composed of flowers of three different heights. I interpreted that as symbolizing the underworld, earth, and heaven. The flowers varied from white daisies to purple asters, with marigolds or lemon yellow poppies or huge sunny chrysanthemums mixed in. Is there a Japanese language of flowers, like the Victorians used? To the Victorians, marigolds symbolized grief and despair. Mexicans think their spicy scent is the perfume of death.

Behind several of the graves stood long wooden blades, notched at the top like stylized flames. "What are those?" Mason asked.

Mayuko became flustered. In a polite Japanese way, she snapped, "You ask so many questions: 'What's this and what's this and what's that?'"

I caught Mason's hand. We hadn't meant to upset her, but she had been such a good guide so far, telling us as much as she could about the shrines and their rituals. She'd made us eager to learn more. How to apologize for asking too many questions? I know so little about Japanese culture, religion, burial practices, belief in the afterlife.... The breadth of my ignorance staggered me. I decided to try to hold my tongue and be content with whatever Mayuko told us.

After an uncomfortable silence, Mayuko relented. She said that she couldn't read the wooden markers. It was an old style of writing. She thought they recorded the "after-death name."

The sky cleared for the first time in our trip. How nice to see blue sky, even a watery blue. Unfortunately, the clearing sky warmed the already humid day. Beneath my black cotton jacket I wore a red T-shirt. The color might have been wildly inappropriate. Who knew? Mayuko wore an oversized white sweatshirt over baggy black jeans. Hiroshi wore blue jeans and a navy and brown plaid shirt. In fact, most Japanese we saw wore dark, conservative colors. Without knowing if red was a sacred color—and without permission to ask—I decided I'd better keep my jacket on.

Changing the subject, Mayuko said that nearby stood a "very sacred place." It looked like a simple cave burrowed into the stone hillside. Inside the grotto stood stone sculptures of more gods than I could count, gods of "fools and drunks, safe traveling, and keeping love." Statues flickered in the darkness, illuminated only by white tapers on which prayers had been written with black marker. The twilight made it difficult to see. Water dripped from the ceiling. An uneven path led around a shallow dark pool.

Mayuko asked, "Do you want to pray for something?"

Mason dodged the question by saying, "Loren might." Mayuko bought me a tiny arch-shaped wooden plaque, an *ema*, painted with a small gold Buddha. She directed me to write my name and wish on the back. She and Hiroshi turned away to give me some privacy. I placed the plaque among hundreds of others on the floor. *Ema* were tucked into niches in the walls, even slipped between the electrical cables bolted to the ceiling.

I wondered if once a year there was a ceremonial cleansing of the cave, when all the wooden prayer plaques were burned. How else could the cave be emptied for next year's prayers? That conflagration would be something to see.

As we left Hasedera, we passed a cat sunning herself on a rock in a little Zen garden. Fascinated Japanese crowded around her. She ignored them. Hiroshi bent down to take her photograph. Why, I wondered, did a sleeping house cat attract so much attention? Here was yet another inexplicable cultural moment, one more thing that I didn't have the references to understand.

Then again, there were things in my own country that I didn't understand, even after a lifetime of study. How could I expect to grasp Japan in four days?

I finally recognized the pressure I'd put Mayuko under. I'd made her the spokesperson for 1,300 years of Japanese history. No wonder she was overwhelmed.

I decided to try to let Japan just flow over me. Curiosity, I'd discovered, even well-intentioned curiosity, could be intrusive. I would have to watch and listen and try to save my questions for only the most important things. It might take a lifetime to understand all that I saw and heard on this trip—and that might be the most important Japanese lesson of all.

Atomic Dome, Hiroshima Peace Memorial Park

DAYS OF INFAMY

Hiroshima Peace Memorial Park, Hiroshima, Japan: April 15, 1994
The USS Arizona Memorial, Pearl Harbor: Easter Day 1997

DURING THAT FIRST VISIT TO JAPAN, I insisted on a day trip to Hiroshima. I'd read about the atomic bombing for so long; I wanted to see the site for myself. After a brief train-ride from another friend's apartment in Osaka, Mason and I found ourselves staring up at the *Genbaku Domu*: the Atomic Dome. The framework structure looked fragile as bleached bones against the swirling gray April sky.

The dome caps the ruins of the Industrial Promotion Hall on the shore of the Ota-gawa River: Ground Zero on August 6, 1945, when the *Enola Gay* dropped the world's first atomic weapon. The bomb exploded, as hot as the surface of the sun, leveling 70,000 buildings instantly. The burning winds set the rubbish afire. Only the Industrial Promotion Hall, at the eye of the storm, survived amidst the devastation.

The building has been shored up over the decades. The Japanese feel it's more important to keep the symbol standing than to keep it historically accurate.

Almost fifty years after the attack, I found it creepy to stand at Ground Zero. I wondered if I was doing permanent damage to my body just by breathing the air. Of course, modern Hiroshima is a city of more than one million people. I'd read that grass sprouted on the scorched earth as early as the spring of 1946. Still, to stand in a place where so many people died, vaporized, their shadows burned into nearby walls... How can anyone comprehend or accept what mankind is capable of?

Before Mason and I made the pilgrimage, our Japanese friends preferred not to discuss the Peace Memorial with me. A number of them had never been to the museum. Among those who had, all visited on field trips from school. In every case, when I mentioned it, I had a moment of direct eye contact with our hosts. Their expressions were as frozen and horrified as my own. "It's a very sad place," Junko Hiroshige, the singer of the noise band Hijokaidan, said. "Very sad."

I thought I was prepared. I don't know if it's possible to be.

Behind the Atomic Dome, the entry to the Peace Museum winds through a darkened hallway. When my eyes adjusted, I saw charred bricks surrounding me, as if I walked through a bombed-out building. Photographs in window frames recorded the surrounding destruction. Here and there buildings huddled amidst the rubble, windows gaping and roofs ripped away. In the black-and-white photos, Hiroshima glowed the color of ashes.

Around the corner into the first room, orange light flickered over mannequins of school children, their clothing in rags. Skin drooped from their fingertips, melting off their bones.

In that room, little cases displayed articles of clothing, still stained with blood five decades later. In clipped BBC English, the narrative tape assured me that the Germans, Russians, British, Italians, and Japanese all had been developing atomic weapons. Whoever won the race and produced the first nuclear bomb felt they had to drop it before the others could. The narration carefully deflected blame from America.

Hiroshima had been chosen as a target specifically because it was an industrial city with a large population that had escaped the firebombing inflicted on the rest of Japan. Any damage Hiroshima received on August 6, 1945 could be attributed solely to the atom bomb.

On that day, children had been released from school to create fire lanes through town in case America dropped conventional bombs. After the daily American fly-over at seven a.m., the all-clear siren sounded. Everyone who could be outside was, leading to the staggering loss of life: 140,000 the first day.

Winds generated by the bomb fanned a firestorm that leveled seventy-five percent of the buildings between the mountains and the sea. Museum cases held a broken pair of eyeglasses or a dented metal water bottle, the sole remnants of children who vanished that day.

One of the cases contained fingernail clippings and dried strips of skin, all that a woman had been able to save of her husband. My imagination faltered at the thought of losing everything so completely that I would treasure a ribbon of my husband's skin.

As I looked around, I realized the museum was crowded with modern schoolchildren: girls in pleated navy skirts and white knee socks, boys in short pants and little caps. The girls clung to each other's hands. I blinked back tears and looked for a place to sit down. These children were traumatized enough without seeing a foreign woman sobbing.

There was nowhere to go: no bench, no secluded corner. The horror was unrelenting. I stumbled toward a brick wall and saw the shadow of a man photographed against it. Such a thing really *existed*. All my life, I'd tried to imagine what it would be like to be photographed by the sun, recorded and vaporized in one searing agony. Here the evidence stood. He hadn't had time to throw his hands over his eyes.

When I turned back, I saw Mason ringed by schoolboys, all eight or ten years old. One of the boys stepped forward and solemnly offered his hand to Mason. Mason, who had been studying Japanese, shook the boy's hand and bowed. With the ice broken, the other boys swarmed in, wanting to shake an American's hand.

If children can reach out to strangers, in the midst of the gruesome evidence of what our country did to theirs... I began to cry in earnest.

Once we left the museum, Mason and I strolled around the Peace Memorial Park outside. I trembled. The world has survived the creation of the bomb. Japan survived the war. Even Hiroshima rose phoenix-like from total demolition. I could not regain my equilibrium.

The park held a jumble of monuments. A polished granite cenotaph in the shape of a bomb recorded the names of the victims. Millions of paper cranes, folded out of bright origami paper, lay in heaps around it. Nearby stood a statue of Kannon, bodhisattva of mercy. The most shocking sculpture emulated a fishlike creature, fallen on one side, supported in midair at the shoulder and hip. Its limbs had been reduced to sticks, its features and flesh chiseled away. It looked like nothing so much as a charred corpse.

The simplest monument touched me the deepest. In the center of the park, a grassy mound rose like the barrows on Salisbury Plain. I stopped before it, understanding without reading the sign that it was a grave. This mound held the remains of such victims as could be recovered, pried out of collapsed buildings or hauled, bloated, from the contaminated river.

Mason told me the plaque said that the barrow contained the ashes of 70,000 victims. In keeping with Buddhist tradition, they had all been cremated. The mound of ashes stood almost twelve feet high.

Nearby, a huge deep bell tolled. In Japan, temple bells are upended cups of bronze. They have no clappers. Instead, a baton— sometimes big as a tree trunk—is suspended outside the bell. Anyone can pull the striker back and let it swing forward to sound the bell. In this case, every peal said a prayer for the repose of the dead.

My sense of guilt was so great that I couldn't ring the bell for the victims of my country's need to prove its superiority. Instead, I hung my head and prayed to see peace in my lifetime.

The visit to Hiroshima made me want to see the USS *Arizona* Memorial in Pearl Harbor. I wanted to understand what could justify the massacre in Japan.

While visiting in Oahu with my mom in 1997, I finally got my chance to go. Unfortunately, I decided to take a tour bus to the monument rather than find my own way on public transit. The thing I neglected to consider was that the tour took just four hours round trip. I should have guessed that wouldn't be long enough to absorb what I'd see, but it seemed enough time to leave Mom alone on an Easter morning. I hoped she'd go to church while I made the excursion.

The tour bus picked me up in front of our hotel at seven a.m. and zipped out of Honolulu before the Sunday morning rush hour began. At Pearl Harbor, I strolled right off the bus into the visitor's center. The *Arizona* Memorial is free, but you have to arrive early to score an entrance ticket.

With the ferry leaving soon for the memorial, I didn't have time to see more than the first room of the museum. It contained a Japanese torpedo discovered unexploded in 1991 during harbor dredging. Workmen accidentally brought it to the surface in the bell of an earthmover. The Navy looked the torpedo over, decided it was too corroded to be safely disarmed, and took it out to sea to detonate. Divers donated what survived the explosion to the museum. Although large holes perforated the steel, a surprising amount of the casing survived.

One display told about a victim of the Pearl Harbor attack who stayed at his gun as the ship burned around him. He died in the hospital the following day. The case held a very nice letter of condolence, along with the ribbons and shards of a champagne bottle with which his wife had christened a ship in his name. It personalized the dead man the way the broken eyeglasses and dented water bottles personified the schoolchildren killed at Hiroshima, except that the sailor's wife had had a body to bury in a marked grave.

There had been talk of turning the shallow harbor on Oahu to American military usage during the Spanish-American War, before the US even annexed Hawaii in 1898. Construction of the Naval base began in 1908. Between Hawaii and Japan stood 4,000 miles of open ocean, a distance too narrow for American hawks.

Out through the back of the museum, a patio surrounded by lush tropical greenery looked out over the placid harbor. The shallow water shone cerulean beneath fleecy white clouds. Park Service plaques held black-and-white photos from 1941, showing where the ships had been moored when the attack began. Gray steel warships were moored around the island in the center of the harbor, encircling it completely.

I know those were different days, but looking back from decades on, it's hard to imagine that anyone could have seen this accumulation of war machinery and believed America's intentions were peaceful. Hostilities might not have been formally declared, but they were clearly anticipated. Historically, the US had long looked forward to quashing Japanese expansionism. Washington simply wanted justification. The Rape of Nanking hadn't been enough.

Men on both sides of the ocean counseled against starting anything. Japan's Admiral Yamamoto had attended university in the US and spoke fluent English. He understood that Americans might be balked by a surprise defeat, but once battle was joined, the larger country would win. He spoke against provoking the US until his countrymen threatened his life. Cornered, Yamamoto lobbied for a decisive first strike to destroy the fleet anchored at Pearl Harbor. With any luck, the US would be completely disarmed until after Japan conquered Asia. By then, it would be too late.

James O. Richards, the admiral in command of America's Pacific

Fleet, called it suicidal to mass the entire fleet in one place. That warning contradicted what President Franklin Roosevelt wanted to hear, so Roosevelt replaced Richards. The shallow waters of Pearl Harbor were considered too for torpedoes to travel. A submarine net easily blocked the harbor's narrow mouth. Radar was only just coming into use, but military consensus was that the Japanese wouldn't dare anything worse than sabotage. To prevent that, Lieutenant General Walter Short ordered American warplanes parked wing to wing and tail to nose to make them easier to guard. That made them impossible to fly on December 7, 1941.

If not for a cascade of American incompetence, the attack on Pearl Harbor might have been no surprise at all. Roosevelt received reports that the Japanese fleet had gone to sea, but his advisors predicted they were headed to the Dutch Indies. The Pacific fleet did not go in search of them.

At four a.m. on the morning of the attack, the USS *Ward* sank a Japanese submarine outside Pearl Harbor. However, its report of the incident was not coded urgent and didn't get passed on to the men sleeping on ships inside the harbor.

Radar trainees had been supposed to shut down their equipment at seven a.m., but because they had not yet gone off-duty, they saw a huge mass approaching Oahu. They reported to a lieutenant on the second day of his command. He expected American B-17s from San Francisco. Even though this swarm came from the south rather than east from San Francisco, he advised the radar men not to worry about it.

When a modified torpedo hit the *West Virginia*, the US fleet was completely undefended. Three minutes later, a bomb cut through the *Arizona* and ignited its forward magazine. It sank in nine minutes, all hands aboard.

Park Rangers loaded us onto a low white ferry for the trip across the water to the memorial. The sound system played "Taps" and informed us that 900 bodies were never removed from the sunken hulk of the USS *Arizona*: "It is considered a cemetery, so keep your voices down." Other instructions included, "Don't throw coins from the memorial." The Park Service still collects coins five times a year, but the metal plummeting through the water damages the old ship. Flowers were okay to cast onto the water, but the lei strings were supposed to be cut so they didn't entangle wildlife.

The tape reported that 110 bodies had been recovered from the *Arizona* and sent home to their families. One hundred more bodies had been removed, but could not be identified. They had been among the first buried in the National Cemetery of the Pacific in the Punchbowl. When survivors of the Pearl Harbor attack die, they can request to be cremated; divers place their urns in the *Arizona*'s gun turret so that they can be buried alongside their comrades.

Once the ferry docked, everyone shuffled down the gangplank onto the blindingly white memorial. Despite the bustle, the monument seemed very peaceful. People kept quiet, moved slowly, were relatively polite to each other—but some men didn't take off their baseball caps. I didn't feel they were being consciously disrespectful. They just didn't know any better.

I kept thinking of my visit to Hiroshima, the bookend of America's involvement in World War II in the Pacific. Pearl Harbor's shipyard had been an obvious military target. Victims here had been warriors. Even if war remained undeclared in 1941, the men at Pearl Harbor were trained and ready to fight. They expected to be called upon to give their lives for their country, if not as soon as they did. These sailors were betrayed by their government and their commanders—and, to be fair, by the enemy—but their deaths succinctly served the purpose the American government had in mind: to goad an uncommitted public into war.

Hymns I recognized from my childhood played over the speakers while people filed through the memorial. The structure is basically an enclosed bridge that straddles the sunken battleship. The *Arizona* rests on the harbor bottom, forty feet down. Its brittle, rusty smokestack is all that protrudes from the water.

As I watched, a rainbow slick of oil drifted from a slowly leaking tank. An older gentleman in military uniform volunteered that the oil had been seeping since the ship went down. "Legend claims," he said, "that the oil will flow until the last survivor dies."

The veteran guide continued to speak, telling us how the memorial received some of its funding. When Elvis Presley came to Oahu in 1961 to film *Blue Hawaii*, he asked to be taken to Pearl Harbor. At the time, a simple plaque was all that marked the spot. Presley performed a benefit in Honolulu and donated the proceeds to the memorial fund.

I wondered how native Hawaiians feel about the monument in the bay where their ancient kings had hunted sharks. More than 5,000 people visit the *Arizona* Memorial each *day*, tossing coins and flowers into the water. It struck me as odd that the Park Service worried about the effect of lei strings on wildlife, but not sixty years of seeping oil.

I leaned through one of the rectangular openings in the memorial bridge, gazing down into the water. I'm not sure what I wanted to see to make the experience real. The men below had long been dissolved and carried away by the ocean. No fish could brave the contaminated water. Below me sat rusting steel bought by the American public, paid for with American blood. What did it mean?

An older woman leaned out from the next opening. I watched her methodically strip pink dendrobium orchids from a lei. The flowers dropped the short distance from her fingers to bob on the wavelets. Tears washed her cheeks. I felt I was intruding and turned away.

Dazed, I considered how I don't have any personal connection to World War II. My dad was an infant at the time of the Pearl Harbor bombing. My mom hadn't been born yet. My grandfathers were too old to enlist. Later in the war, my mother's father moved the family to Virginia to build warships to replace those lost in Hawaii. My mom was too young to recall much of that. My grandmother, who would have remembered, is gone now.

I wandered into the memorial's chapel in the room farthest from the hubbub of the dock. An angular framework suggested a modernist stained glass window, except that the panels were open to the sky and water outside. Bright sunlight only emphasized the gloom in the chapel, highlighting a fraction of the 1,177 names on the wall.

Tourists balked at going more than halfway into the shrine. They clustered toward the back of the room, clogging the entrance. I wasn't sure if that was out of respect or from the same instinct that keeps people out of the front pew in church. I sidled through the crowd to get a picture without baseball caps in it.

On my way back to the ferry, the veteran guide said that scuba had been so new in 1941 that the rescue effort was quickly abandoned, even though they knew people survived inside the sunken ships. Among the tourists he'd spoken to had been a Navy diver. While the man dived that December morning, he heard someone banging for the longest time. They couldn't rescue him. The banging came less and less frequently until it eventually stopped.

Even though I hadn't reached the connection I desired, time had come to return to the tour bus. I kept thinking of the Japanese schoolchildren shaking Mason's hand in the Peace Museum. I wondered if Japanese visitors found such courtesy at Pearl Harbor.

In Hiroshima, the exhibits carefully showed why the city had been chosen. America was not blamed for the atrocity commanded by our government. The sense I got from the *Arizona* Memorial was of the beatification of the dead, helplessly martyred by the foe they had been preparing to kill. America did not seem ready yet to take responsibility for its own contributions to the massacre.

San Francisco National Cemetery, San Francisco

STORYBOOK IN STONE

San Francisco National Cemetery, San Francisco, California: June 12, 1994

I'M NO FAN OF MILITARY CEMETERIES. For me, the rows upon rows of nearly identical white tombstones underscore the soullessness inherent in combat. All the same, of the two official graveyards remaining in San Francisco, one is a military cemetery with a breathtaking view of the Golden Gate Bridge. Always curious to know more about the dead, I arrived one Tuesday morning for a free tour of the San Francisco National Cemetery led by Galen Dillman, a docent for the National Park Service.

I'd seen the tour listed in *Park News*, the free quarterly magazine of the National Parks at the Golden Gate. Only once before had I "toured" a graveyard, but now as I became more interested in them, trailing an expert seemed like the best way to learn about a cemetery that didn't reveal much to interest me on a casual visit.

I was nervous as I parked my car outside the white-painted cemetery gate. What kind of people would I meet on the tour? Would they think my interest in graveyards was strange? I hadn't made peace with being morbid yet. I sipped some water from my bottle, steeled myself, and set off to find the Park Service docent.

As it turned out, no one else showed up for the tour that day, so I got a private escort around the cemetery. Luckily, Dillman quivered with enthusiasm for his subject. He didn't seem to mind that I was his only audience.

The cemetery, part of the 1,480-acre Presidio, provides a link to the earliest European history of the San Francisco Bay Area. In 1776, the Spanish founded a garrison here to guard the mouth of San Francisco Bay. When I visited in 1994, no one was quite sure of the location of the original Spanish wall.

In 1922, thirty-eight skeletons—believed to be the remains of Spanish conquistadors—were discovered in an isolated area of the Presidio. The US Army transferred them to a mass grave inside its post cemetery.

In fact, the American history of the Presidio began in 1847—three years before California became a state—when the US Army took it over from Mexico. The Presidio became a Union outpost to prevent Confederate seizure of the gold fields during the Civil War. In the 1870s, the Presidio served as a staging center for the Indian Wars. Later, the Sixth Army used it as their headquarters as they fought World War II in the Pacific.

The original American post cemetery covered nine and a half acres. In 1851, the hillside on which the graveyard stood was all sand dune and scrub. Prior to the discovery of marble in the Sierras, graves were only marked with wood. Dillman told me, "The wind would come up in a storm and send headboards flying all over the place." Consequently, most bodies lost their identification. Dillman said, "The Army reinterred those that they'd lost track of, plus the original Indian, Spanish, and Mexican burial grounds, in front of the visitor center." Now a monument to the unknowns labels the mass grave, saluting the valiant dead of past conflicts.

In 1884, by order of Lieutenant General Sheridan, the Presidio's post cemetery became the first national cemetery on the West Coast. The graveyard expanded as needed until it now covers almost thirty acres.

After its rise in status, a lot of the burials at the San Francisco National Cemetery came from reinterments. As the US Army closed its forts in the West, they refused to leave their dead behind. Also, when San Francisco evicted its public cemeteries early in the 20th century, any military personnel unclaimed by their families were brought to the Presidio.

I was surprised to learn that people didn't have to be stationed at the Presidio to be granted burial there. Dillman explained, "All you had to do was serve in the military and receive an honorable discharge." If a service person doesn't make a reservation in a local cemetery "pre-need," he or she will be buried in the closest open cemetery. At that time, the national cemetery open closest to San Francisco lay southwest of Sacramento, nearer to the Sierras than to the Pacific.

Despite its status as closed since 1992, burials continue in the San Francisco National Cemetery. In fact, a funeral occurred the morning I took the tour. Dillman altered our route to give the mourners a wide berth. He confessed, "The fellow that runs this place tells me that there's actually lots of space left in the graveyard." Much of it had once been spoken for, but went unused when survivors made other arrangements for their departed.

Dillman's fascination was not with graveyards per se, but with the lives marked in them. He continued to research the Presidio's silent residents. He summed it up this way: "Thirty thousand men and women lie buried here, service people that dedicated their lives. Some answered the call when the country needed them and served two or three years. Some served their entire careers in the military. Some gave their lives in defense of the freedoms that we enjoy today. Their voices are silent now, but what I try to do, in my small way, is to tell a little story about each one: what they did and what the country was involved in at the time."

I realized that graveyards could be looked at as history books with pages of stone. I had the good fortune to tour the San Francisco National Cemetery with a man who has a gift for bringing the stories to life. I won't recount them all here (you'll have to take the tour), but I'll pass along some of my favorites.

As we stood at Charles Varnum's grave, Dillman told me the following story. While the Seventh Cavalry prepared to leave Fort Lincoln to fight the Sioux in 1876, General George Custer's wife had a nightmare. She dreamt that Indians held Custer by his long blond hair and scalped him. He went to Varnum, one of his lieutenants, and ordered him to "Get the horse shears and cut my hair." Returning to his wife, Custer said, "See? It can't happen."

Dillman chuckled. "Custer should have listened to his wife."

At the Battle of Little Bighorn, Custer divided the Seventh Cavalry into three troops. He commanded one, with his brother in it. Major Marcus Reno led another troop. The last division was the pack train. Young Charles Varnum took charge of the Indian scouts. Varnum and his scouts escaped. Reno took fire, but also survived. The Sioux wiped out Custer. Varnum, one of the last survivors of the massacre, died in 1936.

Buried in the same row as Varnum is John Gersham, who received his Medal of Honor the day after Varnum received his. Varnum received his medal for the battle of White Clay Creek. Gersham received his for the battle of Wounded Knee—as a member of the Seventh Cavalry. Ten years after the Battle of the Little Bighorn, the Seventh Cavalry and the Sioux met again. That time, the Sioux Nation was destroyed.

Dillman shook his head over the amount of history represented by these two graves. Both Gersham and Varnum served in the Seventh Cavalry. Both men received the Army's Medal of Honor. Both saw firsthand our country's shameful treatment of Native Americans.

At least one Native American lies buried at the Presidio. The informational sign at the entrance to the graveyard, installed by the Army, calls "Two Bits" an Indian scout. His headstone displays a Christian cross and the date October 5, 1873. His real name, like his service record, is lost to history.

The mystery intrigues Dillman. He dug into the cemetery's records—no easy task, apparently—and discovered that the mortal remains of Two Bits had been reinterred from Fort Klamath. Up near the Oregon border, Fort Klamath closed in 1894, after the Indian Wars ended.

Two Bits died two days after the leader of the Modoc rebellion, derisively called Captain Jack, had been hanged. Chances are that Two Bits served as a scout against the Modocs, but no record survives to show if he was Modoc or Klamath.

While up in Klamath for a wedding, Dillman dropped by the local museum, which displays headstones for Captain Jack and two of his lieutenants. Dillman asked the docent there if she knew anything about the Indian who'd once been buried at the old fort. "She got quite indignant," Dillman reported. "She said no Indian had ever been buried there."

He continued searching. He checked the Fort Klamath post records, now on microfiche, but they never mentioned Two Bits.

Another of Dillman's stories concerned one of the rare women buried at the San Francisco National Cemetery. Sarah Bowman followed Zachary Taylor's army throughout the southwest in the 1840s. "Imagine what the West was like in 1840," Dillman suggested, "especially for a woman."

In those days, the Army didn't provide laundry or cooks, so "camp followers" handled those things for the men. A tall, beautiful woman, Sarah Bowman "married freely and frequently," Dillman said. "She would knock you down if you spoke against Zachary Taylor. She took in Mexican or Indian orphans and taught them cooking or tailoring, so they could make their way in the world, but she was very shrewd in her dealings with the Army."

So respected did this camp follower become that when she died of a spider bite in Arizona, she was immediately—posthumously—sworn into the Army so that she could be buried at Fort Yuma. When that fort closed, the Army transferred her body to San Francisco's Presidio.

"She was quite a lady," Dillman said affectionately.

Also buried in the Presidio is Archie Williams. In 1936, Williams ran the 400-meter at the Berlin Olympics, winning the gold medal. Adolf Hitler snubbed Williams and his teammate Jesse Owens, refusing to shake their hands because they were African American.

Upon graduation from the University of California in 1938, Archie Williams had trouble finding work because, Dillman explained, there was so little call for black engineers. Williams became interested in flying and entered the Tuskegee Institute. The quota system of the time guaranteed that if 100 white pilots graduated from flight school, only ten black pilots could graduate from Tuskegee. Williams made the cut and flew in World War II and Korea.

After his retirement from the Air Force, Williams taught high school mathematics in Millbrae, not far from San Francisco.

Toward the end of our tour, Dillman pointed out one final trailblazer. The San Francisco National Cemetery is the resting place of Congressman Philip Burton, who wrote legislation to create the Golden Gate National Recreation Area. The 75,500-acre national park stretches from south of the city in the San Francisco Watershed (which includes the lakes resting atop the San Andreas Fault) north across the Golden Gate past Point Reyes Station and along Tomales Bay. The park spans redwood forests, beaches, marshes, and grassy hillside meadows. Hawks, deer, and seabirds live there, along with an occasional mountain lion, bobcat, and eagle. Whales visit. The park, a haven for city dwellers, has thirteen million visitors a year.

A clause in Burton's bill said that if the Army ever pulled out of the Presidio, the land would be turned over to the National Park Service. When the bill passed into law in 1972, the Army claimed it would never leave. However, in 1989, budget measures closed the base. Transfer to the Park Service occurred in 1994.

In the midst of the parkland, the National Cemetery itself does not belong to the Park Service. It continues to be overseen by the Department of Veteran Affairs. Still, if you're looking to hear a few stories in a peaceful green oasis, I encourage you to check out the

Golden Gate National Recreation Area web site. Its calendar will let you know when you can link up with Galen Dillman's tour. Ask him to tell you about the Buffalo Soldiers, the Union Army's female spy, and the daring rescue from the submarine. He brings those stories to life.

Seamen's Cemetery, Lahaina, Maui

DEEP IN THE MIDDLE OF THE SEA

Seamen's Cemetery and Wainee Churchyard, Lahaina, Maui: April 2, 1997
Keawala'i Churchyard, Maui: April 3, 1997

I SHOULD HAVE ALLOWED MOM to talk me into visiting the Polynesian Cultural Center on Oahu, even though it seemed pricey. Almost a week into our Hawaiian vacation, I still had no grasp of how the natives lived before the outside world crashed in on them on January 18, 1778.

On Maui I found it was easier to imagine the paradise that once had been. Despite the opening of the first Borders Bookstore in the islands, vast stretches of Maui still *looked* wild—or, at least, underdeveloped. The road that led from the Kahului Airport across the neck of the island passed through sugar plantations gone feral. Haleakala towered on our left, 10,000 feet of slumbering volcano craning toward the sun. On the other side of the road climbed the West Maui Mountains, older volcanoes that hunkered down behind the city of Lahaina.

By design, Lahaina still reflects old Hawaii: not the oldest, pre-contact times, but Hawaii in its "Sandwich Island" days, when libertine sailors and straitlaced missionaries wrestled over the future of the Hawaiian people. Modern city ordinance requires that the buildings remain as they did when Lahaina served as the capital of the American Pacific whaling fleet.

More than half of all humpback whales in the world still winter in the waters between Maui and nearby Lana'i. They travel down from Alaska to calve and breed in the warm, shallow waters. Only since 1966 have they been protected. In the 1800s, they were easy pickings.

Lahaina used to be a loud, lawless town where sailors drank and brawled and died. In addition to the old grog shops (now tourist bars) and the missionary home-turned-museum, the US Seamen's Hospital represents that history. The State Department funded the hospital to serve sailors, particularly whalers, who swarmed the island between 1820 and 1860. In 1859, the government investigated rumors that it was being charged per diems for patients who'd already transferred to the Seamen's Cemetery. No charges were ever filed.

Only a small remnant of the Seamen's Cemetery survives. Most of the men buried there had been young, victims of their rigorous life at sea and primitive shipboard health care. Some sailors drowned as the surf swamped their boats when they tried to land at Lahaina.

Among the dead lies one of Herman Melville's cousins, along with a shipmate of Melville's from the whaler *Acushnet*, a black sailor named Thomas Johnson who died at the Seamen's Hospital of a "disreputable disease."

Markers once crammed the cemetery, but those were of necessity inexpensive and impermanent. Ships came and went from Lahaina, leaving behind sick or wounded men to the mercy of strangers. Charity bought most of the grave markers, so they were usually simple painted wood. Currently, only a handful of tombstones still mark the graves of sailors.

The afternoon grew dark as my mother and I explored the old graveyard. Mosquitoes buzzed around, biting our bare legs and raising welts, but I wouldn't be dissuaded, even when fat warm rain dripped from the steely, pregnant clouds and I ran out of film. The old stones that remain had traveled the world to reach this place. I suspect there is no marble in these volcanic islands—and no one to carve it. Anyone who paid to transport a permanent monument all the way from Vermont or even California to Maui made a declaration of their devotion to the deceased.

I paused in front of the granite marker of Helen Lam Moy E., dead in 1909 at the age of 21. Once a portrait rested between carved olive fronds on the front of her monument, but time or vandals had carried it away. Above the missing picture, a little window seemed to open into the stone to enshrine a low relief of a young woman clinging to a massive rugged stone cross: the Rock of Ages beaten by the waves. Above the woman's head roiled clouds. Around the small boulder from which her bare feet had already been swept, waves pounded in from every side. I hummed the last verse of the hymn: "While I draw this fleeting breath, when my eyelids close in death, when I soar to worlds unknown, see Thee on Thy judgment throne, Rock of Ages, cleft for me. Let me hide myself in Thee."

Not far from the Seamen's Cemetery lays Wainee Churchyard,

established in 1823 as the first Christian cemetery in the islands. Hawaiians consider the ground there sacred, since it encloses Queen Keopuolani, wife of King Kamehameha the Great. As the first native aristocrat to be baptized a Christian, Keopuolani wielded enormous influence in the spread of Protestantism.

King Kaumualii, last king of Kauai, rests here, along with High Chief Hoapili; his wife Hoapili Wahine, governor of Maui; Kekauonohi, one of five wives of Kamehameha II and governor of Kauai in her own right; and High Chiefess Liliha, who led a rebellion of a thousand soldiers against the Western government on Oahu in 1830.

Also in the churchyard stands the oldest Christian gravestone in the Hawaiian Islands, remembering a Maui islander who died of "fever" in 1829. Nearby, a simple tablet stone commemorates Kahale M. Kahiamoe, who lived from 1804 to 1908, 104 years, long enough to see the invasion of the outside world, the end of the kapus and the Hawaiian monarchy, and the establishment of Hawaii as a US territory in 1900. Shell leis draped the rusted iron fence enclosing his grave.

The Wainee Church itself no longer stands. Completed in 1832, it was the first stone church in the islands. A whirlwind tore off its roof and knocked down its belfry in 1858. To protest the annexation of Hawaii, native royalists burned the church to the ground in 1894. After it burned again in 1947, it was rebuilt once more. Another windstorm permanently demolished it in 1951.

I found it strange that faith is a rock, but a church of stone might as well have been a sandcastle.

On our last day in Hawaii, I finally got my mom to slow down. I argued that we needed some time on the beach. We'd packed our days so full that, other than a brief rest in the sand after whale watching, we hadn't relaxed anywhere.

Since the condo where we stayed was so isolated, we constantly drove the Piilani "Highway" north back to Lahaina. We'd never gone farther south than the Wailea Shopping Village (read: mall for golfers). Granted, before too long, the island-circling highway downgraded to a street, then a road, then a trail on which we had been forbidden to drive our rental car. Still, I wanted to see a part of the island where tourists seldom ventured.

We headed toward Big Beach, with its view of Molokini across the water. As the road narrowed, it drew closer to the ocean. Between the blacktop and the water stood a low wall of old rough black lava stones. Inside the wall, a cemetery surrounded Keawala'i Church.

"Like to stop?" Mom asked. She knows me too well.

Although the old church had been founded in 1832, the current building dates from 1855, making it the oldest surviving church on Maui (according to some sources). Be that as it may, Keawala'i Church is one of a dozen missionary churches remaining from the mid-1800s. The churches ringed the island, each a full day's horseride from the next. Itinerant preachers traveled the circuit, visiting each church in turn to bring the gospel to the natives.

Keawala'i Church was built in a low New England style with a wood-shingled steeple rising from its peaked roof. Native Hawaiians fashioned the church out of lava rock mortared together with white coral and faced inside with native koa wood.

Mom and I walked around the old church, but didn't go in. I'm uncomfortable wandering into a church uninvited. Unless a place clearly welcomes tourists, I'm more comfortable leaving it alone. I prefer to treat all houses of worship as sacred.

Perhaps in this case, my avoidance had a deeper cause. When Architects Maui, a preservationist outfit, replaced the original 84-year-old floor, they discovered "sensitive cultural remnants" beneath it. I wondered if that meant bodies. In order to protect the "historic materials below," they built a new floor of native ohia hardwood four inches above where the old one had rested. Had the Hawaiians chosen to sanctify the bones of their ancestors by building a church above them?

The name Keawala'i Church appears on the web mostly in connection with wedding planning. Apparently, its Congregationalist minister will perform ceremonies—partially in Hawaiian—after he meets any bride and groom. One of the wedding planners set me off when they directed, "Don't let the cemetery intimidate you, as most churches have them on their sites." In other words, between the church and the ocean lays the graveyard. You can get married inside the church or on the lawn with the church behind you, but make sure your videographer avoids framing the headstones in the background of your bliss.

Or maybe I'm reading too much into it. To me, marriage and the grave simply seem opposite sides of the coin of life.

The palm tree-shaded little graveyard felt very peaceful to me. A lava stone breakwater shielded it on the ocean side, but the surf made a low, sweet accompaniment as we walked amongst the headstones. Most monuments were simple upright blocks on a granite riser or two, surrounded by a cement curb. Many of the stones had ceramic portraits attached to their faces. One of my favorites was David Kimohewa's, in which he propped a guitar on his knee. He looked like a very genial man.

On the very edge of the land clustered small plaques set flush with the ground. At first I thought they represented people whose ashes had been scattered into the ocean, but as I read the epitaphs, the truth dawned on me. These plaques remembered people lost at sea: fishermen, divers, surfers, children, old men, people for whom the families had no bodies to bury. I stood above them and looked out at the water, fighting vertigo. I struggled with the sense of being on an island in the middle of the wide blue Pacific Ocean, a very small rock in a vast cauldron of churning, unpredictable, dangerous, and completely unsympathetic water. I see how having a rock to cling to might be a very necessary thing.

John C. Anderson's gravestone, Pioneer Cemetery, Yosemite National Park

NATURAL PROGRESSION

Pioneer Cemetery, Yosemite National Park, California: August 19, 1997

AS I CAME OUT OF THE LITTLE MUSEUM beside the Yosemite Valley Visitor Center, my mom asked, "Did you know there's a graveyard here? A sign in the gift shop says you can borrow the guide to the cemetery."

I imagine that most people who go to Yosemite National Park want to see waterfalls, wildlife, or spectacular views. I, however, leapt through hoops to borrow the cemetery guide. They didn't have the book for sale in the gift shop because the information was in the process of being updated. Somebody had stolen the last lending copy of the old guide from the gift shop. Dave, the ranger to whom I was directed, sent me on to Linda, the librarian. She handed me a tattered sheaf of papers marked "Desk Copy." She made me solemnly swear to return hers. I was thrilled to be so trusted. It's good to be a card-carrying member of the Association for Gravestone Studies.

Even armed with the photocopied *Guide to the Yosemite Cemetery*, Mom and I couldn't immediately find the Yosemite Pioneer Cemetery. I didn't see any Park Service arrows pointing to it. Its sign hid behind the grocery story and employee housing, between parked cars. Thank goodness for Mom's keen sense of what would interest me, honed over years of family vacations. Without her sharp eye, I wouldn't have known Yosemite Village had a graveyard at all.

The *Road Guide* I purchased in the gift shop said that Indians in the Valley had come out to attack trading posts after Forty-Niners overran their land. The nearby town of Mariposa had organized a battalion to root out the natives and send them to a reservation. The plan was grander than its execution, but the reports that trickled out after the 1851 incursion provided the first published eyewitness accounts of the splendors of Yosemite. The earliest party of tourists arrived four years later. I hadn't realized how early in California's American history white folk had come to Yosemite.

By 1864, California Senator John Conness introduced a bill to the

US Congress to preserve the Valley and the neighboring Mariposa Grove of Sequoias. While the Civil War raged, President Lincoln signed the bill into law, foreshadowing the National Park system. Yosemite's protection came just in time. By 1877, a stagecoach line reached the Valley. On June 24, 1900, the first automobile arrived. The valley would never be the same.

Shadowed by trees and surrounded by a low split-rail fence, the sad-looking graveyard stood empty on this warm summer day. A flood had scoured it free of grass and greenery in January. At summer's end, things had not been allowed to grow back inside the cemetery fence. The hard-packed dirt looked kind of bleak. The guidebook directed us to start in the farthest corner, past grave markers arranged into a handful of uneven lines.

Mom and I walked into the coolness of the graveyard. My Fleur d'Amour hand lotion didn't keep the mosquitoes from molesting me, so I smeared Avon SkinSoSoft over top of it. Mom had some too. I wondered what the pioneers had done about bugs back in the day. At least they hadn't had to worry about getting West Nile virus.

While I took photos, Mom read aloud from the borrowed guidebook. Where possible, it included portraits of the people buried there. It told a little about their lives, more about their deaths, and some about how their graves had been marked and by whom. Its information came from the oral histories of old-timers as well as accounts from local newspapers.

The pamphlet theorized that this area had been chosen for a cemetery at that time because the natives had already used it as a burial ground. The Miwoks and Paiutes did not mark their graves, but Native American remains have been uncovered during construction projects in the Valley over the years.

The earliest grave marker in the cemetery recorded "A Boy." Jack Leidig, who'd grown up in the Valley, remembered him as the first person to be buried in the graveyard in 1870.

At the time of my visit, most of the graves in the Pioneer Cemetery were marked with plain wooden signboards, painted Park Service brown. Some grave monuments had been carved from Yosemite granite, but contrary to my usual Victorian tastes, I found I preferred the unshaped local boulders. It seemed to me that natural rocks suited the setting best.

Galen Clark, the original guardian of Yosemite in 1866, selected a granite boulder for his tombstone and planted six trees to shade his grave. Dave the Ranger told me later that Clark lived for twenty years after he'd planned his grave. Four of his trees still survive.

An enormous slab of local granite commemorated the Hutchings family. "Daughter of Yosemite" Gertrude (Cosie) Hutchings Mills was born in the Valley and lived there on and off throughout her 89 years. She served as postmaster of Yosemite Valley, then as schoolteacher in the village of Wawona, just outside the park's boundary. When she married, she left Yosemite for 42 years, but after she was widowed in 1941, she returned every summer to work in Yosemite Valley, staying in a tent in Tuolumne Meadows. I admired the simplicity of her lifestyle.

A weathered board commemorated Effie Maud Crippen, who died August 31, 1881, "age 14 yrs, 7 mos, 22 days." "She faltered by the wayside and the angels took her home," it said. According to our borrowed guidebook, Effie moved to Yosemite with her family in 1877. She loved the valley and explored it on horseback, sketched it, and described it in her poetry. A photograph from the year before she died shows a serious girl with a thick dark braid, wearing a shin-length skirt and low button boots. Although hard for me to imagine, humans had already begun to litter Yosemite by August 1881. Wading in Mirror Lake, Effie stepped on a broken bottle and severed an artery in her foot. The fourteen-year-old bled to death.

The *Mariposa Gazette* described her gravesite in its September 3, 1881 issue: "Little Effie now sleeps under the shade of the old oak trees near the Yosemite Falls, and we, who are left behind to mourn her loss, almost envy her the peaceful repose, not broken but lulled by the unceasing murmur of the beautiful river." This is the same river that had done 60 million dollars' worth of damage that January.

Not far away from Effie's grave stood a marble marker "In Memory of Albert May, native of Ohio," who also died in 1881. On his stone, two manly hands clasped, signifying friendship. Marble doesn't occur inside the boundaries of Yosemite; the Sierra Nevada Mountains are granite. This stone must have been brought in by mule train to mark May's grave, a lot of work in those days before paved highways. The effort hinted at the high regard his friend A. G. Black—who erected the stone—must have held for him. May worked for Black as a carpenter and caretaker at Black's New Sentinel Hotel. Rocks the size of grapefruit ringed the grave itself. I wondered who had placed them there, whether they were a modern addition or the recreation of something original to the grave.

Gaudy bouquets of silk flowers flanked a marker so worn as to be hardly legible. All across the surface of the grave lay little crosses made from twigs, one stick placed perpendicular across another. The effort involved in collecting and positioning all those twigs was touching, if mystifying. I've never seen anything like it elsewhere.

As I composed a photograph, Mom read Hazel Meyer's life story to me. Her parents had immigrated to America: Elizabeth (Lizzie) McCauley from Belfast, Gerhardt (George) Meyer from Germany. He first proposed in 1884, when Lizzie was 18 and he 37. Sixteen years later, she finally accepted. Hazel was the first of their three children. She died of scarlet fever in 1905, before she was two years old. When she died, both parents were too ill with the same scarlet fever to attend her funeral. A simple fence of rusting iron pipes, the kind plumbers use, surrounded her grave.

John C. Anderson's marker declared that he "was killed by a horse on the 5th of July 1867." "Beloved by all," it said. On his stone, a willow bent under the weight of its own branches like a person burdened by grief. The faded inscription had sunk into the ground. Luckily, the guidebook recorded it:

> Be ye also ready for ye know
> not the hour the Son of Man cometh
> Dearest Brother, tho had left us,
> Here thy loss we deeply feel.

When gold fever struck him in 1856, Anderson traveled from Illinois to stake a claim in Yosemite Valley. The gold claim didn't pan out as richly as the hotel he and three other prospectors built for travelers to Yosemite. He served as the hotel's coachman on the day he died.

Contradicting the date on the stone, the *Mariposa Gazette* reported that Anderson had been kicked by a horse and died almost instantly on July 13, 1867. In fact, the authors of the guidebook found many errors in the birth and death dates on the gravestones. Either these were a function of the delay in getting the news to Mariposa to be published or, as in Anderson's case, the extreme time required to import the marble stone to mark his grave.

Originally, Anderson had been buried at the foot of the Four-Mile Trail, before being exhumed and moved to the Pioneer Cemetery. Tradition relates that his friends thrust his green locust-wood switch into the ground to mark his first grave. All locust trees in the valley supposedly descend from that green grave marker. I liked the romance of the story, even if the locusts are invasive. Ansel Adams made a beautiful photograph of them shrouded in snow.

In the old days, people had been buried all over the park, where they fell or near places they'd loved. At some point, all the bodies that could be located were gathered together into the graveyard. I should've asked Ranger Dave when that happened.

Before long, Mom and I had thoroughly explored the little patch of ground. Despite the bare dirt, the shaded pioneer cemetery felt very peaceful. At one point, two kids chased each other by, without disturbing the morning. The 10 a.m. sunlight slanted through the leaves. Bright green and dusty yellow light dappled the dark rust-red earth.

How wonderful to be able to be buried in a place you loved so well. I thought of the other Gold Rush-era graveyards I've visited, where people—often children—had been buried and left behind. Here, in this quiet, tucked-away corner in one of the busiest tourist destinations in the country—averaging four million visitors annually—these permanent residents had become part of the living history forever. Even if their lives had been brief and their deaths agonizing or sad, their spirits had been woven into the beauty of the valley. I felt honored to have met them.

When I returned the battered sheaf of paper to the librarian, I left my address so she could let me know when the booklet came back into print. I wanted a memento for my library. After the *Guide to the Yosemite Cemetery* came, I devoured it cover to cover.

Al Jolson's monument, Hillside Memorial Park, Culver City, California

HEROES OF FILMLAND

Hillside Memorial Park and Holy Cross Cemetery, Culver City, California:
August 31, 1997

"WHERE ARE WE GOING?"

"It's a surprise," my old friend Brian promised. He just kept driving. We traveled through parts of Los Angeles I'd never seen before, swank parts. My sweaty back stuck to his pickup's black leatherette seat. Brian's surprises take strange forms, sometimes. I gazed at him suspiciously, hoping he'd cave.

"You wanted to see Al Jolson's grave, right?"

Al Jolson, star of the original talking picture, reportedly had one of the most ostentatious grave sites in Southern California. After Douglas Fairbanks' shrine with its white marble columns and seemingly Olympic-sized reflecting pool at Hollywood Forever, that's saying something.

Trying to worm more information out of Brian, I asked, "Is that where we're going?"

He just grinned. "First."

Just inside the gateway at Hillside Memorial Park, the Jolson monument was impossible to miss. In fact, *Permanent Californians: An Illustrated Guide to the Cemeteries of California* says the monument has become a landmark along the San Diego Freeway. A two-story waterfall (unfortunately, switched off for repairs during our visit) stepped five blue-tiled levels down the hillside. On the grassy knoll at the head of the falls stood a round Grecian-style temple like the temple of Athena at Delphi. The six white marble columns blazed in the SoCal sun. Jolson's third wife paid $75,000 for the monument in 1950.

Brian drove me around to the other side of the public mausoleum behind Jolson's memorial, where we parked. Interred inside the mausoleum are David Janssen (TV's original *"Fugitive"*) and Jack

Benny. Ignoring them, we strolled through the mausoleum with a purpose. Mausoleums, those cubbyhole condos for the dead, are profitable space-savers for cemetery management, but I find them generally too repetitive to explore. Where's the individuality behind matching marble tablets?

Jolson's grave was the antithesis of the modern mausoleum. Its columns soared skyward, supporting a brilliantly colored mosaic of Moses resting the Ten Commandments (written out in Hebrew) against his shoulder. Surrounding the mosaic ran the inscription, "Sweet singer of Israel, man raised up high": King David's last words from the second book of Samuel.

I'd mistakenly expected the nearby bronze statue of Jolson—down on one knee, arms flung wide—to be gigantic. Instead, it was smaller than life-size. He smirked as if he'd just belted out, "Mammy, how I love ya, how I love ya!" His blackface performance is not one of American film's finest moments. It might be justly forgotten, without the benefit of being in the first motion picture with sound—and if not for this amazing display of funerary art.

New mausoleum cubbies stood at the foot of the hill. The poured cement cubicles looked like square nodes in a honeycomb, a hive for the dead. Brian scrambled into one of the vacancies to check it for size, but I'm much too superstitious for that.

"You know," I said, paging through the copy of *Permanent Californians* I'd given him, "Vic Morrow is buried in Hillside."

"Do you want to try and find his grave?"

"Sure. Why not?"

Vic Morrow, star of *Humanoids from the Deep* and *The Bad News Bears*, hadn't made an impression on me until his last film. The 1983 *Twilight Zone* movie wasn't good or particularly scary, but it had the pre-release publicity that Morrow had sacrificed his life to make it. As John Landis illegally filmed his climactic Vietnam sequence one night, Morrow carried two kids across a simulated rice paddy in the Santa Clara River. One of the FX explosions went off too close to the helicopter above them, swatting it out of the sky. The rotors sliced through Morrow, decapitating him and dismembering both children.

The second *Death Scenes* video relived the moment again and again, displaying film from all of the cameras recording that night. The scene had been expensive to shoot and Landis wanted to make sure that he caught the action on film. He certainly did.

Permanent Californians gave us only the vaguest coordinates to Morrow's grave, limiting our search to Block 5 of the Mount Olive section. Brian and I fanned out, each taking a row of bronze markers. If there's anything I hate more than soulless mausoleums, it's bronze grave markers set flush with the turf to ease mowing.

Finally, as we were about to give up the hunt, I stumbled across Morrow's headstone. Eloquent in its simplicity, it said only, "I loved him as 'Dad.' To everyone else, he was 'Vic.'"

I blinked at tears. Here I'd wanted to see the resting place of the man I'd watched die—in horror, I'll admit, although I certainly didn't switch off the videotape. Facing his memorial, I was forced to consider the family and friends he'd left behind. Vic Morrow was loved and missed. My reasons to visit him would have appalled his survivors. Chastened, I asked Brian, "Where else did you want to go?"

He squinted into the setting sun. "We'll have to hurry, but I think we can make it."

Holy Cross, it goes without saying, is a Catholic cemetery. It hadn't occurred to me that Hungarian-born Bela Lugosi had been Catholic. I knew he'd been addicted to morphine and that he'd been buried in his tuxedo and black silk opera cape, but I hadn't known what the man who'd portrayed my first literary crush had believed about his immortal soul.

"I wish I'd known we were coming here," I told Brian. "I would have bought him some roses."

I grew up watching Sir Graves Ghastly host horror movies on Saturday afternoons, never understanding the homage. Sir Graves seemed to be an elderly man in white tie and tails, hosting movies in a thick, obviously fake accent which I now realize he'd cribbed from Lugosi. Sir Graves showed all the classic black-and-white horror movies of the Thirties, Forties, and Fifties. Looking back, I recognize that the show was aimed at children. A "Ghoul Gallery" displayed children's drawings inspired by monsters they'd seen on the show. That part always bored me. I simply wanted to see the heroines in their silk peignoirs swooning in the moonlight to be carried off by Boris Karloff or Lon Chaney, Jr. or Lugosi himself. Even as a child, I wasn't sure if I wanted to be the heroine or the monster, but I knew I wanted nothing to do with the villagers and their torches.

The first vision of Lugosi standing on the castle steps, cape draped around him and eyes twinkling with reflected candlelight, changed my life. I would have died to be there with him, away from the farm and the small Michigan town where I grew up. When I saw Lugosi, I understood that I needed to escape.

I'd stood at a lot of grave sites, but never before at one whose occupant had so altered and inspired my life. The marker was too simple to convey the depth of my admiration for the man below. Illustrating the stone was a polished black granite rose twining around a plain cross marked "I H S," the abbreviation for Jesus in Greek. The epitaph listed only his name, "Beloved Father," and 1882-1956.

Brian slipped away to allow me a few moments to commune with my idol.

As we strolled away from the grave arm in arm, a young man approached us. "Um, please don't think I'm a stalker, but I saw you wandering around the other graveyard. You wouldn't happen to know where Bela Lugosi is buried, would you?"

We laughed and led him back. "Down the row from Bing Crosby," Brian pointed out.

"Really?" The man moved to photograph that grave as well. "I'm a member of the LA Grim Society," he said, by way of introduction. "I want to put a photographic tour of all LA's celebrity graves on their web site."

I told him about *Death's Garden*, the cemetery book I'd published which included one of Brian's essays about Hotel Resurrection, a Venezuelan graveyard wiped out afterward by horrendous mudslides.

"It sounds as if you'd be interested in seeing Sharon Tate's grave," our new friend said. "She's back up this way."

He led us toward the grotto at the top of the hill. A grotto is a small cave, usually artificial, in a garden or park. In Europe, natural grottoes like the one at Lourdes are considered sacred sites, where Christian or even earlier miracles have occurred. In Los Angeles, they build their own grottoes and no one expects miracles. This pile of rocks hosted several white marble statues: the Virgin in prayer, Joseph displaying the baby, and several kneeling angels who looked as if they'd been meant to adore at a crèche rather than gaze at the sod. Someone had placed flowers in front of one of the angels' knees.

Not far from the grotto lay a polished granite slab with incised lettering painted white. The left side remembered "Our Loving Daughter & Beloved Wife of Roman," twenty-six-year-old Sharon Tate Polanski, as well as Paul Richard, "Their Baby."

I gasped. According to *Helter Skelter*, Susan Atkins made a point of stabbing Sharon—who was eight months pregnant—in the belly, intentionally killing the child before it could be born. As horrifying as I found the incomprehensible murders, I could barely grasp that Polanski had named his unborn child before burying him.

The late afternoon sunlight had turned the color of molten copper. Someone soon would come to chase us out of the graveyard, so we said our goodbyes and turned to take a few last photos.

"Was Lugosi's grave a good surprise?" Brian asked when we'd climbed back into the pickup.

"One of the best."

Vintage advertisement for Forest Lawn Memorial Park, Glendale, California

WHAT'S WRONG WITH FOREST LAWN?

Forest Lawn Memorial Park, Glendale, California: November 2, 1997

"I shall endeavor to build Forest Lawn as different, as unlike other cemeteries as sunshine is unlike darkness, as Eternal Life is unlike Death. I shall try to build at Forest Lawn a great park, devoid of misshapen monuments and other customary signs of earthly Death..." — The Builder's Creed

I BLAME FOREST LAWN FOR ALMOST EVERYTHING that's wrong with modern cemeteries. Hubert Eaton, "The Builder," is responsible for reducing headstones to bronze plaques, for placing monuments flush with the ground, giving us the featureless lawns of "memorial parks." That these wrong, ugly elements were pioneered at Forest Lawn meant that I *had* to visit the place and that I should write about it. Clearly, this place comforts some people or it wouldn't have succeeded or been so influential. Still, I'd bet that if you were to visit, you'd agree that everything was off-kilter from the moment you're met at the street by the largest wrought iron gates in the world ("Bigger than Buckingham Palace's!"). Forest Lawn prides itself on its Disneyfication of death.

It wasn't always this way. In 1913, Forest Lawn Cemetery was merely fifty-five peaceful acres on the edge of Tropico (now Glendale) in Southern California. Failed metallurgist and mine owner Hubert Eaton came west seeking another fresh start and took over the small graveyard. One of his former investors gave him a stake, with the understanding that this scheme had better succeed.

Eaton was not the first to sell grave plots to families still living: that had been pioneered by Boston's Mount Auburn Cemetery (America's first nondenominational garden cemetery) in 1832. However, Eaton *was* the first to be aggressive about "pre-need" sales, going door to door to evangelize about the peace of mind one could have, knowing one's family wouldn't be shopping for a gravesite during the sharpest pangs of their grief. To his credit, Eaton adamantly believed that plots at Forest Lawn should not be sold as property speculation (in which the price of burial space increases as the cemetery fills), but that they be purchased as a familial obligation, like buying insurance. Soon afterward, he'd sold most of the original cemetery and bought up the surrounding land. Forest Lawn Glendale now occupies 303 acres.

Finally flush, Eaton undertook a tour of Europe, visiting cemeteries and art museums, looking for "improvements" he could transplant to his own burial ground. For the most part, Eaton—a staunch Baptist—found cemeteries depressing. Strangely enough, he thought they put too much emphasis on death, loss, and pain. Eaton found the fields of sculpted stone ugly. He came back with a revolutionary idea: henceforth, aboveground monuments would be forbidden at Forest Lawn. In their place, the cemetery would provide occasional marble sculptures on authorized subjects like motherhood or valor. The very wealthy could purchase one of these pre-approved monuments to mark their graves. He restricted everyone else to a bronze marker set into the sod, because bronze did not chip when driven over by a lawnmower. It depresses me to see people's lives reduced to a bronze plaque scarcely larger than a laptop: all that they were, all that they loved, reduced to a name and dates and an epitaph suggested by the management.

Not surprisingly, many people felt the same way. Ralph Hancock in his hagiography of Eaton called *The Forest Lawn Story* said, "Forest Lawn underwent the experience of seeing would-be purchasers turn and leave Forest Lawn without purchasing because they could not have a tombstone." Eaton needed another scheme to draw people to his establishment.

He went out of his way to entice the living to use Forest Lawn. Easter sunrise services drew thousands. The cemetery's churches could be rented for weddings and christenings. Among the amenities offered: the Ring of Aldyth, a stone loop through which bridal couples could clasp hands and pledge their devotion, and a Wishing Chair that promised success for everyone exchanging bridal kisses there. In 1955, Hancock wrote, "More people have been married in Forest Lawn's churches than in any other church in America." Of course, that's a comparison of six Forest Lawn churches to any single church elsewhere, but it sounds impressive, doesn't it?

In 1933, Forest Lawn became the first cemetery in the world to offer on-site mortuary services. The innovative idea—that, in addition to a place to stash the body, a graveyard could provide a coffin, embalming, flowers, grave marker: all the accoutrements required for a good middle-class funeral—had to be approved by the Third District Court of Appeals in the California state capital. Evelyn Waugh later sent up the one-stop shopping idea in his comic novel, *The Loved One*, in which Dennis Barlow woos mortuary cosmetician Aimee Thanatogenos under the watchful eye of Mr. Joyboy. It doesn't seem to me, given that speakers broadcasting hymns really do hang in Forest Lawn's shrubbery, that Waugh embellished much.

To this day, Forest Lawn is a cemetery that denies death. "The Builder" didn't want anything challenging or threatening or sad in his masterpiece, so he forbade depictions of grief and sorrow. Even the painting of the Crucifixion that hangs in Forest Lawn's purpose-built hall has no death in it. The thieves have yet to be nailed to their crosses. Christ waits patiently for his sentence to be carried out. Forest Lawn's literature hypes the painting (tall as a twenty-story building, if it were stood on end!) as the only depiction in the world of Christ awaiting his martyrdom. Guess all those images of Christ at Gethsemane don't count.

As an institution used to selling itself to the world, of course Forest Lawn has a gift shop. No, I've never bought anything there. It may be the only cemetery in the world that doesn't sell a single thing I need to have. I'm not sure who would want a glossy calendar of their cheesy marble statuary, or a knockoff tchotchke of their version of David, complete with fig leaf never sculpted by Michelangelo. I'd buy a postcard of W.C. Field's grave marker in a minute, but Forest Lawn's artwork is about as inspirational as a *Precious Moments* figurine, safe as a gift for Grandma and ultimately flavorless.

Although they carefully don't use it as a marketing tool, Forest Lawn is the final resting place for many of Hollywood's famous names. L. Frank Baum (author of *The Wizard of Oz*) rests under a heavy upright granite monument in the original section of the graveyard. Clark Gable and Carole Lombard supposedly lie in the Sanctuary of Trust, but I haven't been able to locate them. Even with *Permanent Californians* or more recently cemetery guidebooks, it is difficult to find anyone. Forest Lawn doesn't sell maps of graves like Hollywood Forever does.

On my first visit to Forest Lawn in 1994, I met a nice older gentleman who had his finger stuck in a copy of *Permanent Californians* as he scanned the grave markers. He'd checked the book out of the library where he lived in Hollywood. I felt less like a tourist when I knew locals went stargazing, too.

On that first trip, we found absolutely no one of interest interred in the Freedom Hall Mausoleum. My friend Brian and I looked and looked while Mason sat on a marble bench and leafed through the guidebook. Some of the alcoves were private, blocked with heavy chains. I contented myself that the marble façade on the walls was particularly pretty, a pink that looked like watered silk.

Outside the mausoleum hung a length of the biggest chain I'd ever seen. The links were definitely bigger that a breadbox. This segment of chain had stretched across Boston Harbor to keep out the British ships during the Revolution. I had the sense that it was there because Eaton could afford it. It must count as a tourist draw for a very small subsection of people.

In a neighboring garden sat a little bronze mermaid. She marked the grave of Walter Elias Disney. *Permanent Californians* acknowledges that he investigated cryonics—having himself frozen until his lung cancer could be cured—but "the best evidence suggests that his ashes are here in the family vault." I can't help feeling that the yeti on the Matterhorn ride might be a more appropriate grave marker. Disney Studios didn't make a mermaid movie until twenty-three years after Walt's passing.

Nearby lies Errol Flynn, whom you probably remember as Robin Hood. In contrast to Douglas Fairbanks' grand marble shrine at Hollywood Forever, Flynn has a simple bronze marker that remembers him as a father. He's rumored to be buried there with six bottles of whiskey.

On a later trip to Forest Lawn, Brian and I admired the monument to Aimee Semple McPherson. Sister Aimee was one of the first evangelists to employ radio to bring God to the masses. In her temple at Echo Park, Aimee produced extravagant sermons, complete with costume changes and live animals. Blinding white marble benches and angels marked her grave, a complete departure from the soulless, nearly invisible monuments surrounding her. I wondered how much the church had paid to bend Forest Lawn's rules.

While we gaped, a woman stopped by to chat. "Do you know Sister?" she asked.

"I've read her sermons," I answered. They'd been part of the text in my history of speechwriting class.

"You ought to come join us at the Temple sometime. Sister's work lives on." With a beatific smile, the woman took her brushes and bucket up the hill to wash the already luminous marble.

She was the only attendant we saw anywhere in the cemetery that Saturday. For all its claims that "Forest Lawn serves the living," the living don't seem to be tempted to spend much time there. Forest Lawn discourages visitors by prohibiting loitering or picnicking. Lying in the grass or even hiking across the lawn is forbidden. Pets are not allowed. The wildlife mustn't be fed. Cut flowers or potted plants are the only acceptable grave decorations—and they must be placed atop the marker to "protect the grass." One might suspect that Forest Lawn has roped its residents in, taken their money, and now their families are an inconvenience that might cause a scene or make a mess. Just as sorrow is banned from Forest Lawn's artwork, grief also seems to be discouraged on its grounds.

The Italian Benevolent Society tomb, Saint Louis Cemetery #1
New Orleans

BASIN STREET BLUES

Saint Louis Cemetery #1, New Orleans: January 25, 1998

I FIRST VISITED NEW ORLEANS in 1988 for the World Science Fiction Convention. A bunch of friends from my class of the Clarion Writing Workshop had planned a reunion. Seeing them was great, but the introduction to New Orleans was even better. When a friend of the group suggested a tour of the old graveyard as a way to see the real New Orleans behind the tourist façade, I leaped at the chance. We met at the tourist bureau after a breakfast I could barely afford at Antoine's.

The original graveyard for the city of New Orleans had been dug at the settlement's edge, near what is now Orleans and Burgundy Streets in the French Quarter. Opened in 1725, Saint Peter's Cemetery quickly filled to capacity. When a royal decree founded the first Saint Louis Cemetery on August 14, 1789, families received six months to move their dead from Saint Peter's to the new graveyard. Despite that, workmen in 2011 found thirteen cypress coffins when digging a swimming pool on the site of the former cemetery. Cypress, which grows in water, never rots. Unfortunately, where there's one coffin, there are probably more.

At least one of the residents of Saint Peter's was moved and still rests in Saint Louis #1. His grave is decorated with a medallion commemorating the Revolutionary War, fought twelve years before the Saint Louis Cemetery opened.

The "new" graveyard, like the Cathedral in Jackson Square, is named for Louis IX, the thirteenth-century king of France. He funded Sainte-Chapelle in Paris, gave alms generously, twice crusaded to the Holy Land, and urged the Greek Orthodox Church to reunite with Rome. He was canonized in 1297.

Both Saint Louis Cemetery #1 and the graveyard that followed it in 1823 (called Saint Louis #2) are situated within the area of New Orleans that came to be known as Storyville. The infamous red-light district operated legally from 1897 to 1917 and gave birth to jazz.

After the parlor houses were torn down, the Iberville Housing Projects, built in 1949, now separate #1 from #2. *Access New Orleans* warns that Saint Louis #1 "is one of the most dangerous cemeteries in town. The only way to see it safely is with a group tour."

When my husband Mason and I visited together in January 1998, Tim and Wendy, who recorded as DogStar Communications, served as our guides. Wendy often worried about our safety in New Orleans. A mutual friend had been robbed at shotgun point while riding through New Orleans on his bicycle. Wendy hadn't been mugged herself, but she'd been home alone in the Faubourg Marigny one night when someone tried to break through her apartment's back door. The summer before our visit, one of the horse carriage *drivers* at Jackson Square shot and killed a British tourist in an argument over the fare. The tourist bureau hushed the story up to protect the primary industry in town.

Wendy, bless her, was a fan of *Death's Garden*, the cemetery book I'd edited. She knew I couldn't come to New Orleans and keep out of the graveyards. She believed that the four of us would be fine braving Saint Louis #1 during the afternoon.

Although Saint Louis #1 is the oldest surviving cemetery in New Orleans, it's only a shadow of its former self. The Varney family pyramid, near the current entrance on Basin Street, once stood at the geographic center of the graveyard. The pyramid, circa 1810, is one of the earliest tombs that survives. The oldest marked grave, adorned with a simple iron cross, remembers Antoine Bonabel, who died in February 1800. Although older graves are known to exist, none still have their original markers.

The oven vaults lining the Basin Street wall also once stood near the center of the cemetery. Called ovens because of their appearance, the wall vaults foreshadowed the drawers in modern mausoleums. Owned by the Archdiocese, these vaults are leased to families who can't afford private tombs. Several restrictions govern their use: the deceased must be Catholic, must be buried in a wooden coffin, and must lie undisturbed at least a year and a day. The specified mourning time allows the tropical heat to decompose the body inside the vault.

After the passage of 366 days, the marble slab may be detached from the mouth of the vault, the brick end cap chipped out, the coffin fragments removed, and another member of the family slipped inside. In deference to the survivors, a black curtain hangs at the back of the vault to hide the reservoir, called a *caveau*, where the bones of all past occupants lie. Also, the newest coffin isn't shoved all the way home, to spare the survivors the sound of the previous tenant's bones tumbling down into the caveau. This reuse of graves is perhaps the most unusual attribute of cemeteries in New Orleans.

Most visitors are struck by the little grave houses beyond the walls of oven vaults. Historians trace the small tombs to Spain, where the soil was too rocky for interment. In New Orleans, the ground is too damp.

Rather than bury their dead in the soggy earth, wealthy Catholics in New Orleans placed the casket atop a slab, then raised a small brick tomb around it. The bricks were plastered over, then whitewashed.

Whereas the oven vaults are leased year by year, these family tombs are purchased from the Archdiocese for 99 years and 364 days. Families take responsibility for their upkeep: whitewashing them, removing graffiti, patching the roof and ironwork. Since the tombs are in a sense private property, the hundred-year deed may be sold. New families usually keep the names of the former residents on the plaques, since the old bones remain jumbled with the new inside the central caveau.

The most famous resident of Saint Louis #1 may or may not be the Voodoo Queen, Marie Laveau. In 1998, the Glapion tomb would have been nondescript but for the trios of brick red X's defacing it. *Access New Orleans* records that the grave is inscribed (in French): "Here lies Marie Philome Glapion, deceased June 11, 1897, aged sixty-two years. She was a good mother, a good friend, and 'regretted' by all who knew her. Passersby, please pray for her."

The death date of 1897 is not the famous Marie's, but closer to her namesake daughter Marie's. Many people believe the remains of the two Maries were switched between Saint Louis #1 and its younger sibling, Saint Louis #2. Robert Florence, author of *City of the Dead*, suggests that Marie Laveau's bones, wherever they once lay, were cleared out of her vault after her entombment, since "bones are one of the most popular forms of gris-gris."

According to the *New Orleans Cemeteries* volume of the *Images of America* series, the "tradition" of breaking a brick off of one of the neighboring tombs to scrawl on the Glapion mausoleum began in the

1960s. The surviving Glapions and the Archdiocese of New Orleans see the ritual as vandalism. Still, encouraged by tour guides, people continue to leave offerings at the Glapion tomb and ask Marie Laveau, wherever she may be, for favors.

Other famous residents in Saint Louis #1 include Homer Plessy (plaintiff in the 1896 Supreme Court case that established the "separate but equal" doctrine, overturned by *Brown v. Board of Education* in 1954), land developer Bernard de Marigny (for whom New Orleans's Faubourg Marigny is named), Etienne de Bore (first mayor of New Orleans and first to granulate sugar commercially, creating the local industry), Mayor Ernest "Dutch" Morial (New Orleans's first black mayor), and Paul Morphy (the first US chess champion). In the city's earliest days, there was no division between black and white in its graveyards or its caveaus. Segregation began only after America made the Louisiana Purchase in 1803.

Segregation of another sort began at the same time. Since the Catholic Archdiocese owned the only burial ground in town in 1805, they leased an unsanctified area to Protestant immigrants to New Orleans. French Catholics called the area "the Cemetery of Heretics." Behind a big ugly spite fence, a fragment of that Protestant section still exists.

In 1819, Benjamin Henry Boneval Latrobe recorded his *Impressions Respecting New Orleans* about visiting the Protestant section of Saint Louis #1: "There are two or three graves open and expecting their tenants; eight or nine inches below the surface, they are filled with water and were not three feet deep. Thus, all persons here are buried in the water."

Which is the strangest thing: Protestants in New Orleans clung to the commandment "Ashes to ashes, dust to dust." They wanted to be buried in the ground, however soupy. Heavy slabs had to be placed atop graves to keep coffins from floating to the surface. In many places in the old Protestant section, the heavy tablets sank into the ground to be covered by grass.

Once buried in the Protestant section of Saint Louis Cemetery, Latrobe's "remains may have been lost" during the exodus to the newer Girod Street Cemetery, according to *New Orleans Cemeteries: Life in the Cities of the Dead.* The venerable cemetery website Findagrave.com has a theory that because Latrobe died of yellow fever, he was hastily buried in a mass grave. Either way, a plaque on the wall at Saint Louis commemorates Latrobe as "founder of the architectural profession in America." He designed the US Capitol Building in Washington, DC after the British burned it during the War of 1812.

Near Latrobe's marker stands a large square marble monument, which Latrobe designed, for the wife and child of the first American governor of Louisiana. Mother and daughter died from yellow fever on the same day. A relief on their monument shows Eliza Claiborne on her deathbed, dead infant at her breast. An angel prepares to place a wreath on the mother's brow while the distraught widower kneels at her feet. The epitaph promises, "For the virtuous there is a better world." Governor William Charles Cole Claiborne was briefly entombed here himself, before being moved to grander digs in Metairie Cemetery in 1880. Two of his wives remain behind in Saint Louis #1.

One of my favorite monuments in the Protestant Section of Saint Louis #1 lies in a bed of concrete. The tablet, once upright, had been erected to the memory of Thomas Slaughter, Shipmaster, who drowned in the Mississippi River. His epitaph reads, "The high roling [sic] Waves & loud Blowing Tempest, I have left to the Living; for here I am anchor'd in Peace, waiting the Return of the Tide of Life."

When the city cut an extension of Treme Street through the Protestant part of the cemetery, it offered land in Faubourg Saint Marie for a new graveyard. Graves were relocated to the Episcopalian Girod Street Cemetery when it opened in 1822. In turn, Girod Street Cemetery was deconsecrated in 1957, then dismantled and partially covered when they built the Superdome. The Girod Street graves formerly stood beneath the Saints' end zone; for four decades, the New Orleans Saints were the only national league team who'd never won a title. Many people believed they'd been cursed by the Protestants they displaced.

The whitewashed tombs in St. Louis #1 were almost blinding in the weak January sun. I wanted to believe that such a bright place must be safe, but even after repeated visits to Saint Louis #1, I still haven't learned my way around. It would be easy to get cornered in a cul-de-sac amidst the maze of tombs, although that assumes the robbers have memorized the tour schedules. There are so many tour companies in New Orleans offering cemetery tours that it seemed another group was always coming along. I wondered if the danger had been overstated as a way to cut down the vandalism of the graves or raise the income of the tour guides.

Since the days of the penny postcard, the aboveground tombs of New Orleans have drawn tourists. I didn't feel the least bit shy about using my camera, with friends along to watch my back.

We prowled among the tombs for a satisfyingly long time. Eventually, Wendy said, "If you want to meet the Voodoo priestess, we'd better get over to her temple."

"We've been to the Voodoo Museum," Mason pointed out.

"That's Voodoo for tourists," Tim said. "This is the real thing."

Wendy was so excited about making the introduction for us that I put away my camera.

Update: Because of ongoing vandalism in the graveyard, the Archdiocese of New Orleans no longer allows anyone to visit St. Louis Cemetery #1 without an official tour. One of the best is offered by Save Our Cemeteries.

Portal of the Folded Wings, Valhalla Memorial Park Cemetery
North Hollywood

WITH FOLDED WINGS

Valhalla Memorial Park Cemetery, North Hollywood, California
March 8, 1998

I'M THE SORT OF PERSON who likes to look out the window whenever I fly. It started as a way to deal with my claustrophobia on a plane, but I soon discovered how fascinating the world is when you float above it. Details reveal themselves that you would never notice on the ground.

The first time I flew out of Bob Hope Airport in Burbank during the day, I noticed a long green field at the end of the runway. In Southern California, the only types of real estate that remain so green are golf courses and graveyards. This field had several fountains and lots of roadways. It obviously fell into the second category.

Next time I came down to visit my friend Brian, I asked about the cemetery. We drove past a Fry's Electronics with a flying saucer motif, then turned down a dead-end road. At the end of the cul-de-sac towered a baroque 120-foot-tall dome, spotlighted against the night sky. It crawled with rococo ornamentation: twisted columns, alcoves, seashells, urns, shrouded female figures: a thoroughly amazing sight.

"What is that?" I asked.

"It's called the Portal of the Folded Wings," Brian answered.

"That sounds ominous, standing so close to an airport."

"Want to come back this weekend and see?"

When we consulted Brian's copy of *Permanent Californians*, one chapter told about Valhalla Memorial Park Cemetery. The dome's full name was "The Portal of the Folded Wings – Shrine to Aviation and Museum," an awkward turn of phrase if ever I saw one. Brian and I needed to investigate exactly what that meant.

When we returned to the cemetery in the daylight, we quickly discovered that—just as it had appeared from the air—Valhalla is a level green field. Grave markers had been set into the ground for ease of mowing. Without the two fountains or rows of cedars, the memorial park looked featureless and unappealing.

The most famous person buried in Valhalla is Oliver Hardy, the rounder half of Laurel and Hardy. His grave lies south of the fountain in the Garden of Hope. His marker said only "Beloved Husband." However, that didn't satisfy The Sons of the Desert (the international Laurel & Hardy appreciation society), who placed a plaque to him on the garden wall in 1977. That read, "A genius of comedy—His talent brought joy and laughter to all the world." It made me smile to see people organize to make such a sweet gesture.

Also buried at Valhalla are Curly Joe DeRita, the "Last Stooge," who replaced Shemp Howard; the psychic Criswell, best remembered now for his part in *Plan Nine from Outer Space*; the woman who played the bailiff on *Night Court*; both Commander Cody, Sky Marshall of the Universe, and Rocky Jones, Space Ranger; silent-era sirens the Girl with the Million Dollar Legs and the Girl with the Bee-Stung Lips; munchkins and flying monkeys; Mae (Violet) Clark, who played the doctor's fiancée Elizabeth in the 1931 *Frankenstein*; and Aneta Corsaut, who played Steve McQueen's girlfriend in *The Blob*. Even performing animals rest there. Circumventing the prohibition against pets being buried with their owners, animal trainer Rudd Weatherwax asked for his casket to be lined with the ashes of his beloved dogs, so they could be together for eternity. He'd trained several of the movie Lassies and twenty years'·worth of TV-show dogs.

In the featureless meadow, we found it difficult to locate individual graves. Brian and I gave up looking for anyone we recognized and made our way back to the towering dome. Built in 1924 as the Valhalla Memorial Rotunda, the structure originally served as entryway to the cemetery. With its pleasant acoustics, it functioned as a concert hall and venue for radio broadcasts. That ended once the Burbank airport opened in 1930. In the heady days of early aviation, perhaps it didn't seem ominous to build an airport beside a cemetery.

The five-story dome soared above us. Its exterior was tiled in sky blue and terracotta, cream and pale orange—colors of a sunset—laid out in a geometric, arabesque pattern. Rococo versions of all the Victorian death symbols frosted the supporting base and cap work, along with the facings of the arched entries: inverted torches, ornate urns, wreaths, robed muses with downcast eyes. Above it all presided a graceful lady with outstretched arms, her gown swept back around her legs. Did she welcome visitors? Hail fallen flyers? Invoke a plane crash?

Six years after his arrival in the US, Federico A. Giorgi received a commission to create decorative castings for the temporary buildings of the 1915 Panama Pacific International Exposition in San Francisco. At the dawn of the silent film era, he designed a scene called "Balthazar's Feast" in D. W. Griffith's *Intolerance*. Valhalla Memorial Park hired him to sculpt its grand entry, which opened in 1925. When he died in 1963, they laid him to rest in the lawn near his masterpiece.

For twenty years, one of the cemetery employees—an aficionado of aviation—strove to repurpose the dome into a shrine to the pioneers of flight. On December 17, 1953, the 50th anniversary of the Wright Brothers' flight over Kitty Hawk, the cemetery rechristened the dome and placed the ashes of some pioneer aviators under its floor: consecrating the space, in a way.

As Brian and I entered the dome, a bronze plaque read, "Welcome to this shrine of American Aviation. The plaques herein mark the final resting place of the pioneers of flight." Golden stars spangled the inside of the dome.

The pillars of the dome held plaques that confused us at first. One remembered Amelia Earhart: "Flew Atlantic Ocean Solo. First to fly Pacific Ocean, Honolulu to California Solo. Most famous and one of the most beloved Women Fliers in History of American Aviation." I hadn't known all that about her, but I did know that her plane vanished over the Pacific Ocean when she ran out of fuel. She left no body to bury. Another plaque recalled Richard Evelyn Byrd, who made the first flight over the North Pole and is buried in Arlington National Cemetery in Virginia. A third commemorated the Wright Brothers, lying at rest in Woodland Cemetery in Dayton, Ohio. Of course Lindbergh's body lies in Palapala Ho'omau Church in Hana, Hawaii, at the end of a long, serpentine road.

We picked up a brochure that explained the memorial plaques. Cenotaphs were available—for a price—to commemorate your favorite aviation pioneer. The National Aeronautic Association had donated the plaque for the Wright Brothers. The cemetery offered a list of other aviation pioneers they would be glad to honor for a total donation of $496.82. (The price has probably gone up since 1998.)

Brian and I wandered across the floor, reading the unfamiliar names of people actually buried at the shrine: Walter Brookins, "first civilian student and instructor for the Wright Brothers." A. Roy Knabenshue, "America's first dirigible pilot. Father of Aerial Transportation. Built first passenger dirigible in the US." W. B. (Bert) Kinner, "Builder Amelia Earhart's first plane. Inventor compound folding wing." (It's tricky to condense a lifetime of achievement onto a brass plaque.) John B. Moisant, "Designed and built first all-metal airplane 1909. First to Fly English Channel with Passenger 1910," who died that same year. Nearby lay his wife, Hilder Florentina Smith, "A pioneer parachute jumper and pilot 1914. In the year 1916 she was the first lady pilot to fly an aeroplane out of the bean patch that later became L.A. International Airport." Carl B. Squier, "13th licensed pilot in America. Co-founder of Lockheed Aircraft. Known as the world's greatest airplane salesman. Sold planes to Lindbergh, Earhart, Wiley, Post, and Getty."

How odd to have a shrine to people whose accomplishments—while undoubtedly paving the way for me to jet in and out of Southern California on a whim—left no celebrated mark on history, outside of this shrine.

Some markers in the floor seemed only tangentially related to aviation. One remembered Lois Hamilton, "Forever Young Floating On A Fluffy Cloud." Findagrave identifies her as one of the top Ford Models of the 1970s, who became an acrobatic pilot in her World War II bi-plane. Another plaque with an even more tenuous connection commemorated aviation historian and Chaplain for the Portal, Reverend John Carruthers. It seemed that eulogizing the pioneer flyers might be enough to find yourself a place amongst them.

Be that as it may, I really liked Reverend Carruthers's epitaph:

> At the grave, when my warfare is ended
> Though no flowers emblazon the sod,
> May a prayer mark the good I intended
> Leaving all decoration to God.

As we mused over the forgotten pioneers, two older men approached us. They wore baseball caps and windbreakers emblazoned with pins with squadron insignia and patches from veterans' groups. They volunteered at the shrine on weekends and seemed very pleased to greet visitors and answer any questions. One of them treated me to a winged lapel pin like kids receive when they take their first airplane flight. A little gold pin with Art Deco wings announced the Burbank Aviation Museum.

The gentleman said he had been a P-38 lightning fighter pilot and a veteran of the War in the Pacific. After World War II, he'd started his own aerial survey firm in the San Fernando Valley. Later, Brian remarked how the docent spoke of his preference for flying certain classic fighters the casual way some men talk about their reasons for being a Ford or GM man.

The retired pilot told us how badly the 1994 Northridge earthquake had damaged the shrine. Restoration had just been completed early in 1996. One of the exhibits in the "paper museum" discussed the post-earthquake facelift. A box of broken dome tiles encouraged us to take a souvenir. I selected a tiny triangle, its cracked glaze the color of crème brûlée.

The free museum inhabited all four legs of the dome. Its displays ranged from mounted photographs to books of clippings, model airplanes, aircraft parts, and posters advertising aviation in the San Fernando Valley. Exhibits discussed aviation and the history of the shrine itself. At the May 27, 1996 rededication, Dr. Tom Crouch, Chairman of the Aeronautics Department of the National Air and Space Museum of the Smithsonian Institution, served as keynote speaker. In 1998, the Portal dome was added to the National Register of Historic Places.

While we poked around, the docent told us that pilots use the dome as a landmark to land at Burbank's Bob Hope Airport, so it still plays a part in aviation. In fact, he said, a plane taking off from the airport once damaged the dome. The pilot died in the crash. The docent brought us a framed newspaper article that reported the story.

Intrigued, I tried to research the crash later. Rumor, posted on the Los Angeles Grim Society's website, said that a flyer landing at Burbank in the 1970s misjudged his altitude and clipped the dome. While aviation records online mentioned two small plane crashes at Burbank that resulted in fatalities, neither accident report referenced the dome. However, a letter in the October 2000 issue of *Los Angeles* magazine said that in the ten years previous, there had been over 600,000 takeoffs and landings at Burbank's airport with out any incidents. That's enough to keep a woman coming back.

To confirm the information on the crash, I turned to Brian, then a researcher at 20th Century Fox. The project turned into a wild goose chase, involving trips to the Burbank Historical Society Museum, a return to the Portal's Aviation Museum, and more, before he found the information misfiled in Fox's own clip files.

In 1969, a twin-engine Navajo Piper lost power on takeoff. It broke apart after ramming into the dome, which stands a mere quarter-mile from the airport. The plane's small cockpit landed in the rose garden. The pilot and one of his passengers died instantly, but another miraculously survived. The story, once I knew its details, no longer struck me as funny.

All in all, Brian and I spent a very enjoyable afternoon chatting with the retired pilots. The exquisite dome is a pleasant place to visit on a hot day in the San Fernando Valley. The museum is open the first Sunday of each month from 1 to 3 p.m. Even if the museum itself is locked, the memorials are open during regular cemetery business hours.

Old Jewish Cemetery, Prague

THOSE THAT HAVE GRAVES AND THOSE THAT HAVE NONE

Old Jewish Cemetery and Pinkas Synagogue, Prague: October 18, 1998

FOR MY THIRTY-FIFTH BIRTHDAY, Mason treated me to a trip to Prague. Several friends had told us how beautiful the city was, but now that the Communists had moved out and it had gotten easier to travel there, the charm of old Prague was being destroyed, they said, overrun by American expatriates.

I don't know how true that is. We never met any other Americans, but that may have been because we traveled in October. Most—but not all, by any means—of the Czechs we met spoke some English. I learned the Czech words for cemetery and ossuary. Despite the lack of common language, Mason and I got around okay. There might have been slightly more wandering than usual as we tried to find our way around in the mazes of streets, but that only led us past more serendipitous beauty than we might have otherwise encountered.

Jews first came to Prague as free traders in the tenth century. They settled along the trade routes below Vysehrad Castle, where they lived peacefully until Christian Crusaders destroyed their settlement in 1096-1098. Afraid to lose the money generated by the Jewish traders, Prague's nobility invited them to shift their homes into the city's Old Town. This area became the first ghetto, three centuries before Venetians coined word.

Medieval Christians believed that Jews had killed Christ and continued to use Christian blood in their rituals. They considered the "Passover lamb" a euphemism for Christ and suspected that, unless Jews were locked behind ghetto walls at night, Christian infants would end up on Passover plates.

As the Middle Ages melted into the Renaissance, interest in the Kabbalah swelled amongst both Jews and Christians in Prague. In this atmosphere, Rabbi Yehudah Loew ben Bezalel (1512-1609) became chief rabbi of the ghetto in 1597. History records that Holy Roman Emperor Rudolf II, who funded research into the alchemical transformation of lead into gold, once summoned Loew (pronounced Lurve) to the palace. (During this same period, Queen Elizabeth consulted astrologist John Dee on similar matters. Dee later studied in Prague, purportedly with Loew.)

Legends sprang up around Rabbi Loew, said to be one of only four men, post-Adam, invited to see the Garden of Eden. While there, he received the *shem*, the secret name of God, which can create life.

This magic came in handy when the ghetto became menaced once again. (The peril varies according to the storyteller, although it's always rooted in Christian bigotry.) Rabbi Loew and two apprentices created a champion out of the muddy banks of the Vltava River. This artificial man served faithfully, protecting the Jews from slander and worse, until something went wrong one night and Loew had to rip the *shem*—variously a clay tablet or a scrap of paper—from behind the golem's teeth.

Little of the Prague ghetto remains. In the late 1800s, when strictures eased, Jews abandoned the cramped buildings of the ghetto for new homes scattered throughout the city. Although new construction replaced most of the twisting streets and little houses, the community chose to preserve important historic buildings. These span architectural styles from Gothic to Renaissance, through Baroque to Art Deco. They testify to a Jewish community that remained in place, uninterrupted, longer than any in Europe.

On our first day in the Czech Republic, Mason and I fought jet lag as the afternoon grew late and we got lost in the Jewish Quarter. We located the wall of mossy gray stones encompassing the Old Jewish Cemetery and followed it around in a circle, missing the cemetery entrance on the first pass. On one street, we could look through a small square window set into a door and see headstones at knee level. As we circled the burial ground, the graves rose up over our heads.

Founded in 1478, the Beth-Chaim (Hebrew for House of Life) served as the sole Jewish graveyard in Prague for three centuries. Penned in by buildings on every side, the Old Jewish Cemetery could only increase in depth. As generations passed, the community filled the burial ground, then brought in a layer of dirt and moved the headstones up to its surface before burying more bodies. The ground contains twelve layers of graves. Twelve thousand surviving tombstones totter over the bones of an estimated 20,000-100,000 people.

A white-painted gate led between buildings to the graveyard. After we paid the admission, a little plastic bucket of yarmulkes waited. A sign in English insisted that men cover their heads. The yarmulkes were bright blue circles of coarse weave, stamped with "Jewish Museum of Prague" in white. The ugly little skullcap didn't want to stay on Mason's curly hair. After it blew off between the graves a second time and we had to stretch over the barrier to retrieve it, he tucked it into his pocket.

A fair number of male visitors brought their own yarmulkes, securing them to their wispy hair with bright silver clips. Velvet seemed to be the fabric of choice. Vendors outside sold crocheted ones. Next time, we know to come prepared.

Stuffed into the irregularly shaped space between buildings, the graveyard was larger than I expected, but very little of it was open to explore. A narrow walkway skirted the outer margin on one side, penning tourists away from the graves. Repeatedly, like clockwork, huge tour groups clogged the narrow walk. Twice I got shoved off the path so people could stay with their tour guides.

After Mason and I shot a roll of film in the cemetery, I saw a sign asking visitors to please respect the place and not photograph it. While we visited, bunches of tourists snapped pictures. Flashes bounced off the gravestones in the late afternoon drizzle. At one point a man with a badge clipped to his blue sweater stepped over the rope and disappeared among the stones, but didn't say anything to halt the photography.

I struggled with the new flash attachment for my SLR camera. Mason suggested we find a place in Prague to develop the film, but I didn't want to. If the photos didn't turn out—or if they got screwed up in development—I might not have had the nerve to come back and take more pictures, after I knew it was wrong.

Between the stones grew bright green grass. Undisturbed by tourist feet, it had grown lush. Tall, strong trees formed an inviting glade. Autumn leaves drifted down, pale green and bright yellow, washing into hollows between the stones. I longed to sit in the grass, put my back against a centuries-old stone, prop my notebook on my knees, and collect my thoughts.

Even if I couldn't relax and absorb the place as I would have liked, I decided to enjoy our visit to the extent possible. I adjusted my attitude and looked around. The gravestones were thicker than I expected, heftier and wider than Christian stones, built to withstand centuries. The stones came in a surprising array of colors: coal black, pale rose, golden white. I had assumed that all the stones would have come from the same quarry, but obviously not.

None of the tombstones had been translated from Hebrew, not even into Czech. Mute text packed the chatty monuments. I craved knowing what had been said about these people.

We saw faintly engraved pitchers first, symbol of the Levites who serve in the temple. Elsewhere we saw a big fat fish, several delicate deer, and bunches of grapes. We found the blessing hands of the Cohenim, the priests. Although the Ten Commandments forbid graven images, ancient rabbis equivocated when it came to hands. Like the Arab Hamsa, the Jewish blessing hands are symbols of power.

Thanks to a tour group crowding the walkway, we missed Rabbi Loew's grave at first. His was the only grave separated from its fellows by the barrier rope, as if you were welcome to touch it. Rather than a simple slab headstone, Loew had a sarcophagus of pink stone, guarded by lions. It held a forest of small white yahrzeit candles. Pebbles, coins, and folded scraps of paper tucked into every niche and covered every flat surface. Of the thousands of graves in Beth-Chaim, Rabbi Yehudah Loew ben Bezalel's was by far the most visited.

According to the Federation of Jewish Communities of the Czech Republic—which oversees the graveyard now—the Old Jewish Cemetery welcomes 10,000 visitors each year. Most bring pebbles in their pockets for Rabbi Loew. I've read several explanations of the Jewish custom of placing pebbles on graves. The simplest appeared in *Mystical Stonescapes* by Freema Gottlieb: "Vegetation fades, but stones are as close as matter gets to Eternity." *Old Bohemian and Moravian Jewish Cemeteries* by Ehl, Parík, and Fiedler traces the ritual back to when the Hebrews wandered in the desert after the exodus from Egypt. Anyone who fell during that forty-year trek was buried along the wayside. Travelers who passed those graves later added a rock as a way of keeping the burial mounds inviolable. These Czech tombstones were feeling the weight of their years. Plastic still shrouded several of them, even though we visited late in October. A sign on the outer wall said that each year, 100 gravestones were cleaned and repaired, at an annual cost of one million Czech pounds. Donations in addition to the admission fee were welcomed.

Our ticket to the graveyard also got us into the nearby Pinkas Synagogue, founded in 1479. Only the second synagogue I'd ever stepped inside, it was certainly the first with a vaulted Gothic ceiling.

Calligraphy on its walls recorded nearly 80,000 names—with dates and towns of citizenship—of people murdered during World War II: the Memorial of Jewish Victims of Nazi Persecution in Bohemia and Moravia. So many names...I found it poignant beyond words. Each first name began with an ochre letter, followed in black. The last names burned red. It looked like a beautifully calligraphed poem, terrible in its repetition and length.

Faced by the wall of names, I thought of 1,200 years of Jewish history in the Czech Republic wiped out in a seven-year period by very determined genocide. Estimates place the modern Jewish community at 4,000, a bare fraction of those who lived in Prague had been before World War II.

While the Nazis demolished 153 Jewish communities in Czechoslovakia during the war, they spared buildings in Prague's former ghetto—including several synagogues and the Old Jewish Cemetery—as part of a museum dedicated to "the extinct race." I wondered why they believed such a museum wouldn't engender pity for their victims. The beauty of the place must have touched some Nazi soul, who made a desperate attempt to be certain something survived,

The Pinkas Synagogue now serves as a receptacle of memory, a building-sized cenotaph for the 80,000 people who left behind nothing but their names.

For Jews, one of the myriad horrors of the Holocaust was the Nazi disrespect of the dead. In Jewish tradition, graves are permanent: none of this unearthing the bones and arranging them in ossuaries. Jewish graves are believed to contain the lowest part of the soul, capable of handing messages up a ladder of grace until they reach God. During the pogroms, villagers gathered in the graveyard on their way out of town, bidding goodbye to their ancestors. The graveyard was the most precious thing they left behind.

I thought about my own family graveyard, where I could visit my grandmothers' graves and feel my forebears nearby. When I knelt before their stones, I could feel their love around me. The graveyard was important to my process of grieving, of grasping the cycle of life, giving me a sense of permanence and continuance.

I whispered a prayer for those who had no graves and no one left alive to mourn. I hoped someone, somewhere, would carry it up to God.

WISH YOU WERE HERE

Terezin National Cemetery, Czech Republic

THE GHETTO AND THE SMALL FORTRESS

Národní Hrbitov v Terezíne, Terezin, Czech Republic: October 21, 1998

JUST OUTSIDE THE OLD JEWISH CEMETERY in Prague, the Ceremonial House displayed children's drawings: simple crayon sketches on brown Kraft paper. Time made the paper brittle, but the illustrations remained bright and clear: happy memories of chasing butterflies, dark reminders of yellow six-pointed stars and the overcrowding in the ghetto, childish renderings of sickness and death and the black figures of the Gestapo.

With few exceptions, the artists died at Auschwitz. They produced their drawings under the tutelage of Friedl Dicker-Brandejsova, a Communist who taught art inside the Terezin ghetto until her deportation to Auschwitz in 1944. The pictures survive only because Dicker-Brandejsova hid them in hopes that something would outlive the war. She knew she was headed to her death.

I'd always sworn that I would never go to a Nazi concentration camp. After I fled in tears from the Holocaust Museum in Washington, DC, I never wanted to subject myself to the emotional echoes of all that misery—or worse, rooms emptied of all memory. But, I told myself, Terezin hadn't been an extermination camp. In addition, it stood close enough to Prague that we could make the round trip on a tour bus in four hours.

The tour flyer I picked up said, "The former garrison town, originally built by Emperor Joseph II as an ingenious system of military fortresses for the protection of the kingdom at the end of the 18th century, was completely changed and converted into a Jewish Ghetto and concentration camp during World War II." Mason, whose Jewish grandfather had died in the US Army in World War II, wasn't sure how much there actually would be to see. I felt like we had to go anyway, to witness.

The bus drove past huge ditches outside the fortress's high brick walls. Our tour guide told us the moat had been designed so that the nearby river could be diverted to flood it. That was the last we heard about the early history of the area.

We parked in a lot beside a huge graveyard, row upon row of identical headstones lying in a flat field before the walls of the "Little Fortress."

The concentration camp Terezin had two parts. The ghetto the Nazis called Theresienstadt, their "model" Jewish town, lay just down the road. We could see its pretty little church steeple from the Fortress's parking lot. After we toured the prison called the Little Fortress, the bus would drive us quickly through modern Terezin, so as not to disturb the townspeople who had resettled there after the war.

During the Nazi occupation, the villagers of Terezin were evicted from their homes so that Hitler could turn the entire town into a Jewish ghetto. The Nazis designed Terezin to refute the world's belief that Germany had Jewish blood on its hands. Jews from Czechoslovakia, Poland, Germany, France, and the Soviet Union were herded into the village, where the Gestapo demanded they "govern" themselves. The town council, elected by the Nazis, was forced to draw up lists—to fulfill Nazi quotas—of Jews to be sent to Auschwitz-Birkenau.

In 1944, the Danish Red Cross visited the ghetto. They pronounced Theresienstadt a model for the care of political prisoners. As they toured, a jazz band (called The Ghetto Swingers) played a catchy tune. Shop windows displayed formal wear. Everyone ate at an outdoor cantina. Money filled the bank. Prisoners wore street clothes, rather than striped uniforms. Everyone had shoes and hats and overcoats. Behind the façade lay reality, which the Red Cross did not examine. Over eighty-five percent of the 140,000 people who passed through Terezin died. Each day, 300 inmates died from "natural causes." Trains carried 87,000 people over the Polish border to Auschwitz-Birkenau. Barely 4,000 "citizens" of Terezin survived the war.

I couldn't imagine moving back into my home after it had been used to corral people, seven out of eight of whom had been murdered.

Before we saw the village, though, we would spend the morning in the Little Fortress, where the Gestapo had imprisoned Communists, prisoners of war, and Jews that they wanted to torture.

A long solemn walkway led past the graveyard under arching

autumnal trees. The sky overhead glowed a deep, flawless blue. Nature had been here long before atrocity.

In warning, alternating bands of white and black surrounded the entrance to the fortress. Our tour group huddled in the entryway for a long time, while the guide who'd come with us tried to arrange for an English-speaking guide to take us around the prison. Apparently, you couldn't tour the grounds on your own, even if you'd paid for a tour guide and brought her along. In the deep shadow of the arch, cold had collected overnight. The October wind rushed through, frosting our breath. Members of the tour group shivered visibly. No one spoke.

Just outside the archway stood the camp's cafe. Our guidebook identified it as the former guards' mess. The guidebook's author didn't suggest one eat there, amid the ghosts, but I wondered if we might have waited there, out of the cold. I failed to imagine how awful that cold would feel if I'd been imprisoned here.

No English-speaking guide was available, so a Czech guide volunteered to accompany us. The guide from our tour bus came along—unhappily—to translate. She didn't really want to tour the camp.

We marched forward into the sunshine, into a pretty little town square. The guides pointed out the beautiful green lawns, the lush shade trees, and the sweet brick buildings where guards lived with their wives and raised their children. Then we turned left down a narrower lane that ended in an ochre wall pierced by another archway. Painted above the arch was the lie "Arbeit Macht Frei": Work Will Set You Free. Only death or the end of the war set anyone free from Terezin. Of the 32,000 people imprisoned in the Little Fortress during the war, 2,500 died. Another 5,000 were sent on to die in the extermination camps. After the Soviets liberated the rest, 500 more former prisoners died of malnutrition and typhoid.

I shivered, as we stood in the dim, cold rooms where people had lived and died. In the mass cells, men slept three or four together on the hard planks of thirty bunk beds. There were no blankets. Each cell had a tiny wood-burning stove, but of course they had no wood to fuel it. Each man received a bowl and spoon, but there was often no food.

Conditions improved slightly in preparation for the visit by the Red Cross. For the sake of appearances, anyone ill or who had been tortured was shot, which eased overcrowding somewhat. Prisoners built a new washroom, complete with porcelain tiles and mirrors over the sinks, but never got the opportunity to use it. The Red Cross delegation, dazzled by what they saw in the ghetto down the road, never set foot inside the prison camp.

Our Czech guide explained the shaving procedure, the delousing procedure, and that imprisoned doctors tried to treat unhealthy inmates but were refused basic medical supplies. We saw a tunnel that served as a mortuary, where corpses of tortured prisoners piled up until survivors could transport them to the nearby crematorium. During the last three years of the war, the crematorium's four trolley-fed ovens burned night and day, disposing of 30,000 bodies from the Fortress, the ghetto, and Flossenbürg work camp over the border in Bavaria. We saw the wall where firing squads executed prisoners. More than 600 of their victims had been buried in shallow graves until after the war, when they were exhumed and reburied with ceremony outside the Fortress's front gate.

The guide led us into another courtyard, where between 400 and 600 prisoners had been crammed at once. He pointed out another guide, an elderly man who'd survived internment there. I shuddered. How did that man nerve himself to get out of bed each morning and return to the prison where he'd seen so much suffering? How did any of the guides find the strength to work in the concentration camp day after day, recounting the horrors?

Jan Leiber, our guide, was a white-haired retiree with the most interesting lines in his square face. He resembled Boris Yeltsin. He didn't smile at all until the very end of the tour, when he thanked us for coming—in English—and said goodbye.

When Mason and I passed back into the area of the fortress where the guards lived, we saw a swimming pool built by Jewish prisoners to impress the Red Cross, where German children learned to swim. We had an opportunity to go into the cinema, also built by prison labor, where Gestapo guards used to watch movies. I had seen enough darkness. I felt like a trapped bird. I needed to get out of the prison.

So we wandered the *Národní Hrbitov v Terezíne*, the National Cemetery of Terezin. After the war, the vicinity of the prison was excavated to recover all the bodies. Gradually, between 1945 and 1958, some 10,000 victims from the Small Fortress, the ghetto of

Terezin, and Flossenbürg were reburied in the National Cemetery. Of those, only 2,400 lie in identified graves. The rest remain nameless. Perhaps one day genetic testing will discover who they were, if they have any relatives left with which to compare them.

A tall cross with a ring of barbed wire at the intersection of its arms towered above the graves. It was erected in 1992. In response, a smaller Star of David was raised closer to the prison wall in 1995. More poignant to me were the uncountable stones marked only by numbers of victims in the mass graves below my feet. Not even the years of death could be guessed or recorded. A low granite tablet with the number *10 000* remembered those who vanished into the crematorium.

I kept horror at bay by gazing at the rows of grave markers through the viewfinder of my camera. I concentrated on composing photos. I felt I had to document this place. I could not, under any circumstances, allow myself to think of these anonymous dead as people with faces and loved ones and brutal, senseless deaths.

A middle-aged woman walked alone among the graves. Pretty ash blond hair hung to her shoulders. She carried a green leather purse and wore matching shoes. Tears streamed down her face. Her silent grief shocked me. She seemed too young to have been imprisoned in the ghetto. Did she have family somewhere beneath our feet? Was her grief for all who had suffered, all who had vanished?

Chastened, I put my camera away. My legs felt rubbery. I turned my back on the prison, on the unforgettable dead, and staggered back to the parking lot. I sat on the curb, near the tour bus, drained and trembling. There was no making sense of this horror, except to cry.

The Slavin Pantheon, Vysehrad Cemetery, Prague

ALTHOUGH DEAD, THEY STILL SPEAK

Vysehrad Cemetery, Prague: October 24, 1998

OUR LAST DAY IN PRAGUE DAWNED DRIZZLY AND GRAY. We wandered the Malá Strana, the historic neighborhood beneath Hradcany Castle, seeking entertainment. A brass band serenaded us as we climbed the old stone steps. We battled the tour groups to see Saint George's Basilica, worth the skirmish to see the ravishing marble statue of *Vanitas* in its crypt: half alluring beauty, half worm-eaten corpse. Over garlicky roasted chicken in an ancient wine cellar-turned-restaurant, Mason and I scanned the guidebook for the perfect experience to round out our trip, preferring something far from the tourist mob.

We'd run through the list of things we felt we *had* to visit: the street of the alchemists, the Charles Bridge, Kafka's grave out in the new Jewish cemetery. We'd drunk absinthe in bars all over town. We'd spent another rainy day in the National Galleries, marveling over the number of crucifixions they owned in which Christ spouted actual fountains of blood. Prague had definitely lived up to its reputation for the beauty of its architecture and the delicious pessimism of its embellishments.

While I'd chosen the *Cadogan City Guide* because it recommended places to go to drink absinthe, it also had a comfortingly morbid sensibility. It encouraged us to visit the ossuary in Kutná Hora. It recommended we search for the mummified severed arm suspended over the door of the Church of Saint James. So when it called Vysehrad Cemetery "an impressive gallery of modern Czech sculpture," I was inclined to be swayed.

By the time we finished our leisurely lunch, the weather had turned. We stepped out into the quintessential autumn day: sky piled high with cottony clouds, the last of the autumn leaves gilding the curbs and gutters, soft yellow sunlight stroking the shoulders of our woolen coats. The day had become a blessing too rare and rich to spend indoors.

Vysehrad means high castle. The rocky promontory that bears the name was the site of the original wooden castle, built around the tenth century. Though no trace remains, *Let's Go* calls the area the Czech Republic's most revered landmark. It was the site where a vision caused Princess Libuse to point to the forest across the river and direct a castle called Praha to be built. She prophesied Prague would become a rich and powerful center of trade. For centuries, the city set about making her dream come true.

Outside the modern-day Vysehrad metro station, a huge Soviet-style exhibition hall waylaid us. We couldn't find our way around the enormous ugly building where the Communist party used to meet. (Fittingly, it was also where the G7 provoked demonstrations in 2000.) Once we escaped its maze of misleading sidewalks, we came across the Romanesque rotunda of Saint Martin, dating from the eleventh century. Although Saint Martin's tower was the oldest surviving building in Prague, we remained goal-oriented and passed it by without more than a cursory glance.

Outside the tall blank beige walls of the cemetery rose the neo-Gothic Church of Saints Peter and Paul, reconstructed in the 18th century after burning to the ground. We bypassed its reportedly fabulous ornamentation. On the trail of a cemetery, nothing could distract me.

Founded in 1869 on the site of a much larger graveyard that no longer exists, Vysehrad Cemetery was conceived as a shrine to the heroes of the Czech Nationalist Revival. It contains graves of more than 600 important Czechs, including Art Nouveau painter Alfons Mucha, composers Antonin Dvorak and Bedrich Smetana, and playwright Karel Capek, who coined the term robot.

We traced the perimeter wall until we located its gate. Once inside, we discovered that a Renaissance Revival arcade ringed the cemetery. Under its covered passageway, curving gothic arches designated each burial plot. Baroque ironwork fences enclosed some of the graves. Others displayed elaborate mosaics, depicting a rain of gold-leaf stars on a cobalt glass background, or a caparisoned knight like something out of Rackham's *King Arthur*. In my favorite memorial, a low-relief blue-garbed ceramic angel leaned against a starburst mosaic in shades of gold and silver. My photograph doesn't do justice to the breathtaking shimmer of those tiles.

Beneath the cloister hunched a marble sarcophagus carved with a gruesome skull. A pair of snakes wove in and out of unnatural openings in the bones, then twined together across the brow to form a diadem. The visceral reference to death startled me. On retrospect, it seemed a logical extension of the exquisite bone artwork we'd seen in the Kutná Hora ossuary.

After all these artistic pyrotechnics, Dvorak's grave seemed less magnificent than I expected. A life-sized bronze bust scowled out from beneath the vaulted arcade. The composer looked as if he concentrated too hard on art to enjoy life.

Enjoying life was not a problem as Mason and I explored the graveyard. From Art Nouveau to Cubism, Vysehrad Cemetery did indeed have an impressive variety of sculpture. I'm not generally a fan of blocky modern art, but I was touched by the Taub monument with its two sturdy, faceless figures supporting each other in their grief. In contrast stood a monument whose family name I didn't note, so captivated was I by the life-sized sculpture of the robed woman bowing forward as if to drop her tears onto the grave. A bearded man draped in a toga or a blanket clasped her hand. Their sadness was as evocative as that of the rough Cubist figures.

Toward the middle of the burial ground, a trio of graves encapsulated the breadth of artwork offered in Vysehrad Cemetery. First, a high relief bust of a woman gazed out of a marble archway as naturalistically as if the stone imprisoned her. Beside her, an art deco bronze of a woman with flowing hair rested her chin against her forearm atop a pink granite monument. Third in line, a high-gloss black granite stone had a gray granite mask inset. Grief distorted the face of the mask, its eyes squinted shut and mouth gaping around a moan. The same gilt that picked out the letters of the deceased's name highlighted the mask's eyebrows.

Since All Souls' Day was approaching, pine boughs carpeted several of the graves. Before the snow falls, families bring a "blanket" made of pine branches to shield their loved ones' graves through the long winters.

Mason and I worked around to the centerpiece of the cemetery, the towering Slavin Pantheon (after which the cemetery is sometimes mistakenly called) designed by Antonin Wiehl. The community mausoleum, topped with an angel laying a palm frond on a sarcophagus, is the final resting place of over 50 Czech artists and sculptors, including Mucha. Even though she stood a long way from any road, soot stained the poor angel.

I ran through the last of my film, so we had to leave the graveyard to find some more. Luckily, the large Vysehrad Park nearby—site of the original wooden castle—hosted a kiosk offering Kodak film, a little souvenir guide, and Becherovka. We'd fallen in love with Becherovka, the Czech national beverage, that was available—as Mason pointed out—anywhere with a glass. We had a glass (a real glass!) at one of the sunny picnic tables before ducking back into the graveyard.

We'd stumbled upon the perfect autumn excursion for a perfect autumn day. Our visit to Vysehrad Cemetery was sheer fate, one of those lucky accidents of weather and guidebook that generate the fondest memories of any trip.

WISH YOU WERE HERE

Zoshigaya Reien, Tokyo

JAPANESE GHOST STORY

Zoshigaya Reien, Tokyo: March 14, 1999

I FINALLY GOT A CHANGE TO GO BACK TO JAPAN with Mason in 1999. When our Japanese friends heard I wanted to see graveyards, everyone suggested a visit to Zoshigaya Reien, Lafcadio Hearn's final resting place. Mason pulled out the Tokyo map and figured out how to get us there. It turned out to be an easy subway trip from Shinjuku, where we were staying, to Ikebukuro. Then it would be a ten-minute walk from the train station.

The *Insight Guide to Japan* describes the Ikebukuro District as "a smaller, less interesting version of Shinjuku." Ikebukuro's heart is a Seibu department store, at one time the largest self-contained store in the world. It fills *blocks*. We skirted the department store on our way to the Zoshigaya neighborhood, a residential area where pink sprays of plastic cherry blossoms hung from the lampposts to celebrate spring. On the bright March day we visited, the sun didn't give much warmth.

Zoshi is an old Japanese word that used to mean odd jobs. People who worked for the shogun once inhabited the area. The land now occupied by the cemetery used to be an estate where the shogun kept his kennels and where his falconers lived. In 1874, Tokyo claimed the land for a graveyard, one of four owned by the city. Public graveyards—unaffiliated with a temple—are a Meiji-era (concurrent with our Victorian Age) import from the West.

Mason and I turned off the commercial street down a little alley, lined on both sides with cement block walls. Halfway down, the wall on our left opened into a vista of retreating vermillion *torii* gates: the Kishimojin Temple, where people have come since the Edo era to pray for the health and prosperity of their children.

Focused on finding the cemetery, Mason and I kept walking. Farther down the alley, bundles of wooden blades, bound together with white string, stacked against the cinderblock wall. In Buddhist ceremonies, those blades—they look like giant tongue depressors—

are inscribed with the name given to the deceased at death, the name she carries into the afterlife. These blank blades waited for people to die.

We reached Zoshigaya Reien's nondescript gate. Inside stood a little garden with statues of the Seven Dwarves. A double swing waited for children to come and play. I wondered if that was intended for public use, or if the caretaker's children lived inside the cemetery walls.

Beside the caretaker's house rose shelves of bamboo buckets, each marked with kanji and a variety of black symbols. Mason reported that the kanji were family names.

One of the guidebooks suggested we buy a map from the caretaker, who was nowhere to be found on this Sunday afternoon. Surely, we thought, Hearn's grave must be marked in English. We would just wander until we found it. The search could provide our entertainment for the afternoon.

Greek-Irish Lafcadio Hearn worked as a writer in the last half of the 19th century. He traveled around the United States as a journalist, then found his true calling in 1890, when *Harper's Magazine* sent him to Japan. Although he soon parted ways with his editors, he loved the country and wrote book after book, describing it to Western readers for the first time.

While his tales have mysteriously fallen out of fashion in the West, Hearn is still revered in Japan. His most famous work is *Kwaidan: Stories and Studies of Strange Things*, a collection of Japanese ghost tales comparable to the work of the Brothers Grimm. It inspired Akira Kurosawa's 1964 movie of the same name, which won a Special Jury Prize at Cannes and received an Academy Award nomination for Best Foreign Film.

Despite living in Japan for fourteen years, Hearn never became fluent in Japanese. In 1891, he married a samurai's daughter, who told him the stories that sparked his imagination.

In order to legally marry her, Hearn had to be adopted by her father. He became a Japanese citizen and took the name Koizumi Yakumo. *That* became important to us when we discovered none of the graves in Zoshigaya Reien had any sort of English characters on them.

Most of the graves were traditionally shaped, with a couple of low steps topped by an upright stone that gave the family name and often featured the round family crest. Our friend Nanjo told us later that the family crests are called *komon*. He said that every family in Japan has one, but only the grandfathers know what they are any more.

Once I started watching for them, I noticed that not every grave had a crest. Instead, some had three large fat kanji in place of the circle. Others had the relief of a lotus on their sides or bases. Three wavy diagonal slashes depicted the water out of which the lotus grew. Above it rose a thin stalk of flowers, one still in bud and the other in horizontal profile. Unlike Western grave iconography, which ranges from flowers to birds, from disembodied human hands to angels and effigies of the soul, these lotus blossoms represented the only illustrations we saw on Japanese graves, other than the *komon*.

Many of the grave sites in Zoshigaya Reien seemed to have private gardens, hedged by small bushes or surrounded by low curbs. Yew trees flanked some monuments. Since yew are often planted in European graveyards because the evergreens point straight toward Heaven, I wondered if those graves belonged to Western missionaries, who would have refused to be buried on the grounds of Buddhist temples. Plane trees or ginkgos grew above other graves.

One repeating motif in the graveyard gardens was a rock with a trough atop it to collect water. I suspected that signified something in Japanese gardening, where a rock is never just a rock. Other grave sites had a large green boulder with its flattened top polished to a high gloss. They looked like benches, or as close to a bench as we saw in the cemetery.

Often graves had a pair of stone lanterns standing right beside the path. The lanterns had a crescent moon cut into one side and a round hole cut out opposite: sun and moon. I wondered if the families lit them at O-Bon, the festival when the dead come back to visit.

As we wandered around, I noticed water cups set on many monuments. Most were turned upside down. I wondered if the families did that or if the caretaker poured the water offering out after a certain time. At first it shocked me to see the cups up-ended. I'm not sure why that struck me so.

I saw similar bouquets on several graves: an orange frilled daisy, a white mum, yellow snapdragons, red carnations, yellow daisies, lavender statice. Some flower shop nearby must be doing great business, selling pairs of this bouquet to stand at either side of headstones.

During our exploration, we tried to keep out of the way of the Japanese visiting the cemetery. Two older ladies stopped short when faced by a huge black bird. Its feathers were glossy, though not as shiny as its bright eye. When I asked later, Hiroshi said the Japanese call it *karasu*, the jungle crow. He imitated its cawing. The bird whetted its matte black beak on the gravestone where it perched.

The old ladies detoured around it and got lost in the graveyard. I was amused to see we weren't the only ones having trouble finding our way around. The cemetery seemed roughly organized into a maze of cul-de-sacs. Mason and I had to keep retracing our steps. Although the cemetery wasn't large, graves jammed every nook.

Still, sometimes getting lost gives one the best look at a place. My senses opened up to every nuance, trying to find a pattern and understand the significances of elements in the maze. We smelled several kinds of incense: something brown and churchy, something green and piney, and plain old Haight Street smoke shop patchouli. It looked as if the family would light a whole pack—or several whole packs—of incense at once. I guess if you bought the incense as an offering, it wouldn't do any good to be stingy with it. It's not like you're going to take cemetery incense home and burn it in your bedroom.

It surprised us to find Zoshigaya Reien so active on a Sunday afternoon. A *lot* of people came and went. Mostly they didn't stay very long for having gotten all dressed up. I wondered if they'd shop at Seibu afterward.

A shrine against the alley wall seemed to draw more traffic than anywhere else. I wondered about the significance of March 14, the date of our visit. One couple after another came to pray. In one pair, the man wore white from his pants to his cable-knit sweater. Later, an elderly couple came in. He wore a navy blazer, so I couldn't theorize about the significance of color.

Fascinated by the incense burning before the mystery shrine, Mason wanted to capture the curling smoke on film. He asked me to stand guard as he framed some photographs. We wanted to leave the shrine if any Japanese came to visit it, so that our presence wouldn't make them uncomfortable. Guard duty gave me lots of time to study the shrine. It seemed to be dedicated to children. Flowers lay heaped in front of it, along with a few small toys, including a sleeping Minnie Mouse in a pink dress.

As soon as Mason had some shots that satisfied him, we moved on. On our quest for Hearn's grave, we came across a brand new tombstone. The slab in front of it had been lifted to reveal an alcove cut into the ground, lined with urns of cremains. A fresh grave! I made Mason take a picture.

We hadn't gone far away when we saw men carrying in the Buddhist wooden blades, already inscribed. They stood them up behind the new headstone.

As we moved away from the burial, I found myself captivated by the variety of the blade racks. Some were very simple fixtures make of plumber's pipes. Others, made of stone, were carved in the shape of *torii* gates. Some new ones were polished chrome.

The blades seemed meant to stay in place until they weathered to gray. I wondered if they were ever burned, or if they were allowed to fall to pieces. Did the eventual decay mean that the soul of the deceased had gone on to another life?

An incinerator hulked in the very center of the graveyard, with a straight tall smokestack. Do they collect up dead bouquets to burn? It seemed unlikely that cremations took place in the cemetery, in the heart of the neighborhood.

We'd wandered the entire graveyard and found no sign of Lafcadio Hearn. If he was buried there, as our guidebook promised in two different entries, only his Japanese name appeared on his tombstone. Mason's spoken Japanese is very good, but he hasn't mastered reading unfamiliar names. If he'd known how to spell Koizumi Yakumo in kanji, he might have been able to find it by matching the characters. Instead, we were out of luck.

As we took our final photographs, a funeral procession filed in. A Buddhist priest led the way. He had a shaven head and glasses and wore a brown kimono with a butterscotch yellow sash. Behind him, the widow wore a black kimono with tiny white circles embroidered on each sleeve and on her back. Around her waist wound a black obi with a large shiny black flower. On her feet, she wore white *tabi* socks and black sandals with a black velvet strap across her toes. She carried a shiny metallic silver-and-black drawstring bag.

Men in the funeral party all wore tailored black silk suits with just a touch of sheen, white button-down shirts, and matte black ties. Older women had boxy black suit jackets, straight black skirts, black pantyhose, and low-heeled black pumps. Their purses were black patent leather. Younger women had on stylish black dresses. They didn't seem too different than what young women might wear for a night out, though these were rather severe in their cut. Little girls wore school uniforms.

The whole group didn't stand at the grave long. I suspected the main funeral must have already taken place and this, as in the West, was just a quick graveside interment ceremony.

Afterward, they all filed out and down the main street. Each man carried a white paper shopping bag with white-wrapped packages inside. Perhaps the widow gave gifts to the people who came to the funeral? I restrained myself from asking our Japanese friends later.

The whole family turned into an alcove off the main street—for a funeral meal?

One of the older men in the family had a camera. After the others had gone, he stayed at the grave to take a photo.

As we tried to find our way out of the cemetery, I thought over my impressions. One grave had two cigarettes on top of its incense burner, burned down to long ashes. I felt touched by the simple offering.

Everything about Zoshigaya Reien looked cared for and spic-and-span. Some of the graves had wire brushes hanging from racks behind their tombstones. Other graves had washcloths draped over their racks or rolled up and tucked into their lanterns or hung in plastic shopping bags stuck into openings in their bushes. I thought of the bamboo buckets hanging near the caretaker's house.

I'd gotten the impression from Mayuko's tour of the cemetery in Kamakura, on my first trip to Japan, that Japanese didn't have much to do with the graveyards. I thought maybe they only went on O-Bon, if then. I was pleased to see that this graveyard still served an important purpose in modern life in Japan.

However, for all the traffic in Zoshigaya Reien, the cemetery remained almost silent. As we left, we heard the wooden name blades clatter in their racks. Lafcadio Hearn would have loved the eerie sound. The breeze didn't seem that strong, but the sound made me think of bones rattling.

WISH YOU WERE HERE

Jack London's grave, Jack London State Historic Park
Glen Ellen, California

NOT FADE AWAY

Jack London State Historic Park, Glen Ellen, California
September 5, 1999

"I would rather be ashes than dust. I'd rather that these sparks should burn out in a brilliant blaze than that I should be stifled by dry rot. I would rather be a superb meteor, every atom of me in magnificent glow." —Jack London, quoted in *The House of Happy Walls*

I HAD BEEN WINE TASTING WITH MY PARENTS. We ended up in Glen Ellen, in California's Sonoma County, and turned into the Jack London State Historic Park. The little museum drowsed quietly on a weekday, so we had lots of time to poke around. I found it all fascinating. As a child, I'd dreamed that someone would create this sort of museum in my memory: handwritten manuscripts, picture postcards from my trips, unusual items I'd collected, rejection slips from editors proven shortsighted by time.

The museum made me want to read London's work. The only thing I'd ever studied was the short story "To Build A Fire," which my eighth grade English teacher read aloud to illustrate Man vs. Nature. That's the story where the Yukon adventurer wants to slice open his dog so that he can warm his hands enough to get a fire going. With my morbid bent, I'm surprised that I never followed that up and read any more of London's work.

Anyway, after my parents and I finished exploring the museum, we decided to walk up to the ruins of Wolf House, the huge mansion London had built on his property. He meant it to be his permanent home, where he could withdraw from the world and write. As envisioned, Wolf House would have contained twenty-six rooms grouped around an interior reflecting pool. Once it was practically complete and waiting for London and his wife Charmian to move in, a fire destroyed it on a blazingly hot day in August 1913. London suspected arson, but in reality, linseed oil-soaked rags probably spontaneously combusted.

Decades later, the ruins looked majestic. Stone walls like bare ribs poked up into the azure sky. The woods drew close around the house. The museum said that the savor left London's life after the house burned down. He wandered around lost for several years. Finally, he and Charmian left on one last sailing adventure. London came home ill with intestinal problems and kidneys damaged by years of drinking. In November 1916, he overdosed on morphine. It might have been suicide. He was forty.

One September weekend when I couldn't stand another day of San Francisco's summer fog, I asked my friend Jeff if he'd chauffeur me up to Glen Ellen. It suited him, since he was looking for a reason to take a drive in his '65 Barracuda, to blast AC/DC on the CD player and absorb some heat.

I don't think either of us realized how hot Sonoma County in September could be, until we stepped out of the un-air conditioned car into the parking lot at the State Historic Park. Dust hung suspended in the breathless air. Nothing moved: not a bird, not a grasshopper. Gratefully, we ducked onto the oak-shaded path and strolled up the trail to the House of Happy Walls.

After my first visit, I hadn't realized that Charmian London built the "cottage"—which now houses the museum—after her husband's death. Jack never actually wrote at the desk while it sat upstairs. He never inhabited the museum building at all. His spirit was merely conjured by the items he had collected, the everyday things he had touched. Some of the books on display had come from his brag shelf: the shelf every writer keeps of her own works, the one she looks at to remind herself that she did the work before and should be able to do it again. In his forty years, London had published nineteen books.

I told Jeff how my last visit to the museum had motivated me to read *The Iron Heel*, London's dystopian novel about the Oligarchy, comprised of foolish churchmen and greedy factory owners, crushing the labor movement. London imparted a sense of hope to the book by including footnotes, ostensibly commentary from the future written during the peaceful labor state inspired by events in the novel. Of course, Jeff pointed out, London died before communism turned ugly, when everyone spied on everyone else and the politburo lived like kings.

We moved through the museum more quickly than I had with my

parents, then left the air-conditioned building specifically to visit London's grave. The woodland canopy gave us respite from the sun, but the shade barely cooled the stagnant air. I was glad we'd brought water with us as we hiked up the powdery trail to the slight ridge where London finally found rest.

A plaque near the grave related how the gravesite had been chosen. Before his death, Jack told Charmian and his sister, "I wouldn't mind if you laid my ashes on the knoll where the Greenlaw children are buried. And roll over me a boulder from the ruins of the Big House."

Four days after his death on November 22, 1916, Charmian London carried her husband's ashes up the rise in a small copper urn wreathed in primroses, one of the hardy flowers that don't shrivel in winter's chill. She placed the cremains in a cement receptacle. Four horses pulled a large lava rock up from the area around the Wolf House, where it had been left aside by the architect as unsuitable. Using rollers and a crowbar, workmen from the ranch shifted the boulder into place. London's old friend, San Francisco's Poet Laureate George Sterling, attended the ceremony. He reported, "No word, aside from a brief whisper, had been said."

The boulder marking the grave is strangely shaped: a weird, worn, organic form for a rock. Moss covers it like velvet, softening its broken edges. If it hadn't been for the fence of peeling pickets surrounding it, the boulder could have been any natural rock, so well did it suit its environment.

Inside the fence, crispy brown oak leaves lay in a mat amidst the dead grass. September in Northern California is a time of brown and dust.

Near London's grave stood another smaller picket fence surrounding the trunk of an oak. Tall green weeds drowsed inside the fence, blanketing the graves of two settler children. Not much is known about David and Lilli Greenlaw, who died in 1876 and 1877, although the park has a file on them, if you ask. The graves have always been marked with redwood boards, replaced whenever they deteriorated by each successive owner of the land.

Why did this lonely spot appeal to London? Did he expect that Charmian would live alone on the ranch, overseeing the men who fed the stock and farmed the land? Did he look forward to the day when they would be together again, when she died and had her ashes placed alongside his?

Did he recall the care each landowner had shown the graves of the Greenlaw children? Did he expect that whomever bought the land from Charmian would eventually care for his grave?

The State Park's website says, "Jack was deeply moved by the feeling of loneliness at the children's graves." He felt that they would be less lonely if he were buried near them. It's an odd sentiment for a man who abandoned his first wife and two daughters to chase a life of adventure.

Mostly I wondered if London chose a boulder to cover him so that he could fade into the landscape he loved and vanish with memory. He had lived through the tail end of the Victorian age, with its excessive stages of mourning and the elaborate cemetery monuments that I love. London was among the most widely read authors of his time. He might have guessed his grave would become a place of pilgrimage, with grateful readers wanting to commune with him as they offered a rose. I suppose he strove to be too much of a man's man to want any sentiment. The boulder, the isolation: those were conscious choices on his part.

Of all the graves I've visited over the years, London's is the most isolated. Of course George Washington and Thomas Jefferson lay entombed on their own properties as well, but those grave sites stood in settled lands, easy travel even in Colonial days. In 1916, Sonoma County was sparsely populated, a place of ranches and vineyards. London might as well have been buried on the edge of the earth, like Robert Louis Stevenson in Samoa or Charles Lindberg in the churchyard at Hana. At least Lindberg had more company than a couple of nearly anonymous children.

I framed a couple of quick sun-struck photos while Jeff loitered under an oak tree.

When we returned to the main path, a ranger pulled up to us on a little flatbed pickup. "How are you?" he asked.

"Fine," Jeff answered skeptically.

"I've been offering people a ride back to the parking lot," the ranger continued. "It's too hot to walk."

"We're okay," Jeff said, looking to me for confirmation.

"It isn't much farther, is it?" I asked. "We've got water." I held up my bottle.

"Not too far. Look, I'm going to drive up to the ruins, see if there's anyone up there that needs help. Don't want anyone keeling over from heatstroke. If you're still on the trail, I'll pick you up on the way back."

"Sounds good," I said.

Jeff and I didn't talk about fame or isolation or abandoned pioneer children as we ambled back to the car. The heat made it difficult to talk at all as we trudged through the dust.

The Aldigé angels, Metairie Cemetery, New Orleans

A BUS NAMED CEMETERIES

Metairie Cemetery, New Orleans: November 1, 1999

"They told me to take a streetcar named Desire, and then transfer to one called Cemeteries..."
— Tennessee Williams

SINCE TENNESSEE WILLIAMS WROTE HIS PLAY in 1947, a '42 Cemeteries' bus has replaced the streetcar named Desire down Canal Street. "Where else would you see a bus marked 'Cemeteries'?" Mason asked.

Mason, our friend Paul, and I rode it past the place where Blanche Dubois would have disembarked for her encounter with Stella and Stanley Kowalski. We continued out to the edge of New Orleans.

At a corner beside Odd Fellows Rest, across the street from Greenwood Cemetery, Mason and Paul followed me off the bus. We scurried across the street toward Cypress Grove Cemetery. As much as the area full of graveyards enticed me, it was not pedestrian-friendly. No crosswalks or walking signs interrupted the busy traffic.

We scuttled through the gloom under the Pontchartrain Expressway to reach Metairie Cemetery. When last Mason and I stayed with Tim and Wendy and visited Saint Louis Cemetery #1, I'd seen the Metairie Cemetery from the rush-hour traffic on the highway overhead. On that trip, it felt strange to look down on the graveyard, which seemed to stretch for miles. Actually, Metairie Cemetery abuts Lake Lawn Memorial Park, which it joined in 1969.

Metairie Cemetery opened in 1872 on the grounds of the old Metairie Race Course. Legend holds that the graveyard's owner, Charles T. Howard, had been barred from betting on the ponies by the Creole aristocracy for being a crass American who'd made his fortune in the corrupt Louisiana State Lottery Company. At his first opportunity, Howard bought the land, closed the track, and charged the Creoles money to be buried on it. New Orleanians love a good story. Even though this one is not historically accurate, the oval shape of the track still dominates the modern cemetery. Exquisite mausoleums line its concentric drives.

Old postcards show the grand entrance to the cemetery as an ivy-swathed archway. Unfortunately, that got demolished when the state chopped the Pontchartrain Expressway through. While we approached Metairie Cemetery from the same direction that the old New Orleanians would have come, the former grand entrance now serves as the back exit. Despite the lack of sidewalk, cement stairs still lead upward to a simple gate.

Right inside the brick fence rose the thirty-foot high tumulus of the Louisiana Division of the Army of Tennessee. The tumulus, a man-made hill, is perhaps the most ancient form of grave monument. Bronze Age barrows rise throughout Northern Europe, usually enclosing the remains of warriors. I'd cried over the tumulus in the Hiroshima Peace Park.

The burial mound at Metairie Cemetery belonged to a "Benevolent Society" that provided burial space to veterans of the Civil War. Inside the grass-blanketed tumulus lay forty-eight crypts full of old soldiers, including Confederate General Pierre G. T. Beauregard, who ordered the first shot fired on Fort Sumter and later commanded the Army of Tennessee. When the last Civil War veteran was buried in the tumulus in 1929, the tomb finally knew peace. I had to get creative to take a picture of the gravesite without power-lines and the freeway behind it.

The most famous person ever buried in Metairie Cemetery had been Jefferson Davis, sole president of the Confederate States of America. He died in New Orleans in 1889 and was laid— temporarily—to rest beneath the 38-foot granite column marking the tomb of the Army of Northern Virginia. Davis's funeral was the largest New Orleans has yet seen. Even so, Louisiana could not hold him. Several years after his death, Davis's widow Varina allowed his remains to be removed to Hollywood Cemetery in Richmond, Virginia. The Army of Northern Virginia's column in Metairie remains dedicated to Davis's memory, since the bronze letters that recorded his name and dates discolored the marble before they were pried off.

Mason, Paul, and I timed our visit to Metairie Cemetery specifically to arrive on All Saints' Day. Historically, November 1st saw a citywide celebration in New Orleans. Businesses closed, people swarmed the graveyards, the blind and orphaned solicited donations, bands played, and families prepared their ancestors' tombs for winter. They scrubbed the marble, re-plastered the bricks, whitewashed the plaster, and weatherproofed doors and windows. Fresh flowers, often yellow mums, adorned every grave. The holiday was a joyous one, bringing generations together to celebrate their history, their permanence.

In the modern era, All Saints' Day is no longer the grandest holiday in New Orleans. Mardi Gras, the Jazz Festival, even Halloween have eclipsed it. On All Saints' Day 1999, we saw a fair number of women visiting graves, usually alone. One woman huddled on the steps of her family's mausoleum, crying. Another genuflected quickly in front of a tomb, crossing herself before offering her flowers. All the men we saw were retirees. One older family spread a blanket on the grass near the lagoon so they could picnic. They had a bag of oranges. I heard their wine glasses chime together as we passed.

Perhaps people with children had come the previous weekend. Perhaps the celebration has shifted—as is the case in San Francisco—from communing with your dead in graveyards to praying for them in churches. Holy mass consumes less time than working in the cemetery, even if I personally don't think it's as good for the soul.

Despite the lack of All Saints' decorations, we found a hundred wonderful things in Metairie Cemetery. My favorite monument—as hard as it is to choose a single favorite—belonged to the Egan family. Designed to look like a ruin, its Gothic archway yawns open to the sky, just like the chapel that inspired it on the Egan property in Ireland. New marble blocks had been distressed to appear cracked and broken. Even the family's nameplate looked as if it had been dropped. I loved the intentional devastation.

Another candidate for my favorite was the jaw-dropping Brunswig tomb. The granite pyramid rose taller than wide, stabbing its point into the November sky. The German family name beneath the Egyptian solar disk amused me. A maiden in Greek drapery and elaborate curls raised her hand to knock on the tomb's door. Behind her stood a tall Roman urn with ornate handles and a marble eternal flame frozen in its mouth. Across the entryway crouched a sphinx whose broad shoulders dwarfed her impassive face. The book *Going Out in Style*, which examines the "architecture of eternity," attributes the inspiration for the tomb to one that stands in the Cimitero Monumentale in Milan, Italy. I just liked the juxtaposition of the German drug magnate retiring into eternity with a Greek maiden inside an Egyptian Revival tomb decorated with a Roman urn beneath the humid Louisiana sky.

Paul coveted an astounding grave inspired by one in the Basilica of Santa Croce in Florence, Italy. The baroque monument in Metairie had been built by Eugene Lacosst, a successful Bourbon Street hairdresser who made his fortune in the stock market. His rococo sarcophagus stood inside a blinding marble archway with a half-dome like a band shell. Lacosst is buried alongside his mother.

Behind that stood a row of mausoleums with angels surmounting their roofs. I'd seen it in antique postcards. I loved the pair of marble angels atop the Aldigé monument. Mrs. Jules Aldigé, her daughter, and granddaughter drowned in 1898 when the steamship *Bourgoyne* sank in the Atlantic Ocean. Atop their cenotaph, two angels stood inside the prow of a boat. One angel clasped her arms around her companion, either clinging to her or holding her back. The other angel had thrown her arm over her head in distress as she lifted off. Of all the angels I've ever photographed, these were the most dramatic.

Just beyond that, a little retired woman sat before the opened doors of a mausoleum. As I neared, she looked up from reading a glossy brochure. She smiled graciously, startling me; everyone else we'd seen in the cemetery completely ignored us. "Are you photographing graves?" she asked.

She must have known that we were. I had my Pentax with its telephoto lens slung around my neck. Mason and Paul both carried point-and-shoots. "Yes, ma'am," I said. "I've driven by the cemetery before, but I've never been in."

She asked if I came from New Orleans. San Francisco, I told her. "Y'all are buried in the ground out there?" she asked.

I nodded and told her we had nothing as grand as the cemeteries of New Orleans.

Her whole family lay in the mausoleum at her back. She believed it was one of the oldest ones in the cemetery. Perhaps she meant that as an invitation to photograph it and her, but I didn't take the liberty.

"My family is buried in Michigan," I said.

She nodded sagely. "I'm the last of mine," she confided. "When I'm gone, they'll seal this tomb up and we'll all roll around in there together."

Not much I could say to that, but I didn't feel she was looking for comfort: just relishing the fact. As I tried to figure out how to politely excuse myself, she asked if I'd seen the dog. "There are several stories, but I heard that when its master died, the dog vanished for a couple of days. They found it guarding its master's grave. Eventually, they buried it in there with him. I couldn't say if that is true, but that's what I've heard." She fanned herself languidly with the brochure. "Nowadays, someone comes into the cemetery at night to tie bows around the dog's neck on the big holidays: Easter, All Saints', and Christmas. The cemetery posts guards, but no one's ever seen doing it. On Mardi Gras, they leave beads."

"Ooh, I need to see that," I said.

"Now, I don't remember where exactly it is, but if you go up and around the curve," she gestured toward the lane, "you'll find it."

After some wandering around, we did. My guide had neglected to mention that the Masich dog sculpture had engraved curls, like a childish lamb. Fat, almost angry, tears hung like pearls from the inner corners of the statue's eyes. Someone had tied a bright pink bow around his neck and placed a bouquet of yellow carnations between his paws. I was glad to see the guardian of the dead hadn't been neglected on All Saints' Day.

Of all the graveyards I'd visited, I couldn't remember ever speaking to a plot owner about where they planned to end up. I wished I wasn't so shy. I sensed I could've sat and chatted with the lady, that she would have welcomed the company and the audience. The brief conversation we'd had added so much to my appreciation and enjoyment of her eventual home. It made me long for the old times, when All Saints' Day would have brought throngs to graveyard. Just imagine all the stories you could have heard then!

Update: Since it occupies low ground close to Lake Pontchartrain, the Metairie District was completely inundated after Hurricane Katrina in 2005. The photographs of mausoleums barely cresting the water broke my heart. I haven't had the opportunity to return to New Orleans since then, so I can't report how well everything has been restored. The disaster just underlines the fragility of these old cemeteries, full of history and one-of-a-kind artwork.

Unknown Soldier, Post Cemetery, Mackinac Island, Michigan

TOMBSTONE TALES

Post Cemetery, Sainte Anne's Catholic Cemetery, and Protestant Cemetery
Mackinac Island, Michigan: August 22, 2000

JUST NORTH OF MICHIGAN's LOWER PENINSULA lies Mackinac Island, the #1 tourist destination in the state. When I was a kid, my folks took me and my brother up several times to explore the old fort—complete with costumed soldiers doing marching drills and cannons fired out over the water—and a museum dedicated to a doctor who had studied digestion through another man's abdominal war wound. We loved it.

In 1898, the island banned motorized traffic, so the chief modes of transportation remain bicycles and horses. Horse-drawn taxis deliver tourists from the ferry docks to their hotels. Horse-drawn tour buses circle the island, lecturing about the island's native history, the time it served as a hub in the fur trade, and the two battles fought on its soil during the War of 1812. Since those exciting days, Mackinac Island has become a quiet, relaxing retreat, where life moves at a slower pace.

I hadn't been up to the island in twenty years when my mom suggested a trip. My parents and I reached the Mackinac (pronounced mack-in-naw) Island Visitors Center ten minutes before it closed for the afternoon. Mom asked if they offered the night tour of the village, led by a schoolteacher, which she'd taken on a previous visit. The answer was no. Not missing a beat, Mom asked, "Is there a tour of the graveyard?"

I couldn't have been prouder of her for thinking to ask. Lucky me: there was a one-time cemetery tour. Tickets were ten dollars. I would have happily paid for Mom and Dad to join me, but they didn't seem inclined. It was hard to decide to go alone, since the tour didn't start until dusk and I wasn't all that familiar with the island, but I really wanted to take a night tour—my first—of a cemetery. I bought an advance ticket, so that the tour wouldn't be called off for lack of interest.

As the afternoon wore on, I grew progressively more anxious. I don't like to explore unfamiliar places alone. Fifteen years earlier, I was attacked by a man my university had on suicide watch. He grabbed me in a busy hallway in my dorm as I walked with a girlfriend. Since then, my sense of safety requires the presence of other people. I have no illusion that just being with them would stop an attack—but maybe, like the last time, they could chase down my assailant. Still, my parents had no desire to climb to the top of the island to reach the cemeteries. If I went, I would have to go alone.

After dinner, I walked my parents back to the hotel to get Mom's umbrella. They planned to stroll through the village and watch the sunset, but rain clouds threatened from the north. We said our goodbyes and I marched off like I wasn't a coward.

My heart thudded in my chest as I climbed steep Bogan Lane. The street dead-ended at a wooden staircase that led upward for more stories than I could count. I wouldn't have chosen such an isolated path, but I didn't have time to find another way up the bluff to the cemetery. I paused at the foot of the stairway, trying to calm down. I would be safe, of course. This was an island. No one would dare molest me because they'd have no way to escape. The ferries stopped running at sunset.

Unless they owned a boat, I thought, realizing that it would look suspicious to sail away after dark.

It crossed my mind that I could just eat the ticket price, go into "town," and have a drink somewhere until I could slink back to the hotel. Mom and Dad need never know that I was afraid to wander the island alone. All the same, I really, really wanted to attend the graveyard tour.

I would be safe, I promised myself, then started upward. Trees shadowing the stairs made them feel enclosed. Even though I didn't pass a soul as I climbed, I couldn't allow myself to pause and rest. When I reached the top of the staircase, my knees quivered.

A handful of mansions lined a paved street that stretched off to my right. I'd expected to find a bench at the summit, where I might catch my breath and load film into my camera. There wasn't anywhere to sit. I guess the locals didn't want tourists loitering in front of their houses. An old-fashioned street lamp stood there, so I knew I'd have at least one light on the walk back. I checked my backpack to be sure I'd brought my mini flashlight.

The path turned left, into the forest. I felt like I should leave a trail of breadcrumbs, so I could find my way back after dark. The lonely road dwindled to what seemed like a bike path between the trees. My nerves twanged again. I wished my sixty-year-old parents had come along, although my dad could never have made the climb.

I'd left the island map with Dad, but remembered that I wanted Garrison Road. When I reached the path that ran behind the fort, I found a sign pointing to the cemeteries half a mile away. Cemeteries, plural, I noted with excitement. I picked up my pace. I didn't have any sense how long I take to walk half a mile. Usually distances aren't so carefully measured for me. I hustled, since the ticket said the tour started at 7:30, instead of the 8 p.m. printed on the flyer I'd cajoled out of the clerk at the Visitors Center.

I reached Sainte Anne's Cemetery first. Its stone gates opened on the left side of Garrison Road, where a sign forbade riding horses in the graveyard. It struck me as sad that tourists needed to be asked to behave.

I stopped in the shadows at the side of the road to load my Pentax K-1000. My watch said 7:15. I felt sticky in the August humidity, even in a T-shirt. My hands shook as I tried to thread the film. The light was fading, but I thought if I hurried, I might be able to take some pictures with the aperture dialed all the way open. Hopefully I could hold steady enough, once I calmed down.

Mosquitoes whined around my ears. I needed to get some bug lotion on *fast*. While I slicked myself up, a couple of costumed players wandered by, discussing whether they would have sex. The woman asked cheerily if I could share some "bug juice."

After I gave her a handful of lotion, I ducked into the Catholic cemetery. Sainte Anne's sprawled across an irregularly shaped piece of land, bounded by the curves of Garrison Road on the north. The oldest graves seemed to lie on the Garrison side. I didn't see any angels, but lots of stones dated from the last half of the 19th century. I knew they must have been ordered and shipped from the "mainland," so finding them was a nice surprise.

As the afternoon light failed, the colors looked very strange. Everything took on a yellowy pallor as the setting sun tinged the overcast. I attached my huge flash and tested it a couple of times, but it took forever to recharge. I hoped my battery would last. If only I'd come prepared for this, instead of rushing around. I wondered if I could settle down enough, once the tour began, to enjoy myself.

I watched people come into the Catholic Cemetery, then climb over its low fieldstone wall to get out, rather than backtrack to a gate. Probably these were same people who needed to be told not to ride their horses through the graveyard.

About 7:30 I crossed Garrison Road to the Post Cemetery. The burial ground lay in a slight depression, surrounded by a white picket fence. Even though summer hadn't ended yet, a tree inside the graveyard blazed orange. Regulation military headstones stood at attention in straight lines, joined by a variety of other sorts of tombstones. I liked seeing a military cemetery with personality.

A sign listed some of the people interred there. German-born Civil War Private Ignatius Goldhofer came to Mackinaw Island in 1869. In 1872, his wife buried him in the Post Cemetery. Josiah and Mary Cowles buried two children here, leaving them behind when Lieutenant Cowles got stationed elsewhere. Also in the Post Cemetery lay civilian Edward Biddle, who'd served as village president, sheriff, and surveyor.

Currently, both the Park Service and the Bureau of Veteran Affairs oversee the cemetery. It stands with Arlington, Gettysburg, and the Punchbowl as one of four cemeteries in the United States who always fly their flags at half-mast. I didn't think to ask why. Instead, I noted the faded Stars and Stripes on the flagpole and the crisp miniature flags thrust into the graves.

My camera crapped out. It was too dark to figure out if the battery had died or if I'd screwed up loading the film. One more reason to switch to a digital, I thought. Scowling, I put the heavy Pentax into my backpack. I'd have to come back in the daylight, if I wanted photographs.

I needn't have worried about the tour being cancelled. People kept arriving on foot and by horse-drawn taxi until eventually sixty people clustered around. The organizers split us up. My group of fifteen went off with a good-looking college boy named Brian.

Rather than touring just the Post Cemetery, we saw all three graveyards. My group started in the Protestant Cemetery, the farthest one west and the most recently opened. Oaks, pines, and beeches separated the Protestants from the military graveyard. A low wall of openwork stone, pierced like lace, surrounded their graves.

Originally, Mackinac Island had only a Catholic cemetery, set up by French fur traders in the 18th century. It lay down near Sainte Anne's Church, closer to the water. For nearly one hundred years, Mackinac Island simply had no Protestant community. Once the fishing industry began in earnest, Calvinist missionaries came to preach to the fishermen and convert the natives. In 1823, they'd built their first cemetery near the Mission Church, now a museum. By 1856, the village banned burials in town. The original Protestant cemetery, long since abandoned by the mission, was declared a public nuisance. The current plot of land was borrowed from the military about that time. The first known graves in the Protestant Cemetery (its official name) date from the 1850s.

Fragrant with cedar and pine, the Protestant Cemetery was one of the best smelling graveyards I've visited. I had to watch my step as acorns rolled under my feet.

The first grave we visited belonged to the man who'd made Mackinac Island a nationally recognized resort. An actor with a silver mustache and a long black coat played Eugene Sullivan, social director for the Grand Hotel, who reminisced about his boss, Jimmy "the Comet" Hayes. James R. Hayes had managed the Grand Hotel during the Victorian era. He decided that Michigan alone couldn't support the hotel, so he courted the wealthy of Chicago. When he heard Theodore Roosevelt planned to tour the country, Hayes invited the President to be a guest of the hotel. Before Roosevelt could decline, Hayes wrote all the major Midwestern newspapers to announce the President's visit. Roosevelt never came, but the press attention cemented the hotel's reputation.

I knew from the flyer that there would be costumed characters on the tour, but I liked that they didn't play the dead people at our feet. Instead, actors played friends and family reminiscing about the dead.

One of my favorite stories in the Protestant Cemetery regarded William Marshall, Mackinac Island's longest serving soldier. During the Civil War, Marshall manned the fort alone, guarding three soldiers from Tennessee imprisoned there. When his term of service expired, he reenlisted himself.

More recent burials included G. Mennen "Soapy" Williams, heir to the Mennen Company. (Mennen made Speed Stick and Teen Spirit deodorants, before Soapy's children sold the company to Colgate-Palmolive.) As Michigan's governor for two terms, Williams arranged funding for the suspension bridge that links Michigan's Upper and

Lower Peninsulas. The Mackinac Bridge opened in 1957.

I enjoyed several epitaphs: "The whole world is my neighbor," from the headstone of Lina Kurowski; "His music built bridges from man to man," on the marker for George McAlpine Fraser; and Logan Herbert Roots, Bishop of Hankow, China from 1904-1928, whose gravestone said, "The Indians have a saying, 'Whom God loves, he gives a home at Mackinac.'" His tombstone called him a pioneer in the world fight for moral rearmament, but I couldn't guess what that meant. That's one of the things I like best about graveyards: you never get all the answers. Some things simply remain mysteries.

Our tour group returned to the Post Cemetery, where interments may have begun in the mid-1820s. Records show that forty American soldiers died at the fort between 1796 and 1835, but only a dozen graves remained marked in 1835. Those who fell during the War of 1812 probably still lie under the Wawashkamo Golf Course, where the British buried them.

Of the 109 burials in the Post Cemetery, 76 have headstones labeled "Unknown." Phil Porter, in his Park Service pamphlet *Mackinac Island's Post Cemetery*, blamed post commanders for the number of unknown soldiers. They kept poor records and didn't maintain the site. Some of the unknowns have since been identified.

In 1835, Dr. C. R. Gilman described the picket fence around the Post Cemetery and reported that a former post commander built it at his own expense. Gilman noted only two wooden headboards then, one for Private Andrew Lawrence who drowned in the harbor the previous year.

I halted beside by the lamb sleeping atop the monument for William A. and Frank M., sons of William and Matilda Marshall, aged "2 years, 4 months, 9 days" and "2 years, 3 months." While it's rare for wives to be allowed burial in military cemeteries, I don't think I'd ever seen children buried amidst the soldiers. Their presence testified to the isolation of inhabitants of the island. Their epitaph made me sad: "Short pain, short grief, dear babes were they, now joys, eternal and divine."

The last military funeral on the island celebrated Private Coon Walters in 1891. Four years later, the US Army abandoned Fort Mackinac, leaving behind the military burial ground. The cemetery fell into disrepair until the Mackinac Island State Park Commission began maintenance in 1905.

This didn't end the cemetery's troubles. Caretakers in the early 20th century made mistakes on replacement headstones. Unfortunately, as in so many other graveyards, caretakers lined the markers up for ease of mowing. The current placement of the headstones bears little connection to the bodies in the ground.

The final graveyard on our tour was Sainte Anne's, where I'd begun the evening. The cemetery had originally been called Bonny Brae, or goodly meadows. It contained older graves moved up from the first Catholic cemetery on Hoborn and Market Streets, just north of the Village Inn restaurant, where I'd had dinner with my folks. That earlier cemetery, created in 1779, had filled to capacity before being disassembled.

As early as 1852, islanders buried their dead on military reserve land near the Post Cemetery. The Army eventually ceded the land to the church. The reason the three graveyards clustered together was that this was one of the few areas of the rocky island with topsoil deep enough to dig graves.

By the 1880s, most bodies from the first Catholic cemetery had been moved to Sainte Anne's. Phil Porter's leaflet on the Post Cemetery reported, "the old Catholic burial ground showed signs of neglect: a 'forlorn, unkempt, ragged-looking, little spot,' according to one 1889 newspaper account." Not all the graves were transferred, however. Several stray headstones have been discovered in the weeds in town over the years. One now resides in the village museum.

The oldest marked grave in Sainte Anne's Cemetery belongs to Mary Biddle, who died in December 1833. Her parents, Edward and Agatha Biddle, paid for a stone carved by W. E. Peters in Detroit (he signed his work) to mark her grave, which had been moved from the earlier cemetery. Her father Edward, who had served as the village president, was buried in the Post Cemetery across the road.

Mary's epitaph summed up the brevity of many children's lives at the time:

> As the sweet flower that scents the morn
> but withers in the rising day,
> Thus lovely was this infant's dawn
> Thus swiftly fled its life away.

Also buried in the cemetery was Lieutenant G. A. Graveraet, a 22-year-old who oversaw Confederate prisoners of war at Camp Douglas, the notoriously unsanitary camp near Chicago, before leading the 1st Michigan Sharpshooters Company K into battle at Spotsylvania. His tombstone said he died in Washington of wounds received before Petersburg. Sharing his monument was 1st Sgt. Henry G. Graveraet, 57, one of the "boys" in Company K, who died in the battle. How agonizing it must be to have your father die under your command.

Another ghost evoked by the tour was Matthew Geary, an Irish immigrant who became a government fish inspector and made his fortune. He was remembered by Jim Union, a cooper, who had a "wooden marker because he couldn't afford a stone like Mr. Geary." Coopers made barrels to crate up whitefish to ship to Chicago. Their necessary labor didn't pay as well as the bribery fishing captains could offer the inspectors. Union's grave, now unmarked, had been the first in Sainte Anne's Cemetery in 1852.

When the graveyard tour ended, people drifted uncertainly off into the twilight. I'd hoped to meet some nice women with whom I could walk back to town, but the tour had been such a whirlwind that there hadn't been time to speak to anyone else. The group simply hustled from actor to actor, heard the stories of the people whose graves we clustered around, and rushed on.

I still didn't have a map of the island. I suspected that I could walk down past the fort and into the village below by following someone, but I wondered if I'd remember which street my hotel was on if I came at it from that direction. Better to go back the way I'd come.

I trailed a French Canadian couple down the road that wound past the back of Fort Mackinac. The fortifications glowed ghostly bluish white in the half-light. Oak branches strained toward the path, trying to close out the darkening sky.

When we reached the row of mansions at the crest of the hill, the French Canadians turned left, leaving me to face the staircase alone. Down is always preferable to up, but I stood at the landing, looking out over the village below. Old-fashioned streetlights twinkled in the darkness. The breeze carried me a breath of laughter. Somewhere, a dog barked. Other than that, the lack of automobiles on the island made for a kind of quiet that I'd forgotten existed.

I felt more peaceful now. I didn't mind being completely alone in this strange place—and I felt entirely alone in the quiet darkness. I'd been calmed by exploring the graveyards. Nothing bad had ever happened to me in a cemetery, I realized. I'd always felt safe there.

A guttural engine revved up as the last ferry chugged out of the harbor. Once the boat left, we were trapped on the island for the night.

The wind blew colder, raising goosebumps over my humid skin.

Time to climb down.

Bodie as seen from Wards Cemetery, Bodie State Historic Park, California

GOOD, BY GOD, I'M GOING TO BODIE!

Wards Cemetery, Masonic Cemetery, Miners Union Cemetery, Bodie State Historic Park, California: September 16, 2000

I'D WANTED TO GO TO BODIE FOR SO LONG that I don't remember how I first heard about the place. I've known for years that it's a ghost town on the eastern edge of California, over the Sierra Mountains and past the tufa spires of Mono Lake. That the desert site was excruciatingly hot in the summer and unreachable in winter (when the pass through Yosemite snows closed) just added to Bodie's allure. Its inhospitable site preserved it and kept it glamorous.

In its brief heyday, 10,000 people lived and worked in over 2,000 structures in Bodie. Miners who'd chosen to take stock rather than wages brought home $880 a week. Over the course of a single month in the 1880s, miners dug out $600,000 in gold and silver. The total haul reached thirty million dollars in gold, one million in silver.

A ghost town does not die all at once. Folks were lured away when the next mine opened, promising more money for easier labor. Fancy girls and gamblers trailed their marks. Some people stayed, because the town had become their home. Their clapboard houses encompassed all their worldly wealth. They no longer had the cash to hire a truck to move their belongings elsewhere. Many people—when finally forced to leave Bodie by its isolation, its extremes of temperature, or the inability to farm their own food or even water their cattle—simply walked away. They took what they could carry on their backs, or mules, or pickup trucks, and left the rest behind.

As a functioning town, Bodie survived into the modern era. It sports a Shell gas station and the hulks of several cars. It had the first power-generating station in the West. Power lines still etch the empty desert sky. But Bodie, which had once been fabulously wealthy and the "meanest town in the West," offered no amenities to middle-class families traveling in the Eisenhower years. It stands a long way from anywhere. It still boasts no lodging or working restaurants. The washboard road into town continues to be passable only to motor vehicles traveling at five miles per hour. Despite the rage for Gene Autry, Roy Rogers, and the cowboys of early television, Bodie survived in a West too wild to be reclaimed. The wilderness gradually swallowed the dirt track. Few people traveled the valleys of the eastern Sierra foothills to loot the antiques away.

Between the time the last working mine closed in 1947 and the ghost town's induction into the state park system in 1962, it effectively vanished from the map like Bonny Doon. The outside world forgot about the boomtown. It amazes me that the memory of the city was so completely erased.

Currently, Bodie has been designated the best-preserved ghost town in America. Up to 200,000 people visit it annually. Its 170 surviving buildings stand in a state of arrested decay. Nothing is being restored; at the same time, nothing is allowed to tumble to the ground. Overseen by the California Park Service, Bodie State Historic Park's highlights include an undertaker's parlor, complete with coffin showroom; the last standing church, scoured of whitewash by the gritty winds; several gambling houses, still furnished with roulette wheels and billiard tables; and one of the gold mills which day and night pounded the city's wealth from the hard quartz.

Most of the buildings in Bodie are no longer open to tourists. Instead, their windows have been sealed with Plexiglas so that the curious can stare in on dust-softened beds and cast-iron cook stoves, oak pews and grand pianos, crystal chandeliers and zinc-topped bars: all manner of furnishings too heavy or costly to haul away when the economy failed.

I found that the strangest, most appealing aspect of wandering through Bodie: so *much* remains in place. It's as if a neutron bomb went off and vaporized the inhabitants, leaving their daily lives to await their return. Rather than a city's skeleton of rotting buildings, Bodie looks as if it could be spiffed up and inhabited even now.

During the boom times, gunfights broke out weekly, if not daily. Mine accidents occurred repeatedly. Childhood could be brutal. With life so uncertain in Bodie, the extensive graveyard that overlooks the town is in fact five cemeteries adjacent to one another. The first is Wards Cemetery, the main city graveyard. Directly behind that lies the Masonic Cemetery, followed by the Miners Union Cemetery.

West of the perimeter fence remain the Chinese, excluded from the proper graveyards. Whenever Chinese immigrants died in California, they wanted to be buried only long enough for their remains to skeletonize. The surviving Chinese in the area were supposed to open the graves, collect the bones, and return them to their homeland, where they could rest with their ancestors. Unfortunately, because of violent prejudice and the transient nature of the Gold Rush boomtowns, many Chinese linger in their original graves. The Friends of Bodie's cemetery brochure estimates that several hundred Chinese were—and are—buried in Bodie.

The final cemetery on the hill shelters the outcasts: gunmen, illegitimate children, prostitutes, all those shunned by "respectable" folk. Only wooden posts or heaps of rocks ever marked most of those graves. Now the only marker visible is fairly modern. A cement tablet, stamped with a rough cross and her name handwritten in shaky letters, remembers Rosa May, a prostitute who died while nursing miners during a pneumonia epidemic.

Inside the proper cemeteries, a surprising amount endures. Some of the plots still sport split-rail fences. Beautiful ironwork, imported from as far away as Terre Haute, Indiana surrounds others. Lonely fences, like the frames of vacant beds, punctuate the sagebrush-covered hills and underscore the vast, silent isolation of the dead who've been left behind.

One of the most beautiful monuments has a child-sized marble angel leaning against a scroll to the memory of Evelyn Myers. A month shy of her fourth birthday, Evelyn's folks had a drainage ditch dug around their home. Curious little Evelyn leaned over the railing on the porch to watch the workman. Without looking over his shoulder, he brought his pick back and crushed her skull.

Bodie's museum in the former Miners Union Hall displays a clipping from the *Bridgeport Chronicle,* which reported, "A sad accident occurred in Bodie...which has enlisted the sympathies of the people of the entire county for the bereaved parents.... The funeral took place on Wednesday, the attendance showing the deep sympathy of the people, with whom she was a great favorite, being a most beautiful and lovable child." Although her name wasn't mentioned in the story, her father Albert K. Myers operated the general store, according to a bookmark I picked up in the museum's gift shop. Everyone in town must have known him.

If Evelyn's parents lie in the graveyard, they're in unmarked graves. More likely, they moved away and left their beloved child behind.

The little museum also includes several of the hearses that worked in Bodie. The carriages were kept in such splendid condition that I wondered if they are pressed into service when any of the old-time inhabitants of Bodie return to their final home. In the Wards Cemetery section of the graveyard, I had been startled to see the marker of Mary A. Miller, who died in 1963. Apparently, people born in Bodie or who can prove they resided there are still allowed to retire to their family plots. That custom explained a curious wooden sign on the cemetery fence that read, "Cemetery Still In Use. Please Show Due Respect."

Bodie's namesake has only been shown proper deference in later years, although confusion lingers over his real name. When "Bill Body" made his initial discovery in 1859, richer diggings in Virginia City and elsewhere overshadowed it. In the winter of 1860, Body (or Bodey) got caught outside his cabin by a snowstorm and froze to death. Coyotes stripped his flesh before his partner found him in the spring. Not until 1879 did the city fathers reclaim his body from its shallow grave and transfer it to Wards Cemetery. Townsfolk ordered a granite monument to celebrate him, but before it could be placed on his grave, US President James A. Garfield was assassinated. Swept up in the national mourning, Bodie's citizens co-opted Body's monument and rededicated it as a cenotaph to the slain president.

In 1976, Boone's Memorials placed a large black granite marker on the founder's gravesite. On it, the founding father is referred to as "Waterman S. Bodey," but the other details of his story remain the same. In that monument's shadow stands a cement wall erected by the historical society E Clampus Vitus to "William S. Bodey," which prays, "Let him repose in peace amid these everlasting hills."

My visit to Bodie was everything I'd dreamed. The dry air immediately stripped the curl from my hair. The altitude of 8400 feet played mischief with my photographs. Even though I intentionally underexposed the film to counteract the bright desert sunshine, the sky in the photos is a luminous turquoise behind the dazzling marble monuments.

A sign in the museum remarked that nature reclaims the graveyard even as the gritty desert wind polishes the monuments. I worried that the grit would scratch my lens or gum up my shutter release. The heat, dryness, relentless sun and wind wore me out early in the day. It's difficult to imagine how exhausting it must have been to struggle to feed a family in those conditions. Undoubtedly, the arid natural surroundings contributed to the rowdiness of Bodie's nightlife.

Mason, our friend Samuel (with whom we'd traveled to Paris and who had become a cemetery photographer himself), and I returned to our tents beside a stream half an hour's drive away. We dozed beneath the pines, listening to the songs of birds leaving the mountains as autumn wound down. Soon we would leave the ghost town to its ghosts when we migrated back to San Francisco. We could travel in hours what would've taken Bodie's citizens days. Sometimes it's good to live in the modern era—especially when the past still welcomes visitors to enjoy its mysteries.

Shelley's grave, The Protestant Cemetery, Rome

HALF IN LOVE WITH DEATH

Il Cimitero Acattolico, Rome: April 21, 2001

*"The cemetery is an open space among the ruins, covered in winter
with violets and daisies. It might make one in love with death, to think
that one should be buried in so sweet a place."*
—Percy Bysshe Shelley's introduction to "Adonais"

DURING THE LAST YEARS OF THE ROMAN REPUBLIC,
after Caesar conquered Egypt and vanquished Cleopatra, Egyptiana
became fashionable in Rome. *Access Rome* says, "Numerous pyramids
sprouted all over Rome." I don't know if that's true. I do know that
the only Roman-era pyramid still in existence sits across the street
from the *Piramide* stop on Rome's subway line B.

The estate of Caius Cestius built his pyramid in 12 BC. His tomb
announces he was a praetor and tribune, as well as an epulo: one of
seven priests who offered sacrificial meals to the gods. Other than
the pyramid, he left no mark in recorded history. Only his tomb
ensured the survival of his name.

Unlike the other tombs—long destroyed—which once lined the
road to Ostia, Cestius's pyramid survived because it was incorporated
into the eleven-mile wall Emperor Aurelian built to protect the city
from barbarians in 271 AD. During the Middle Ages, people believed
Cestius's tomb belonged to Romulus, founder of Rome. I'm
fascinated by how different ages mythologized the pyramid to suit
their needs. Their veneration kept the tomb intact. In fact, the
pyramid owes its continued existence to serving as a landmark as
much as to the protection of the Popes, even though it was as pagan
as pagan could be.

Mason and I came up out of the Metro to see Cestius's hundred-
foot-tall pyramid directly across the road. Aurelian's old brick wall
connected right up to it. The crumbling bricks looked fragile in
comparison to the older pyramid.

Half of the pyramid lies lower than the modern surface of the ground, which seems strange because the Protestant graveyard beside it rises much higher. The cemetery was built on a hill where Rome dumped its garbage, I understand. For how many hundreds of years had this area served as a dump? What treasures lie in the soil accumulated around the pyramid?

Outside the moat around the pyramid, a plaque said that in his will, Cestius stipulated that he wanted his Egyptian mausoleum constructed before a year had passed after his death. The project bankrupted his heirs.

A frescoed burial room inside the pyramid spans twenty by fifteen feet. Apparently, one can enter the pyramid through an entrance cut into its walls during its restoration in 1663. Unfortunately, I didn't know that when we visited. It probably wouldn't have helped if I had. My sources, published over a span of forty years, disagree on how one might get permission to visit the interior of the tomb.

When we visited, the pyramid's marble façade glowed bright white in the late April sunshine. Although Cestius's inscription was still legible, grass and wildflowers had sprouted from toeholds between the stone blocks, bright crimson and lavender and deep pink. I hoped my photos would capture the colors.

We knew we were supposed to follow "the wall" around to the cemetery's entrance, but the wall came to a point by the pyramid. In one direction, it went straight down the street away from the station. In the other, it turned a corner beyond the Porta San Paolo. On the way to his beheading circa 65 AD, Saint Paul (author of all those letters in the New Testament) walked past Cestius's pyramid. Now the gate near the pyramid bears his name.

We decided to try that direction. Through an iron grate in the wall, we could see old, crumbling gravestones amongst the trees. I caught a breath of the Judas trees in magenta bloom and sneezed.

Around the next corner, down a little residential street, we found the cemetery gate. It's funny how bold I've gotten about wandering foreign neighborhoods. Mason and I have searched out so many graveyards that we no longer try to triangulate on a map.

Permanent Italians warned that we would have to ring the bell to get the gardeners to let us in. The bell hung just inside the doorway, a real bell that swung back and forth. The people ahead of us rang it and we followed them in. Throughout our visit, the gardeners kept busy running back and forth to let people in. Most visitors seemed to be tourists with cameras, but families came to attend graves. Small children pirouetted beside the tombstones, warbling as their parents conversed.

The entry lay on the low side of the hill so that the graveyard rose gently to meet the old city wall. Birdsong filled the air, which was rich with the perfumes of cypress and roses. The space danced with light and color, shades of green and stone.

Il Cimitero Acattolico di Roma dates to 1738, when an Oxford student named Langton was buried under a lead shield near the pyramid. Prior to that, the Vatican forbade burial of unbelievers and foreigners inside Rome's city limits. Bodies of Protestants either had to be transported to Leghorn, one 160 miles away, or buried with the prostitutes below the Pincian Hill. That changed only after a British ship captured one of Napoleon's vessels and returned its cargo of looted treasures to the Vatican. In gratitude, the pope set aside a field beside the old pyramid for the burial of non-Catholic foreigners.

That was the limit of papal generosity, however. For years the Vatican stalled, claiming that a cemetery fence would obscure the view of the pyramid. Finally, in 1824, Pope Leo XII allowed the oldest part of the graveyard to be surrounded by a moat. The Italian Catholic populace promptly filled it with dead dogs and cats.

Until 1870, a Vatican commission reviewed every monument proposed for the cemetery. Since they believed there could be no salvation outside the Mother Church, they forbade the epitaph "Rest in Peace." In addition, according to *Permanent Italians*, crosses could not adorn gravestones. The limitation must have been lifted at some point, but for the most part, it led to a graveyard that looks like no other.

Mason and I turned left inside the cemetery gate to pick our way through the luxuriant green grass. It wasn't difficult to find John Keats's grave beneath the elderly shade trees in the *parte antica*, the old section of the graveyard. Little daisies spangled the grass.

Keats had come to Rome in September 1820, already suffering from the tuberculosis that would kill him five months later. As he lay dying, Keats sent his friend Joseph Severn to visit the graveyard. Severn wrote later, "On being told about the anemones, violets, and daisies, the poet whispered that he could already feel 'the daisies growing over me."" I wonder if this is where we get our euphemism "pushing up daisies." The *Oxford English Dictionary* doesn't mention the phrase, so I suspect it's American. I'd love to know its genesis.

Twenty-five-year-old Keats published the poems for which we know him over a period of four years. He felt he was dying without leaving a mark on the world, so the epitaph he chose for himself claimed, "Here lies One whose Name was Writ in Water." A lute with missing strings adorns his tombstone.

I thought about the young poet, dead these many years, whose works are still studied by college girls searching for something eternal. Did he have such an incorrect sense of himself, I wondered, or was the epitaph consciously ironic? Probably not. Probably it was as desperately composed as any freshman girl's face when she goes out dressed as *La Belle Dame Sans Merci*.

Keats's name doesn't appear on his own monument, but *is* carved into Joseph Severn's beside him. Severn, *Permanent Italians* says, was an undistinguished painter, but a terrific schmoozer. An artist's palette, down-turned brushes thrust through its thumbhole, decorates his gravestone. In his own epitaph, Severn called himself "devoted friend and deathbed companion of John Keats, whom he lived to see numbered among the immortal poets of England."

The sky overhead shone an amazing potter's blue, deep and glossy, heaped with huge white clouds like a galleon's sails. I pulled out my notebook and sat in the grass to record some impressions, but the wind stuck cold fingers down my collar. Mason and I decided it would be better to find a sunny place to sit.

Despite his poor estimation of his enduring worth, Keats's grave brought distinction to the burial ground. It isn't too much to claim that Keats made the Protestant Cemetery the exquisite place it is today.

Signs pointed us up to Shelley's grave at the back of the graveyard. At the foot of the crumbling brown wall, his ashes lie far from Mary and separate from their son William, whom they'd buried in the old section. Shelley's Latin epitaph translates to "Heart of Hearts." His heart was all that remained whole, when his friends cremated his body, but it doesn't lie in Rome.

In July 1822, Percy Shelley disappeared off the Italian coast while sailing the *Don Juan*, named for Byron's poem. Two weeks later, Shelley's body washed up on a beach near Viareggio. Despite the flesh of his face having been eaten by fishes, Edward Trelawny, another literary adventurer, identified the corpse because Shelley had books by Aeschylus and Keats in his pockets.

Per Italian law, anything that washed ashore had to be buried immediately, as a precaution against the plague. A month later, Trelawny, Byron, and Leigh Hunt exhumed Shelley's body from the beach. An errant mattock blow cracked open Shelley's skull. Byron wanted to keep the skull as a memento, but the other poets forbade it.

They doused the body with wine and set it afire. The corpse split open in the blaze and Trelawny snatched out the unburned heart, which he later presented to Mary. When she died in 1851, the shriveled heart was found in her writing desk, wrapped in a copy of Shelley's poem "Adonais." Mary wanted to be buried in Rome with Shelley, but her parents didn't allow it. Instead, she lies in Saint Peter's Churchyard in Bournemouth. Shelley's heart was buried with her.

Back in 1822, once Shelley had dissolved to ash, the poet-undertakers collected up his cremains. For several years, his urn waited, stashed in the wine cellar of the British consul while negotiations for his burial dragged on. Mary wanted Shelley buried with their toddler William, but new burials had been forbidden in the *parte antica* after August 1822. Finally, Joseph Severn purchased a plot in the new section and Shelley was laid to rest a second time.

The plan had been to disinter William and rebury him in his father's grave. However, when they opened the grave under the child's headstone, the skeleton inside was five and a half feet tall. In the gap between burial and placing the marker, a mistake had been made. Severn wrote, "To search farther we dare not...it would have been a doubtful and horrible thing to disturb any more Strangers' Graves in a Foreign Land."

Be that as it may, when Trelawny saw Shelley's gravesite, it didn't suit him. He purchased a double plot near the Aurelian wall and had Shelley's ashes reburied there.

Years later, when Trelawny himself passed on, his ashes were sent from England to be buried beside Shelley's. His stone reads: "These are two friends whose lives were undivided. So let their memory be, now they have glided under the grave. Let not their bones be parted, for their two hearts in life were single hearted."

It's an unusual boast, since Trelawny scarcely knew Shelley for six months before the younger man's death. After Shelley passed on, Trelawny traveled with Byron to fight in the Greek War of Independence.

Near Shelley's grave knelt an angel I recognized from larger copies in California: guarding Jane Stanford's brother at their namesake university in Palo Alto and over the grave of Teddy Roosevelt's cousin Jenny in Cypress Lawn in Colma. There are many more copies around the world. In Rome's Protestant Cemetery stands the original "Angel of Grief Weeping over the Dismantled Altar of Life." It represents sculptor William Wetmore Story's last work, made to mark the grave of his wife Emelyn in 1895. What a rare honor to have an original monument carved in stone by the man who loved you! When Story died later that same year, he joined her there. Their son Joseph, named for his grandfather, was also reburied there. He had died of a mysterious fever at the age of six a full forty years earlier.

Story's father had inspired his son's career as a sculptor. The senior Joseph Story had been a Supreme Court judge, when he spoke at the opening of Mount Auburn Cemetery, outside of Boston, in 1831. When Judge Story passed away, the cemetery hired William— who had trained as a lawyer—to carve his father's bust. To carry out his commission, William traveled to Italy to study sculpture.

The change of vocation suited him. Nathaniel Hawthorne praised Story's image of Cleopatra in his story, "The Marble Faun." Hawthorne called the likeness "fierce, voluptuous, passionate, tender...one of the images that men keep forever, finding a heat in them that does not cool down through the centuries."

When Mason and I stopped by the Angel of Grief, a tabby cat hid under her wings. The poor feline looked flea-bitten and scruffy, but happy enough to sun himself on the warm white marble. In fact, as we explored, we discovered dozens of cats living in the cemetery, gray and orange and black, all friendly, each pleased to make our acquaintance when we passed through its territory.

At one point, we saw a parade of cats, tails lifted like proud banners, climb one after another up the center path. At the top stood a slim elderly lady, dressed in elegant black. An article I read later in our hotel's tourist magazine said she had fed generations of cats, taking them in to be fixed to limit the population. The concept of birth control in the Catholic nation intrigued me. I wondered how such a thing was even thinkable outside the confines of a Protestant cemetery.

In addition to the living denizens and the famous dead, exquisite artwork crowded the cemetery. One of the first monuments to catch my attention featured a pair of stone doves chasing each other down toward the ground. Despite my usual preferences, I liked a cubist couple that perhaps represented Adam and Eve, since their hips were girdled with stone leaves. Their heads leaned together as he offered her his heart. Was this the first time I'd seen Original Sin depicted in a graveyard? A life-sized dog waited atop another grave with an eager expression, as if he'd just heard his master's voice. I also liked the relief of a bare-chested man tenderly touching the arm of a woman in a transparent toga, which seemed an echo of the pagan funeral monuments of Rome.

Several of the graves had guardians that caught my eye. I especially liked the relief of a toga-clad winged angel of death grasping the arm of a nude musician with a lyre upon his knee. Another masculine angel, nude save for the sheet draped through his belt, stood on a pillar over one grave. A boy in military garb perched atop another headstone. The grave guardians I am used to tend to be female, as in David Robinson's *Saving Graces*. I was surprised to see male figures taking time away from the bustle of the world to keep company with the dead.

The Protestant Cemetery held the first examples of modern Italian mosaic I was privileged to see. A mosaic wreath of forget-me-nots hung at the heart of a cross. Nearby, delicate mosaic-work formed a pair of roses on a field of gold on another gravestone. I hoped that somewhere the dead enjoy the beauty created in their honor.

One of the most unusual grave markers I've ever seen was a marble cross set inside an archway filled with the thinnest sheet of alabaster. Sunlight glowed through the alabaster stone like stained glass. Streaks and ribbons of light wreathed the cross. I've seen few simple monuments as lovely.

The sense of humor in the graveyard surprised me. General Nicola Chiari's epitaph read, "Rosebud. What does that mean?" I smiled at the sort of man who would choose a joke about an American film as the only thing strangers would remember him by.

By the time we'd each shot three rolls of film, the day had grown chilly. My mind chased half-formed thoughts of expatriates who came to die in the former center of the world, but the wind had too much bite for me to sit and write. Tall white clouds piled together in the sky, looking menacing. Mason and I returned to the Metro to seek lunch near Coliseum station. Poking around cemeteries makes me ravenous.

WISH YOU WERE HERE

Entry ticket for the Catacomb of Saint Sebastian, Rome

THE ORIGINAL CATACOMB

Catacombe di San Sebastiano, Appian Way, Rome: April 23, 2001

ON OUR LAST MORNING IN ROME, Mason and I wandered around the Piazza Venezia, trying to find the Archaeobus that would take us out to the Appian Way. I was sick with a cold I'd picked up in the Vatican (go figure) and we'd had no time for breakfast. As we rushed down the stairs near Trajan's column, I missed a step. When I painfully straightened my legs, I discovered I'd skinned both knees. Miraculously, the fall hadn't torn my slacks. I limped to the bus stop to be swept off on our adventure.

The ancient Christian catacombs hadn't initially been on my "must-see in Rome" list. However, the more I read, the more it seemed I should overcome my skepticism. A lot of history had been buried in the old tunnels.

Beyond the third mile marker, the Archaeobus dropped us off near the Catacombe di San Sebastiano. A crowd already loitered in the plaza. Mason and I hurried into the cloister on the right side of the small yellow basilica to be near the entrance when the catacomb reopened after lunch.

We bought our tickets at a window barred like an old train station. The lobby occupied a long, low room full of fragments of marble and terracotta, many clamped tightly to the brown walls. Each item had a relief on it: a bird, a fish, a lamb: symbols of Christianity to people who couldn't read.

These shards of ransacked sarcophagi saddened me. The bodies have been removed from their rest, whether portioned out by the Church or otherwise disrupted. For me, the grave is not the person, but I feel that the spirit of the person enlivens the grave. A vacant tomb has lost something that a rock never owned. Whoever they were to those who loved them, these people have been swallowed by time.

A German-speaking guide summoned a small group of tourists to follow him down the steps, leaving Mason and me in the chilly gallery of shattered tombs. A busload of chattering American tourists filed in behind us. Mason wondered if we should follow the Germans, even without understanding the guide, just so we'd be able to see everything without the horde.

An English-speaking guide appeared. A cheerful Turkish woman, Maria spoke with a mélange of British and Middle Eastern inflections. She glowed with inspiration. She had clearly been "called" to talk about the catacombs, her faith strengthened by the history of the martyrs who'd lain below our feet. I was relieved that she felt no need to testify. Instead, she assumed we were all Christians, that we began with the same point of view.

Maria led us partially down the steps so that she could count the group. Thirty-seven of us would muddle through the tunnels together. Some were frail old people: ladies as fragile as birds, an elderly gentleman who leaned heavily on his middle-aged daughter. At the risk of gross generalization, many of the others appeared to be teachers on spring break. Other than a knot of African American women in bright flowered dresses, ninety-five percent of the group was white. Mason and I represented the low edge of the age curve.

Our guide promised that there would be no ghosts in the tunnels. There were no longer any bodies, either. Most had been removed in the fourth and fifth centuries, when the catacombs suffered at the mercy of barbarian hordes who couldn't breach the walls of Rome.

Maria ran through some figures for us: thousands of graves in four levels comprised the seven miles of Saint Sebastian's catacombs. The tour passed through only a fraction of the second level. The other levels were unlocked only to archaeologists blessed by the Pontificia Commissione di Archaeologia Sacra, a bureau of the Vatican.

The steps reached a landing, then turned to continue downward. We had to take care not to jostle each other on the stairs. I had visions of some lady breaking her hip. Before long, the group reached a level and surged forward. The air, already cold and still, lost another couple of degrees.

Yellow light globes, hung at intervals near the tunnel's ceiling, did little to brighten the gloom. Other tunnels, also lighted, branched off at right angles. They tempted me, but I dreaded getting lost.

Our guide directed our attention overhead with the beam of her flashlight. A pickaxe had scarred the ceiling. "They excavated the catacomb by hand," Maria explained. "The ground here is called tufa, a lava rock that is easy to dig. Fossores, special miners in service to the early church, planned the excavations and did the digging. They carried the earth away in baskets."

She turned our attention to the walls of the tunnel. It looked as if bunks had been carved into the stone, irregular indentations that appeared comfy enough to crawl into. The bed of each cubbyhole lay reasonably flat. The shallow niches spanned just large enough to tuck a body inside.

Maria said, "The dead would be wound in a sheet and placed here, without a coffin, then a slab of marble—if they were wealthy—or terracotta would seal them inside. You may wonder how the fossores reached the graves at the top." She swept her flashlight beam upward. "They filled the graves on top first, then dug the floor down below them." In the tunnel where we stood, the floor had been lowered five times.

She gestured to another hole. Carved between columns of larger holes, this one spanned only as long as my arm, barely deep enough for a bed pillow. "You'll see a lot of graves for children," she warned. "Infant mortality was high."

Maria set off at a pretty good pace into the maze of tunnels. We used Mason's flashlight to peer into graves as we passed. Each featureless hole had been stripped of mementos.

We walked by low arched compartments that began level with the tunnel floor and reached hip-high. Eventually we passed one with its sarcophagus still in place. Did you know that the word sarcophagus means flesh-eating stone? The original Greek sarcophagi were so named because the kind of limestone they were made of speeded up dissolution of the corpse within.

That's the sort of thing I knew going into the tour. I'm sure we could have had more lecture if there hadn't been approximately forty of us in the group. Few areas were large enough that our group could coalesce. The guide spoke only when all of us could hear, which I don't dispute, but I'm sure we passed treasures she never mentioned.

In some places, the tunnel expanded into small rooms with low, vaulted ceilings. The configuration made me think of a snake that had swallowed an egg. Those rooms had once entombed families. We jammed into one, dark as a cave. I huddled into the hollow where a shadowy altar stood, more concerned about cobwebs than ghosts.

Then again, what would spiders eat so far underground?

I tried to conjure a sense of what the place must have been like when bodies filled it. There was, of course, no embalming in the Roman world of the second and third centuries. When people died, their survivors had to cart them out of Rome, since the Law of the Twelve Tables forbade burial inside the city walls. Most Romans would not have owned a horse or an ox, especially not Christians, who tended to come from the lower and slave classes. I suspect that transportation of a cadaver presented a pressing concern in the Roman summer.

So here we have a cool—though unrefrigerated—compound of seven miles of un-embalmed corpses. I envisioned early Christians negotiating the tunnels by the flickering light of clay oil lamps, through air clouded with myrrh and the inescapable, cloying sweetness of rot.

The pagan majority of Romans disposed of their dead by cremation. They burned corpses on a pyre, then collected the ashes into an urn. These urns of ashes were placed in tombs that lined the Appian Way, the road to Ostia through the Porta San Paolo, and all the other old roads leading out of Rome.

Jews practiced inhumation—burial in earth—in observation of Genesis 3:19: "Earth you are and to Earth you shall return." We hear it most commonly as "ashes to ashes, dust to dust" from the funeral service in the Book of Common Prayer. Early Christians pursued this custom, burying their dead because Christ had been placed whole in his tomb. Early Christians anticipated bodily resurrection, just like Christ.

Romans called a collection of graves a necropolis: a city of the dead. Christians, many of whom spoke Greek rather than Latin, referred to their burial places as *coemeteria*, equivalent to dormitories. The root of dormitory means to sleep. Christians believed that their dead were merely resting (ideally in peace) until Christ came again and ushered them into heaven. This is why we refer to a graveyard as a cemetery.

So the catacombs were a vast maze of rotting bodies where the souls were believed to linger, awaiting resurrection. Some of these dead did not go gently to their graves but had been martyred, dying for their faith. How could there not be ghosts?

Maria led us into a room unlike any we'd visited. Marble sheathed its floor. Its walls were whitewashed. In contrast to the rest of the catacomb, this room was brightly lit. It seemed spacious until our tour group spread out into it.

On my left stood a simple stone table, draped with a spotless white cloth edged in lace. Across from that, on a pedestal, balanced a polished marble bust of a man in pain or ecstasy. The bust was so wonderfully crafted that my fingertips tingled, wanting to touch that emotion.

Maria explained, "Sebastian was a Roman soldier who decided he could no longer persecute Christians. The other soldiers tied him to a tree and shot him with their arrows. They left him to die, but he recovered from his wounds and started to preach. They captured him a second time and killed him. Christians buried his body beneath this altar. This has always been known. This room has always been a place of worship. When Constantine converted to Christianity in 312, he had a church built above the catacombs and Saint Sebastian's bones moved into the basilica, directly over our heads."

A friend of mine (who hadn't grown up Catholic) believed Sebastian to be the most homoerotic saint. Bound mostly naked to his tree, his soldier's body straining against the ropes, mouth open in passion: Sebastian's image has inspired artists for centuries. Bernini, the architect who decorated Saint Peter's Basilica, had carved the bust before us. I wondered that such a rare and valuable piece of art remained out where people might touch it. It had to be a copy. I didn't dare ask.

The tour group flowed into a room with a low, arched ceiling. Glass encased its carefully lighted far wall. "This is another holy place," Maria said reverently. "For a while, the Saints Peter and Paul were buried here."

That seemed unlikely to me. Saint Peter's Basilica, at the heart of Vatican City, claims to have Peter's body in its crypt. The legend is that Peter was crucified upside down by Nero and buried nearby in the pagan necropolis on Vatican Hill. I'm not clear why the early Christians would have moved his body to this catacomb so far from Rome, then moved it back (where they promptly lost it) until the excavations to build the current Saint Peter's in the 16th century. It's not impossible, but it's a lot of lugging for his bones to end up buried back where they began.

Paul also was supposed to have been brought from the site of his martyrdom and buried in this room, only to be transported back to the Via Ostiense where Emperor Constantine later built a basilica in his honor.

The evidence for these postmortem migrations? Graffiti. Scratched into the plaster were prayers in Greek, addressed to the Apostle and the Evangelist.

I had been willing to accept all else as history, if perhaps churchified history, but the temporary burials tweaked my skepticism. Our incandescent guide glowed with faith.

The tour made one final stop. At some point during the excavation of the catacomb in the late 1800s, church archaeologists had discovered three Roman-era tombs. These little villas had been perfectly preserved when the low area where they stood had been filled with rubble to support the church above.

I waited for the crowd to move ahead so I could peer into the Roman tombs. Beautiful delicate mosaics brightened the surprisingly roomy interiors. One tomb had a staircase that stretched down to the tunnels below it. I found it hard to conceive that the Christian architects had just thrown rubble down on these lovely tombs.

"Here is the origin of the word catacomb," Maria said before we left the area. "This place was called *cata cumbas*, meaning the low place near the quarries. Here stood a crevice between the tufa hills where the Romans cremated their dead. Since it was already a necropolis, it made sense for the Christians to bury their dead here also."

From this place, the word catacomb spread to refer to any hall of Christian tombs, from the ossuary in the quarry under Paris to the aboveground mausoleum complex at Cypress Lawn Cemetery in Colma, California.

I got all excited. Though I had been ill and injured, it was a thrill to visit a place that inspired so much of what I've studied. I suppose the feeling must echo what the Christian tourists felt as they completed their pilgrimages.

Casentini monument, The English Cemetery, Florence

PERMANENT FLORENTINES

Il Cimitero degli Inglesi, Florence: April 27, 2001

MASON AND I ARRIVED AFTER NINE A.M. to find the cemetery gate locked. Since the publication of *Permanent Italians* in 1996, the graveyard's opening hours had apparently changed. The only name on the buzzer was Holloway, a strange name for the caretaker of a cemetery in Florence, but this *was* the English Cemetery. We pressed the buzzer. No answer.

Disappointed, Mason and I sat on the steps with our *Access Florence*, trying to figure out where to go next. The old Pinti gate once stood nearby, part of Florence's fortifications in the Middle Ages and Renaissance. Like the Protestant Cemetery in Rome, this area once lay outside the city wall. Now it remained outside the city's heart. Our guidebook didn't suggest much nearby to interest tourists.

Traffic whipped by on the street beyond the cemetery's small plaza. The road circumnavigated the cemetery, isolating it like the wall once had. We'd taken our lives in our hands crossing the street in the first place. If a crosswalk existed, we hadn't found it. I wondered how funeral parties managed.

The cemetery felt like an island. One of the guidebooks mentioned Arnold Boecklin's paintings of the "Isle of the Dead," which he painted in his studio nearby. (One version hangs at the Metropolitan Museum of Art in New York.) A small island near Corfu had inspired those paintings, but here at the edge of the graveyard, we had a very definite sense of being set apart from the bustle of life.

A telephone truck jumped the curb from the Viale Antonio Gramsci and parked on the flagstone plaza in front of us. The repairman stepped past us without a word and pressed all the buzzers on the gate. A woman in a simple habit came out to let him in.

In halting Italian, Mason asked if the graveyard would be open in the afternoon. She answered, "Si."

He sat back down on the steps beside me. I wanted to visit Santa

Croce, where Michelangelo, Galileo, Machiavelli, and Rossini were buried. Unfortunately, that basilica stood all the way across the old part of Florence. The plaque on the gate behind us said that English Cemetery didn't open at all over the weekend; we planned to leave Florence Sunday morning. Mason was starting to suffer from the cold I'd caught in the Vatican, so he wasn't thrilled about hiking all over town and back.

Initially, the English Cemetery hadn't even been on my list of must-see destinations in Italy. In Florence, the most important thing for us to visit had been the Museo La Specola, the medical history museum crammed with wax models of human anatomy. I supposed I could forego this cemetery now, if Fate and the Italian system of opening hours kept me out of it. We'd just have to return to Italy someday.

Once we'd decided to move on, the caretaker came back out of the gatehouse. She startled us by asking, in British English, "What language do you speak?" Then she said it was absurd for us to sit outside since she had to be there while the phone man worked. She would allow us to come in for a quick look around, but we mustn't dawdle. She had a lecture to present at noon.

As we followed her through the breezeway of the gatehouse, she told us briefly about the cemetery, pointing up the hill toward the grave of Elizabeth Barrett Browning. The caretaker's name was Julia Bolton Holloway, we discovered from the flyer she handed us about her lunchtime lecture, and she was a Browning expert. She apologized for the condition of the graveyard, which had been closed to new burials for decades and, consequently, neglected. In fact, an Allied bombs had exploded near the English Cemetery in World War II. Much of the damage still needed repair.

I asked if we might make a donation for our entry fee. She said it would be fine to do that on our way out.

Past the gatehouse, the path led up a gentle hill. White marble sculpture jammed the cemetery. They climbed the hill in ranks of stone like chess pieces, an army mustered at attention. At first I had trouble differentiating between one memorial and the next. Since we'd promised not to dally, Mason and I pulled out our cameras and marched up the incline between the boxwood hedges.

Part way up, just to the left of the path, stood the monument to Elizabeth Barrett Browning. With her husband Robert Browning, the poet came to Florence in 1847 to escape the cold damp of England and her possessive father, who'd declared that none of his children would ever leave home. Elizabeth celebrated her new residence in the poem "Casa Guidi Windows." She and Robert hosted salons and publicized the Florentine charms so well that the city became a stop on the Grand Tour.

In 1861, Elizabeth succumbed to the weakness in her lungs. Robert saw her buried in the ground here, then immediately left Florence, unable to bear it without his wife. He lies in the Poets' Corner in Westminster Abbey in London. Her fear of abandonment came true for eternity.

A marble sarcophagus supported by six classical columns marked her resting place. I'd never seen a grave monument so determined to hold itself clear of the ground. A cameo of the muse of poetry ornamented the box.

In part because Elizabeth's grave became a place for pilgrimage—no person of sensitivity could go to Florence in the 19th century and not visit her—the cemetery became known as the English Cemetery. Officially, it's called the *Cimitero Protestante di Porta di Pinti*: the Protestant Cemetery of the Pinti Gate. The Swiss Evangelical Reformed Church owns the land.

Just behind Elizabeth's marble confection lies the grave of Fanny Waugh Hunt, wife, model, and muse of the Pre-Raphaelite painter W. Holman Hunt. He immortalized her radiant beauty in his "Isabella and the Pot of Basil." Fanny died in childbirth and was buried beneath a sarcophagus sculpted by her husband. It's a rounded capsule of marble with a peaked lid that seems to float on stone clouds above a granite base.

Walter Savage Landor, poet-leader of the early English Romantic movement, is also interred here, under a simple marble tablet.

As Mason and I wandered, it quickly became clear that the iconography here was different than we'd seen anywhere else: lots of butterflies, more than one ouroboros, pelicans feeding their young, and hourglasses winged with swan's wings, bat's wings, and everything in between.

Italians created the hourglass in the late 14th century to measure the passage of time. By the 17th century, Protestants adopted the symbol to decorate their graves, adding wings to indicate how quickly time flies. Juxtaposed against the Protestant work ethic, the concept of no man knowing the hour of his death struck very real fear into them.

The pelican appears in the writings of Saint Augustine. For some reason, early Christians believed that the pelican tore open her breast to feed her young on her own blood. For centuries, the pelican symbolized Christ, spilling his blood to nourish his believers with eternal life. On the graves in the English Cemetery, the pelican seemed to speak of sacrifices made for faith.

After our visit, I read in the little booklet available from the cemetery office that many of the people buried in the "English" Cemetery were in fact Italians, who had been persecuted for their Protestant beliefs. Challenging the Pope's authority in Italy in the 19th century had been a criminal offense, punishable by imprisonment. They were also forbidden to be buried in sanctified ground. I wondered if the Swiss Evangelic Church had ever been allowed to bless their land.

In this sea of sculpture, the most amazing monument marked an Italian's grave. A larger-than-life skeleton brandished a scythe, about to slice down a clump of stone lilies. The Reaper wore his shroud like a cloak, tossed jauntily over one shoulder. The raw bones of his shin and thigh peeped out at the bottom. A rag blindfolded his eye sockets but didn't mask his grimacing teeth. I'd never seen anything like him. I haven't been able to discover any information about Andrea di Mariano Casentini (1855-1870), but clearly Mama and Papa had some message to give the world when they lost their child.

Not far from the Grim Reaper, we found vandalism, which I understand has since been repaired. At the time of our visit, marble slabs were tilted and cracked, resting at crazy angles. Crosses rested against their bases. Columns lay in the dirt. It made me sad to see those broken gravestones.

Mason and I shot four rolls of film in less than half an hour. I would have liked to linger, to savor the birds singing in the cypress trees and the sense of isolation from the bustle beyond the cemetery walls. It would have been nice to explore the stones with my eyes and fingertips, rather than through the lens of my camera, but we'd promised Ms. Holloway and I didn't want to make her come searching for us when she needed to leave.

We loitered outside the cemetery office, looking at the postcards taped up inside the window.

"Thank you for letting us come in," Mason said as he handed her a donation.

Peering at the bill, Ms. Holloway protested, "This is much too much."

It was equivalent to twenty dollars. Clearly, the cemetery needed support, and restoration of marble—even in Italy—must be expensive. "I wish we could do more," I answered.

"Would you like to see the library and gallery?" She pushed open a door on the opposite side of the gatehouse and ushered us inside. She had pinned a series of postcards and reproductions of paintings to a velvet curtain. "I'm trying to collect up images of all the people interred here, as well as of the art they created." She showed us a library of books related to the graveyard and the people buried there. She told us that she'd gotten the caretaking job because she'd edited Elizabeth Barrett Browning's poetry.

Since the area used to lie outside the city walls, it had previously been used as a dump. Ms. Holloway showed us a shard of pottery, part of a hand-painted plate. It had a pretty blue pattern on a cream background. "The rain uncovers them from time to time," she said. "I ask visitors to bring the fragments to me for the museum."

She was working with *Istituto per l'Arte e il Restauro* to have students study conservation of the statuary in the graveyard. Several students became as passionate about the cemetery as she is and were now working to clean the stones in their free hours. To my surprise, she said the most dedicated students were female.

Or maybe it's not surprising at all. I'm finding that women tend to be deeply interested in restoring graveyards. Perhaps caring for a burial ground is the opposite face of midwifery and childbirth. When I retire, I want to be caretaker of a cemetery. Maybe I can even make my own museum.

The grave of Igor Stravinsky, Cemetery of Saint Michael
San Michele in Isola, Venice

A DREAM OF MELANCHOLY

Il Cimitero di San Michele, San Michele in Isola, Venice: April 29, 2001

THE OWNER OF OUR PENSION IN FLORENCE hoped that we would arrive in Venice during the day. "It's like a dream," she promised.

Lunchtime loomed as the train from Florence sped across the lagoon from the mainland. Mirror-flat water spread out as far as I could see. It looked as if the train skated across the lagoon like a water bug. Ahead of us, the old city rose from the water like a magician's illusion.

The train pulled into Santa Lucia station and we disembarked. Like any European terminal, people streamed off the train in a single direction. The sense of having stepped into a mirage evaporated as we dragged our book-filled suitcases up a short flight of stairs. The ordinary windows to change money or buy espresso or purchase junk food disappointed me.

At the crest of the stairs, we faced another flight of steps back down to the surface of the water. From the threshold, it seemed again as if we'd strayed into a dream. The Grand Canal stretched perpendicularly in front of us, bustling with low narrow speedboats, boat-buses called vaporetti, even a gondola or two. The houses across the canal seemed made of wedding cake, heavily decorated with frosting columns and swags and nosegays.

My head swam in the glare and humidity, but I didn't want to miss a single impression. I fumbled my sunglasses on. My chest filled with that sense of magic I felt on walking into "New Orleans" in Disneyland, except *that* was an illusion designed to overwhelm you with wonder and this was the real thing. I felt like a child again, hungry to rush in every direction.

Luckily, Mason kept his head. "Let's figure out which vaporetto we need," he suggested, leading me down the steps toward the bus stops. "The hotel shouldn't be very far away. Then let's have lunch and go out to your graveyard."

I appreciated his level-headedness. If I'd been alone, I would've bought a lemon granita from a cart by the water, sunken down onto a marble step in the shade of the lone olive tree, and watched the people. Really, though, the island of San Michele, where Venetians buried their dead since Napoleon closed the city's churchyards, was the goal of our visit. We needed to remain focused. We only had three partial days in Venice and a lot of ground to cover.

I pulled the suitcases into a little cluster at the edge of the canal. Something iridescent swirled in the green water, spelling runes that broke apart before I could decipher them. I watched rainbows play across the wavelets. While I was mesmerized, Mason figured out the transit system and bought our tickets.

The hotel room had a comical green glass chandelier and white French provincial furniture like my childhood bedroom. It wouldn't matter: we didn't have long to stay there. We grabbed lunch on the street that led to the Fondamente Nuove, the northern edge of the city. From there, we'd catch our shuttle out to the cemetery island.

When we got on, people on their way to Murano to visit the glass factories jammed the vaporetto. Mason and I didn't want to go far from the boat's doorway, since the stop at Saint Michael's Island came first. I felt queasy as we motored across the lagoon. While normally I'm comfortable on boats, I worried the narrow vaporetto might capsize under its uneven load of passengers.

Four or five of us stepped off the boat on the cemetery island. The other visitors hurried up the ramp away from the water and through the brick gateway, but I lingered behind, pulling out my notebook to copy down the historical plaque at the boat landing.

The plaque said there had originally been two islands: San Michele in Isola and San Cristoforo della Pace. The Venetian churchyards had been emptied onto Cristoforo, but when that clearly wasn't going to provide enough space, engineers joined the two islands by filling the canal between them. To this day, San Michele in Isola serves as the main civil cemetery for Venice.

The cemetery island takes its name from the Church of Saint Michael, which had existed on the island since the tenth century. In 1212, it became a hermitage of Camaldolesian friars. Mauro Codussi built the "new" church—the first Renaissance chapel in Venice—in 1496. Dedicated to the archangel Michael, who will hold the scales on

Judgment Day, it was restored in 1562 and several times since.

Before venturing into the graveyard, Mason and I explored the crumbling mortuary church. The empty sanctuary was chilly inside. It smelled of age and damp, dark and full of old tears. I shivered at the sound of the water lapping against the corpse-door, where a body would be sent into the church from its water hearse. I debated taking a photograph of the church, but Mason found a display with Kodachrome postcards. We left some coins in the box and took one.

The Cadogan guidebook suggested we get a rough map from the caretaker, but since the chapel seemed completely deserted, we decided to roam at random. After all, we were on a small island. How lost could we get?

You'd think I would eventually learn to stop asking that question.

Leaving the chapel, we passed through the ancient cloister. Plain wooden coffins stacked three high along the brick wall. I'd never seen so many coffins in one place. There didn't seem to be any pressing need for them; in the course of our visit, Mason and I never saw anyone working at the cemetery, let alone digging a grave. The coffins seemed simply to be stockpiled. We wondered if Venetians were brought out to the island without a box. I had a romantic notion of a pale beauty dressed in her wedding gown, shrouded in her bed sheets, lying in state on a gondola as cloaked mourners sang a requiem.

The monuments lining the wall of the cloister had amazing decorations. We found a Romanesque stele with a winged angel gazing at a shrouded mourning portrait. (Most stelae I'd seen to this point were large stone tablets used by the Romans as grave monuments, illustrated with low reliefs of people going about their daily lives. The Romans took the stele concept from the Greeks.) Another stele in the cloister showed a seated scholar being crowned with a wreath by an angel. The most breathtaking relief depicted a seated nude holding a book across his hips; the pages read "Sacred to the Honor of" in English. Death, wimpled like a nun, grasped his shoulder and leaned close to whisper in his ear.

We wandered through an archway into a garden with a green lawn. This was the first grass we'd seen in Venice, which seemed—to our fresh eyes—to consist strictly of pavement and water. What a luxury grass must be to Venetians.

The graves in this garden belonged to servicemen. One trio of tablet stones remembered aviators lost in World War I. The first tombstone held a bronze wing, the next Icarus, the last a figure mending a pair of wings. Beyond them stood a pillar crowned with life-sized eagles at each cardinal point. The torso of a pilot in a belted bomber jacket and leather helmet stood beneath them. In addition, three lions' heads protruded from the column, which balanced on the arc of a globe. I was amazed once again by the skill of Italian sculptors, creating one of a kind artwork that would live unprotected from the elements, unguarded from vandals, in a cemetery where few people would ever see them.

In the city, the air had been humid and summery, even though it was barely May. On Saint Michael's Island, the sun-warmed bricks drained the moisture from the air, turning it arid as a desert. I flinched as I photographed the marble monuments inside the brick-walled garden. As I sighted through the viewfinder, the reflected sunlight scraped my eyeballs like a knife.

A brilliant Murano glass mosaic sparkled on a monument dedicated to the ambulance drivers of World War II. The colors glowed more vividly than the grass covering the graves or the robin's-egg blue sky overhead. On a field of gold, four white-coated men leaned above a bleeding soldier. It was one of the most graphic tombstones I'd ever seen.

As Mason and I wandered the island, we found signs directing us to the Reparto Greco, the section for the Orthodox faith. Inside lay composer Igor Stravinsky and his wife Vera. We easily located their graves along the back wall. A pair of white roses with their long stems crossed adorned the slab over Stravinsky's grave. A red silk poinsettia, anchored in a pile of stones, burned like crimson flame on the lower left corner. Above that, a curving stalk of lavender reminded me of a treble clef.

The entire arrangement of flowers looked composed, like a stage set or a painting. I snapped a photograph, knowing that, in the bright afternoon light, my camera could not do it justice. The unfiltered sun on the white stone would bleach the colors out.

Not far from Stravinsky rose the monument to Sergei Diaghilev. Among the unusual offerings on his grave clustered a trio of plastic pots of miniature cactus. While I puzzled over their significance, a little lizard darted out from behind them and ran off into the grass.

Atop Diaghilev's grave rested a pair of weathered pointe shoes, wrapped in their own faded pink satin ribbons. What a beautiful tribute to the impresario of the Ballet Russe. I'd been a huge fan of the ballerina Anna Pavlova when I was a dance student. I wished I'd thought to bring my last toe shoes as an offering to the man who delivered her talent to the West and thereby changed the history of ballet.

The Reparto Evangelico seemed the saddest part of the graveyard to me. Tucked away in a tattered garden lay Protestant foreigners who died while visiting Venice. It struck me as poignant to see graves in Italy that read "Hier ruht" and "Here lies" instead of "Requiescat en pace." A rusted iron cross, tilted against the weathered brick wall, bore the simple legend "Auf wiedersehen." Another monument along the wall was a very sharp pyramid perched on lion's feet that remembered a man who'd died at Alexandria, Egypt.

A stele on one grave showed a praying mother, shrouded from head to ankles, begging as a Pre-Raphaelite angel led her child away. Even though the girl stretched a hand back toward her mother, her feet had already left the surface of the earth. A gang of cherubim sang above. Their false cheer seemed mocking to me, cruel.

Mason and I both loved an angel who looked like a young Eleanor Roosevelt, with bobbed hair and a square-necked dress and a string of pearls. One of the few three-dimensional figures in this section, she placed a garland of roses on a tablet stone.

Rather than the yews that stood in rows inside the other gardens, oaks shrouded the Reparto Evangelico. It had more shade, which made it seem more mournful than the other gardens. Dirt showed through its patchy grass. Still, the guidebooks described it as overgrown and weedy, which was not the case while we were there.

We searched and searched for a poet's grave, not because I'd read any of his work, but because he was famous. I can't even remember his name now. We peered beneath every bush, every tuft of grass, trying to find his stone. While we looked, one of the graves that caught our attention was bounded by a low curb and blanketed with ivy. It belonged to the Russian poet Josef Brodsky, whose life had been turned upside by reading Dostoevsky's *Notes from the Underground*. Venice seemed a long way away from Leningrad, where Brodsky was born, and Brooklyn, where he died.

Eventually, the fruitless search for the poet's grave grew tiresome.

Maybe someone had stolen the gravestone, although I couldn't imagine trying to lug it away on a vaporetto. My gaze lifted to the brick walls encircling the Foreign Section. Beyond them rose the roofs of family mausoleums. One of the most magnificent—a brick fantasy with flat Corinthian pillars and almost Byzantine brickwork—had plants sprouting on its Spanish-tiled dome. The decay made me think of New Orleans, where families reuse tombs until they fall down.

We wandered briefly into the newest section of the cemetery, the part utilized by modern Venetians. Condo-like stacks of mausoleum drawers rose up over our heads. They stretched off toward the outer wall of the island. Perspective shrank them like some kind of Escher painting.

The only things of interest we found amongst the modern burial ground were the exquisite Murano glass mosaics end-capping each bank of crypts. The one that creeped me out the most depicted Saint Lazarus, back from the dead. On the relief, Lazarus still wore his shroud, bound tightly around his body, but his eyes gazed at his sisters. The bodily resurrection was not something I wanted to contemplate on an island covered with graves.

The afternoon's shadows had grown long, so we decided to head back toward the boat landing. Neither of us thought to ask how often the vaporetti ran, so we weren't sure when the last one might pass. Of all the graveyards I've ever visited, San Michele in Isola would have been worst one in which to be locked overnight. Because of the heat, we'd quickly sucked down all the water we brought with us. We hadn't carried jackets. At night, the isolation would have been very chilling indeed.

On our way out, we passed one of the most touching grave offerings I'd yet seen. It's common to see a symbolic anchor on the grave of a fisherman or sailor. In Christian iconography, the anchor recalls that Christ himself was a fisherman. It also signifies faith that tethers one through life's tempests. Atop this grave, marked with a simple stone cross, rested a real anchor: not a cartoon anchor with two barbed tails, but an iron bar with four hooked prongs. The anchor didn't appear to be broken or beyond use but, whoever the survivors were, they chose to decommission the anchor to mark their loved one's passing. More than a mere boat had lost its anchor, it seemed to say. The family struggled without its anchor as well.

Mason and I returned to the lagoon, tired and quiet, trying to make sense of all we'd seen. The island behind us lay silent, except for the quiet lapping of the waves. I'd never felt so melancholy on leaving a graveyard before. The isolation here had gotten to me. Coming to visit loved ones on San Michele in Isola wasn't as simple as turning in to the graveyard on your way home. One needed to plan the excursion. When the last boat left, the dead would be truly alone on their island, nothing but the sound of the water and the occasional lizard to keep them company.

When we rejoined the living on the Fondamente Nuove, Mason bought me the lemon granita I'd been craving since we stepped into this dream.

Douglas Fairbank's monument, Hollywood Forever, Hollywood

SHADES OF FOREVER

Hollywood Forever, Hollywood, California: June 17, 2001

I DON'T KNOW IF I'VE EVER knowingly visited another graveyard after it's been sold. This time, difference was visible immediately. When I visited Hollywood Memorial Park for the first time in January 1994, its sparse brown grass had shriveled in the Southern California sun. The potholed streets were roughly patched. One of the marble muses had been tarted up with nail polish and red paint. Holes in the sod marked places where survivors had uprooted their loved ones to move them to another, better cared-for cemetery.

Hollywood Memorial Park had once been the height of fashionable final addresses in the Los Angeles area, before Forest Lawn in Glendale inexplicably thrust it aside. Once called the Cemetery of the Immortals, Hollywood Memorial served as the final resting place for Peter Lorre, Cecil B. DeMille, Mel Blanc (whose gravestone reads, "That's all Folks!"), director John Huston, two of the Little Rascals, William Randolph Hearst's mistress Marion Davies, and many others from the film industry. The necropolis—like the stars buried there—seemed like a memory quickly blurring toward erasure.

Since I don't live in Southern California, I hadn't kept up on the financial state of the apparently bankrupted cemetery. To me, Hollywood Memorial simply seemed to symbolize the way the past in America is so quickly discarded in our society's search for the next big moneymaker. I found nothing romantic about this object of vandalism and neglect. All I could think was how the mighty had fallen.

What seemed to scandalize Angelenos more than the slow dissolve of their cinematic past was the sale of the cemetery to Tyler Cassity, who already owned graveyards near Kansas City and St. Louis. He had grand plans for making cinematic history turn a profit. Reports got back to me that he had legally changed the name to Hollywood Forever, shedding the dignified (if funereal) Memorial

Park.

I also heard a rumor of talking gravestones. I imagined a sort of "zoo key" system, in which a visitor could buy a bright plastic key, insert it into a headstone, and hear the deceased dispense wisdom from beyond the grave.

As I understood Cassity's vision, Hollywood Forever would become a form of theme park, using the fame of its permanent residents to draw visitors to shop for gifts or flowers, mementos or tribute. The graveyard wouldn't need to depend on selling burial space to survive.

In my layman's way, I understand the economics of running a graveyard. A manicured lawn in the desert valley of Los Angeles is foolish, but that's what people expect in their cemeteries: eternally green grass juxtaposed against the arid brown hills beyond the cemetery fence. Used liberally to keep nature at bay, water is expensive. A healthy lawn demands maintenance, which necessitates equipment and a crew. The crew requires payroll, so money must come in. Acquiring new residents means hiring a sales staff, which will demand a secretary to file the pre-need plans. Hollywood Memorial had slipped so far already; it would require gardeners, a skilled monument restoration team, glaziers, road workers, and someone to dredge the pools in order to make it presentable. Most of all, it needed security to halt the vandalism before real restoration could proceed.

Cassity purchased the land for a song. On property valued at eight million dollars, Cassity offered $375,000. The prime real estate lies alongside Santa Monica Boulevard, abutting Paramount Studios, not far from the trendy area of Melrose. These 62 acres—cleared of dead people—could have commanded a princely sum. Of course, organized destruction of the graves might have roused public ire, leading to costly court battles against historic preservationists or family members who'd paid into the looted perpetual care fund. The Memorial Park's creditors took the only offer they got and moved on.

When I visited post-sale in 1999, the gift shop and theme park angles of the new Hollywood Forever seemed to have been postponed, pending cosmetic improvements to the graveyard. My friend Brian and I saw marble angels with professionally reattached wings. Slanting headstones had been straightened and reset. Marble had been cleaned; granite polished. Trash receptacles stood everywhere. Garbage no longer blew across the grounds.

One of the most inspiring restorations was the spiffed-up Douglas Fairbanks monument. In true Hollywood style, Fairbanks' widow paid $75,000 for a marble sarcophagus raised in front of a classical Greek wall adorned with a bronze silhouette of the actor. Running up to it all is a hundred-foot reflecting pool. In the past, the pool had been full of litter rotting beneath a scum of algae. Now bright healthy water lilies bloomed in clean water. Over the years I'd come to Hollywood Memorial, I'd never seen it look so nice.

I was also impressed by the pink granite column standing on the edge of the central lake. At her death in 1952, Hattie McDaniel's last wish had been to be buried at Hollywood Memorial. After all, she had been the first African American woman to sing on the radio. Her cinematic career spanned over 300 movies. For playing Scarlett's Mammy in *Gone with the Wind*, McDaniel became the first African-American recipient of an Academy Award. She belonged among the cinematic pioneers—and had been rejected by Hollywood Memorial because of the color of her skin.

In October 1999, nearly fifty years after her death, that indignity was commemorated—if not made right—by the placement of a cenotaph to her memory in Hollywood Forever. McDaniel's grave remains undisturbed in Angelus Rosedale Cemetery, but now she has a monument among the immortals, as she wished. When I visited, someone had placed a garland of bright silk flowers around the column's foot.

Another legend has long had a cenotaph in Hollywood Forever. Articles in the *New York Times Magazine*, *LA Weekly*, and *LA New Times* have perpetuated confusion about where Jayne Mansfield rests. After she died in a car crash in 1967, her body was buried with her family in Pennsylvania. In Hollywood Forever, the red granite marker with its epitaph "We live to love you more each day" was often vandalized by purported Satanists, who remembered her membership in the Church of Satan back when Anton LaVey recruited celebrities like Sammy Davis, Jr. On one of my early visits, black candle wax heaped Mansfield's stone and her porcelain portrait had been defaced. Unfortunately, its replacement—a color photograph plaque of Mansfield in white fur and shimmering jewelry—had faded under the merciless sun. I hoped the cemetery would contact her family for yet another replacement.

When I'd visited in 1997, I hadn't been able to see Rudolph Valentino's grave in the big Cathedral Mausoleum. After the 1994 Northridge earthquake threw over the marble statues of the apostles and shattered the stained glass skylights, the locked mausoleum was opened only for family members.

This time, the stained glass windows were clearly under repair. One of them had a new panel. The modern glass didn't match the rich deep colors of the original, but the replacement vastly improved on the plywood I remember.

Valentino lies in a vault toward the back of the building. When he died after surgery for a perforated ulcer and ruptured appendix in 1926, mourners thronged the graveyard. For years, women in black left roses at his marker. On this visit, Valentino had no flowers and someone had appropriated the glass vases outside his niche.

The video scrapbook Hollywood Forever has assembled to Valentino's memory more than made up for that lack of respect. Consisting of a slide show of publicity stills, newspaper clippings, film clips, all accompanied by a musical soundtrack, the short video tribute (available for viewing at *www.hollywoodforever.comstories*) gave me a greater appreciation for the beauty and talent of the legendary screen lover. Newspaper stories, clear enough to be legible, floated above a background of mourning badges and film reels. My only criticism? It would have been nice to have the film clips labeled, so I could track down the complete movies myself.

The day of zoo keys—or even video screens out on the grounds—hasn't come yet. A viewing console stood in the mausoleum, unfortunately unplugged. Brian and I went into the graveyard office to ask about it, only to be directed to a mini four-seat theater where we could watch the memorials in comfort and privacy.

The video system offered several introductions to the cemetery. One of them was an advertisement for the Forever video tributes, which offered such epigrams as "Every life's struggle is to be remembered" and "You are one chapter in the story of life." The historic basis claimed for the current technology seemed shaky: yes, Egyptian pictograms teach us about the lives and beliefs of the Pharaohs, but that wasn't their intended purpose. Their creators never expected them to be seen by mortal eyes after the tombs were sealed. I found it odd that Hollywood Forever offers what's essentially grave robbing as justification for what it sells.

Continuing in that strange vein was a segment about the Taj Mahal, which—true—commemorates a Sultan's great love. However, I'm not sure that the average mourner understands that the Taj Mahal is a tomb. The correspondence between the grandest mausoleum in the world and an ephemeral monument in video seems tenuous. Worse yet were the video clips of the Central American pyramids. Granted, many of them have contained bodies, but those pyramids were used mostly as temples, not as tombs. They honor religious beliefs, not individual lives.

The introductory video found its métier when it turned to the modern era. Yes, our memories of John F. Kennedy, Martin Luther King Jr., and Princess Diana have been formed and kept alive via video memorials. The spirits of the dead *do* seem to persist much stronger because we can watch their expressions and hear their voices.

Not all of Hollywood Forever's permanent celebrities have video biographies yet: Peter Lorre, Darren McGavin, Mel Blanc lack them. Tyrone Power's tribute had movie clips narrated by a costar's reminiscences. A number of unfamiliar names appeared in the listing. I was curious to see how they were remembered, but the hour grew late. As it was, the receptionist went home at five o'clock, locking us in the building, and we had to find someone to lead us out the employee exit.

Update: 2010 was Hollywood Forever's 110th year, which makes it the oldest surviving graveyard in Los Angeles. One of the most popular ways it draws people into the graveyard is by showing movies on its mausoleum wall on summer evenings, bringing its permanent residents back to life.

Another popular event is its Dia de los Muertos celebrations. The community comes together to build huge altars. Attendees are encouraged to dress up as skeletons. South and Central American dancers and musicians perform. Even with an admission price of $10, the event sold to capacity when I attended in 2011.

Show biz icons of the current day are now calling Hollywood Forever their final home. Rozz Williams, singer for Christian Death, has a niche covered in lipstick kisses in the new columbarium. Both

Johnny and Dee Dee Ramone have monuments near the lake. Icons are dying to get in.

While many people—including me—were skeptical when Cassity took over the graveyard, Hollywood Forever has obviously been pulled back from the brink. To my surprise, I approved heartily of what the new management is doing. I look forward to visiting again to see what else can be accomplished. A cemetery that's used is a cemetery that's loved and appreciated. It's cared for and kept up. Visitors keep a cemetery safer than guards.

Of course, I'd also gladly add a zoo key to my collection of cemetery memorabilia.

Rose Hill Cemetery
Black Diamond Mines Regional Preserve, Antioch, California

PIECING HISTORY BACK TOGETHER

Rose Hill Cemetery, Black Diamond Mines Regional Preserve
Antioch, California: August 10, 2001

PERCHED HILL ON A HILL above the Black Diamond Mines Visitor Center, the cemetery looked like broken fangs of marble jutting through the dead grass toward the cloudless cerulean sky. No roses flourished on its baked surface.

I've never seen a graveyard in the process of being rescued from the brink of oblivion before. Oh, I've been in graveyards that had live re-enactors reading the words of people buried below. I've visited graveyards across a span of years, like Hollywood Forever, and seen them turned around. Rescued from the brink, if you will. Before my visit to Rose Hill Cemetery, I'd never seen a graveyard reassembled from near-total destruction. It's hard to put words to my wonder.

Rose Hill Cemetery lies in the Black Diamond Mines Regional Preserve, near Mount Diablo in the eastern part of California's San Francisco Bay Area. Rose Hill has seen a lot of change since its first burial—a teenaged girl named Elizabeth Richmond—in 1865. Not so long ago, it was a sad patch of ground on a hill in the middle of nowhere. A county road used to run right by it, making it accessible to anyone from the inland towns of Antioch or Concord who wanted an isolated place to drink beer and smash up gravestones. The worst of the vandalism began in the 1950s, according to Park Supervisor Roger Epperson. Even before that, however, ranchers allowed cattle to graze among the old monuments. Occasionally Bessie might bump a fragile marble tablet and knock it over on the steep slope.

When the East Bay Regional Park District took control of the land in 1973, its well-meaning "preservation" tactics did as much harm as good. First, they used herbicides to sterilize the soil around the graves. The intention had been to ease maintenance by removing the need to mow. Unfortunately, once the native grasses died off, winter rains carved gullies into the bare dirt hillside. Volunteers collected the chunks of broken headstones and set them in concrete, level with the ground, where they could be walked on—or worse, stomped on—while collecting pools of water whenever winter came to California.

According to Park Supervisor Epperson, the graveyard suffered more abuse in the 1990s after Antoinette May featured it in *Haunted Houses of California*. Psychic Nick Nocerino reported that the desecration had caused the tolling bells, laughter, and crying often heard in the cemetery at night. Would-be ghost hunters often sneaked into the graveyard to hear for themselves. Some of them took more than photographs as souvenirs.

The current Black Diamond Mines' Visitor Center resides in the old Hazel Atlas Mine, where it's naturally air-conditioned against the broiling inland sun. Naturalists lead tours of the mines on the weekends, journeying 400 feet underground into the darkness. A collection of photographs and artifacts gives a sense of life in the mining days. When I visited, Supervising Naturalist Traci Parent narrated a series of slides for visitors, illustrating the five towns that once thrived within the park's 4,677 acres.

As one can guess from the Black Diamond moniker, former residents of the area mined coal. Starting in the 1860s, the area eventually supplied coal to most of Northern California, including the state capitol of Sacramento, 60 miles away. Black Diamond became the largest coal mine in California. By the dawn of the 20th century, the best-quality coal had already been removed. All five settlements gradually became abandoned.

The area had a slight resurgence in the 1920s, when another company mined sand for glass manufacturing and steel casting, but the towns never recovered. According to Parent, the buildings were dismantled "stick by stick" for their valuable redwood timbers. Little evidence of the boom time remains in the area, other than heaps of mine tailings and exotic plants like Italian cypress and pepper trees, planted by the townspeople.

Back in the day, the population of Nortonville, the largest town, topped 1,000 people. It lay slightly west of the cemetery, over a ridge. Closer to the cemetery stood Somersville, whose population peaked at approximately 900. For many years, residents called the cemetery after the nearest town, although local newspapers referred to it as the Nortonville Cemetery. Later, after townsfolk abandoned the area, the graveyard was identified as the Old Welsh Cemetery because so many

Welsh immigrants rested there. Eventually it came to be called Rose Hill, after Andrew Rose, who ranched the area. His widow Emma deeded the land to Contra Costa County in the 1940s.

Since the mining pioneers were buried, nearly all of their grave markers have been toppled or stolen. Park Supervisor Epperson has a theory about the psychology of vandalism: that cemeteries are especially vulnerable as symbols of society for children who may have been incompletely socialized. Once kids see no future, they attack the past.

The park staff labors to undo the abuse. They are removing the concrete "repair work" from the stones which remain in place, then cleaning and restoring them. Their goal is to return as many of the stones as possible to their proper upright positions. At the time of my visit in August 2001, they'd reset eleven stones, three that year alone. Once I looked more closely, I noted that almost all the standing monuments have been returned to their places by the current staff.

The park's brochures solicit help in returning items that have been looted from the graveyard, including a beautiful double stone commemorating a husband and wife. Some stones have already been returned: one anonymously to the nearby Walnut Creek Police Department; one by a rancher who had rescued it from the dirt decades ago, then stored it in his milking barn.

I visited Rose Hill Cemetery with members of the Association for Gravestone Studies who were in the area for a conference. AGS volunteers helped the park staff demonstrate a variety of conservation techniques.

Ta Mara Conde showed how to wash a gravestone. She recommended plenty of fresh water. At home in Massachusetts, she always carries several gallon jugs of water in her car's trunk, in case she comes across a graveyard. She urged conservators to wash stones from the bottom upward. If the stone is very dry, it can become stained by run-off from the washing water. When the process starts from the bottom of the stone, the soiled water drains into the ground. As washing proceeds upward, the lower part of the stone has absorbed enough clean water to be protected.

Ta Mara stressed that it's important not to sit in front of a headstone as you clean it. Old stones can be unstable and dangerous. Ta Mara usually stands to one side and reaches across the stone. She pointed out that, to prevent the monument from loosening at the base, you shouldn't lean against it, even to keep your balance. You definitely shouldn't push hard as you wash it. She uses a soft nylon vegetable scrubber to brush away dirt without scratching the surface of the stone.

Fred Oakley, another AGS member from Massachusetts, had visited Rose Hill Cemetery several days in advance of our tour to apply a "poultice" to a tablet stone. He'd hoped to kill the lichen that attacked it. "Black lichen is the devil's own tool" for destroying gravestones, Oakley proclaimed. When he cut the plastic wrap from the stone, the lichen had been loosened, but not entirely eradicated. With a sigh, Oakley combined diatomaceous earth, kaolin (white clay), glycerin, and water into another poultice and directed that it be left on for several more days.

With all the years of erosion in the graveyard, some of the heavy granite bases have slipped out of place. While we watched, Park Ranger Doug Fowler and Naturalist Kathleen Young reset the base for one of the old stones. Fowler dug around the base stone, then began to prop it up from underneath. Once he had it leveled, he shoveled fresh cement into the hole to support it.

Elsewhere in the graveyard, Epperson and Oakley reset a marble base atop a granite stone that had been leveled earlier. Epperson repeatedly sponged water onto the granite and marble blocks while Oakley mixed up the mortar. Epperson explained that when they do stonework in the inland graveyard, it's important to soak the stones before they're set into place. Otherwise, the stone wicks the moisture out of the mortar, which dries so quickly that it won't hold.

C. R. Jones, a conservator for the New York State Historical Association, demonstrated how to patch a crack in a stone. He combined a special repair mortar with marble dust in order to match the color of the stone: a skill one learns only after much trial and error, I'm certain. Eventually, Jones said, the mortar may darken in the sunlight, but it prevents water from getting between the broken edges of the stone and doing further damage.

Near the foot of the cemetery, I found Georg [sic] Adam Ott's stone, which had been damaged so completely that it couldn't be reassembled. The rangers had reinforced the broken pieces with a backing of white Portland cement, which is anathema to some cemetery preservationists. Epperson defended the practice, because it is reversible—a major issue for conservationists—and allows badly broken stones to be set upright again. If there's ever a better way to return these stones to their places, Epperson is fully in favor of it. In the meantime, he believes it's important that the stones stand over the graves to which they belong. "Once something is out of context," he said, "it's the same as an stuffed animal in a museum."

Finally, the park crew led us to their pickup to see a stone that had been lying in the dirt for decades. In the year prior to our visit, they'd pried it up, removed the old rough concrete, washed the tablet stone thoroughly, and now they would return it to the grave it had guarded for nearly a century. Ranger Fowler said that he usually rides in the back of the pickup when they bring stones up from their workshop. He would hate to have a tool chip the marble on the rough ride.

After the base stone had been drilled, the restoration crew filled the hole with epoxy. A brass screw, which won't oxidize like the original iron pin, connected the upright tablet to its base. The men rocked the tablet into place, then tapped it gently with their fists until it stood straight and true. Fowler said he sometimes sits with a stone for hours in the hot sun, just to make sure it doesn't shift as it dries.

Although the conservation workshop was a wonderful learning experience, I don't feel confident enough to begin restoring gravestones on my own. My fear is that I'd do more harm than good, damaging something with the best of intentions. Still, it was amazing to see the professionals at work, returning history to its place to teach future generations. As Ranger Fowler told me, "I'm bouncing off the walls for days after we reset one. People think I'm crazy, but it's exciting. We're putting history back together."

Mary Baker Eddy's monument
Mount Auburn Cemetery, Cambridge, Massachusetts

GARDEN OF GRAVES

Mount Auburn Cemetery, Cambridge, Massachusetts: April 15, 2002

*"The natural features of Mount Auburn are incomparable for the
purpose for which it is now sacred. There is not in all the untrodden
valleys of the West a more secluded, more natural, or more appropriate
spot for the religious exercise of the living; we may be allowed to add
our doubts whether the more opulent neighborhood of Europe
furnishes a spot so singularly appropriate for a 'Garden of Graves.'"*
—the *Boston Courier*, September 24, 1831

I PUBLISHED MY FIRST CEMETERY TRAVEL COLUMN on
Gothic.Net In March 1999. For the next forty-five months, I wrote
about cemeteries both important and forgotten, urban and rural,
tourist graveyards and family burial grounds. At some point in the
middle of the adventure, I started to consider collecting those travel
tales into a book.

After that, I wanted to travel not merely to fulfill my curiosity but
also to close gaps in my knowledge. Some cemeteries, particularly in
the northeast, were historically important, both as part of their
communities and in the scope of national events. These cemeteries
were emblematic of the way American society came to terms with
death.

Mason and I planned a graveyard tour for April 2002. To make
the best use of Mason's vacation time, it made sense to fly to Boston,
rent a car, and drive as far west as Gettysburg, with stops along the
way at the Old Dutch Churchyard in Sleepy Hollow, Grant's tomb in
Manhattan, and anywhere else we passed that had headstones and
looked inviting. In addition to colonial burying grounds in Boston, I
wanted to visit garden cemeteries, urban graveyards, and family plots.
With any luck, we'd find spring along the way.

In the end, Mason and I visited twenty-two cemeteries in
seventeen days. They ranged in age from pre-Revolutionary to 21st
century, and in condition from the exquisite to the shameful. It was a

wonderful trip, educational and lovely. The company could not have been better.

Primary of all the graveyards in America that I felt it necessary to visit was Mount Auburn Cemetery in Cambridge, Massachusetts. Chief of Mount Auburn's innovations was the liberation of the dead from the overcrowded municipal burying grounds and churchyards to rest in the peaceful arms of nature. This had already happened in Europe, after city officials feared contagion from churchyards that were centuries old: first with Père Lachaise, then with Highgate and the other Magnificent Seven cemeteries of London. In the United States, it took a couple of decades for businessmen to see the advantage of buying attractive land to sell for permanent burial spaces to prosperous families. Mount Auburn, America's first garden cemetery, proved nothing less than a paradigm shift on the soil of Massachusetts.

Dr. Jacob Bigelow, the foremost botanist in New England and a professor at Harvard Medical School, began the discussion of opening a country cemetery in 1825. A possible site was quickly chosen. Outside Cambridge lay undeveloped land where students from Harvard came to walk, contemplate nature, and take a break from their studies. The poet Emerson walked there nearly every day when he studied at Harvard. Students called it Sweet Auburn, after a poem by Oliver Goldsmith called "The Deserted Village." Auburn was "where smiling spring its earliest visit paid." The land belonged to George W. Brimmer, a nature lover, who'd purchased the land originally to protect it from development. In 1831, he sold it to the Cemetery Corporation for $6,000.

Mount Auburn had hillocks and dells, valleys and promontories. With Bigelow's assistance, the Horticulture Society designed the cemetery to give a very real sense of space and privacy. They selected plantings to turn the cemetery into an arboretum of unparalleled loveliness.

Mount Auburn was the first "planned" landscape open to the public in America, so it became "immensely popular," according to David Charles Sloane in his landmark book *The Last Great Necessity: Cemeteries in American History*. The cemetery became so popular that it not only inspired garden cemeteries across the United States, but also the urban park movement in America. Central Park, a direct descendant, didn't open until 1857.

While visitors were welcomed to Mount Auburn from the start, carriage drives were so popular that the Board of Trustees banned horses from the cemetery—except for funerals—as early as April 1832. They reversed themselves three weeks later, allowing lot holders to ride at any time. That strikes me as a canny advertising strategy. If you wanted to ride in the park, you paid a one-time fee of $60 and got yourself a pass, as well as a permanent resting place for your whole family.

The first burial in Mount Auburn—a child—took place in July 1831. The first monument placed in the cemetery belonged to Miss Hannah Adams. Adams was the first female author in America to make a living through her writing. Her works included *The History of the Jews: from the Destruction of Jerusalem to the Present Time* and *Letters on the Gospels*. When she died in December 1831, Adams became the ninth permanent resident of Mount Auburn.

After Bigelow became President of the Cemetery Corporation, he designed the cemetery's Egyptian Gate, which still stands. The gate is twenty-five feet high and sixty feet long, including the lodge that serves as an office and gift shop. Bigelow took his inspiration from the gates at Denderah and Karnac, which were discovered by Napoleon's troops at the turn of the 19th century. Bigelow crowed in his *History of Mount Auburn Cemetery* that "The size of the stones, and the solidity of the structure, entitle it to a stability of a thousand years."

The same could not be said for his lovely Gothic Revival chapel, which needed to be rebuilt repeatedly in the 1840s and 1850s. While a respected botanist and medical professor, Bigelow was not a trained architect. He believed, however, that "the Gothic style imitated the groves and bowers under which ancient Druids performed their sacred rites." His chapel helped introduce Gothic into the cemetery vernacular in the US.

By 1846, a guide to the cemetery was for sale. In 1893, the Cemetery Corporation itself published maps to the graves "most inquired for." "Guidebooks," Sloane explains in *The Last Great Necessity*, "provided routes for visitors, information on notable families, and appropriate poetry...relating to the melancholy atmosphere of cemeteries." After a tour Longfellow gave of the graveyard, an Englishman quoted in Tom Weil's *The Cemetery Book* wrote: "Cemeteries [in America] are all the 'rage'; people lounge in them and use them (as their tastes are inclined) for walking, making love, weeping, sentimentalizing, and every thing in short."

At 72 acres, Mount Auburn Cemetery was the largest burial ground in the United States when it opened. (The New Haven Burial Ground, considered large at the time, encompassed only six acres.) Mount Auburn has now swelled to 175 acres, too large to explore completely in a single day. Luckily, the cemetery office offers an app for your mobile device to guide you.

In addition, the Friends of Mount Auburn Cemetery host guided walking tours, slide lectures, and special events at the cemetery from time to time. The Friends explore the history, horticulture, art, and architecture of the cemetery, in addition to the celebrities buried there.

With so many other things to see and do at Mount Auburn, the graves serve as adornments, not as the distinguishing features. *Famous and Curious Cemeteries* by John Francis Marion calls Mount Auburn the "Westminster Abbey of America." Its permanent residents include Oliver Wendell Holmes, Henry Wadsworth Longfellow, the poet James Russell Lowell, Amy Lowell (who won the Pulitzer Prize for poetry), John Bartlett (compiler of the *Familiar Quotations*), publishers George H. Mifflin, Charles Little, and James Brown, as well as Dorothea Dix, who pioneered humane treatment for insanity, painter Winslow Homer, Julia Ward Howe (author of "The Battle Hymn of the Republic"), and Mary Baker Eddy, founder of Christian Science.

When we visited, a sign on the Egyptian Gateway announced that the cemetery closed at six. We arrived around three, as the sky cleared after a rainstorm. The sun shone brightly on the grass. We could not have timed our visit more perfectly. We parked beside an apple tree that showered petals across a lovely round Greek Revival temple. I wanted to get a map from the kiosk inside the Egyptian Gate. In fact, the cemetery offered a large variety of leaflets, including flyers highlighting a "Person of the Week," featuring poetry by the resident bards, or designating the State Champion trees. Some brochures were for sale at thirty-five cents; others were free. We stocked up. Then we marched into the office to see about buying Blanche Linden-Ward's *Silent City on a Hill: Landscapes of Memory and Boston's Mount Auburn Cemetery*. Once we dropped fifty bucks for the book, the receptionist gave us a couple of postcards of Longfellow's grave for free.

I told him I wanted to see Mary Baker Eddy's tomb, but asked what else we should see. He explained the different eras of the landscaping and sent us to see the dell where the cemetery's consecration address was given, Bigelow's Gothic chapel, and the Washington Tower.

The lay of the land felt more interesting than any cemetery I'd seen before. The rises and valleys made it romantic in the historic sense of the word: cozy, almost. This cemetery had a spirit of its own. I began to understand why the original owner wanted to preserve its beauty.

Of all the old cemeteries I've visited, this was clearly the most loved and cared for. Every road had an ornate black-painted street sign. Every footpath did, too. The map undoubtedly has to be poster-sized to make all those threads of pathway legible. Before the creation of Mount Auburn Cemetery, people were buried in their local churchyard, which spanned perhaps an acre. Even if you didn't know where Uncle Jonathan lay buried, it wouldn't take long to read every stone and find him. At Mount Auburn, the trustees named every pond, hillock, and cranny, so that survivors could find their predecessors. Once the plantings filled out, the cemetery assigned every grave plot a number. Many of the tombs had addresses carved into their stones, but like addresses in Europe, consecutive numbers didn't lie side by side. I grudgingly admitted that the modern grid pattern of marking cemeteries is more helpful and makes it much easier to find what you're looking for.

Probably Mount Auburn could not have come about before the 1830s. As long as most of the people in the United States were working class, spending large sums of money for an architect to design a permanent memorial could not have been a priority. Once Bostonians attained a comfortable economic level, the concept of a monument to proclaim their names and wealth into the future was as unmistakably attractive as it was bourgeois. Families strove to outdo their neighbors.

The cemetery trustees even encouraged this competition. They didn't want to "fill" the landscape with graves, so the bylaws strongly suggested that each family build a central monument to itself as a whole, then mark each individual grave within the family plot with a smaller stone ("Mother," "My Husband," "Little Frank").

We had to stop the car so I could photograph an enormous armload of harvested wheat draped over a headstone, something I'd never seen before. The implication of a life fallen before the reaper seemed achingly lovely.

With the unsettled sky overhead, Mary Baker Eddy's large round temple made a beautiful reflection on the ruffled waters of Halcyon Lake. She was the "discoverer and founder" of the Church of Christ, Scientist in 1879. Inspired by the accounts of healing in the New Testament, she taught that all healing occurred by the power of God, not because of the human mind. She died of a cold in 1910.

During her life, Mark Twain called Mary Baker Eddy the most interesting person on the planet. In 2002, the Women's National Book Association nominated her book *Science and Health with a Key to the Scripture* as one of the seventy-five books by women whose words have changed the world.

Her Greek Revival grave monument is a circle of columns open to the sky. It quotes the Bible several times (including references to being martyred for one's belief) and includes text of Eddy's own, which defined science as God's law. The upper ring of her decidedly pagan temple proclaims her authorship of *Science and Health*: an advertisement graven in stone. Urban legend has long held that a phone had been installed in her grave so that she could call back from Heaven with instructions. The Mary Baker Eddy Library site and Snopes.com both debunk this.

When we visited, a field of daffodils gilded the shore of the lake. Fruit trees and dogwoods were in exuberant blossom. Everywhere I looked, I saw highlights of snowy white or pale pink. I realized I needed to revise my idea of the most beautiful cemetery. Mount Auburn in springtime had all the others beat.

In Mount Auburn's earliest state, plot owners were encouraged to "improve" their investment by planting a tree or a shrub, available for sale from a gardener employed by the cemetery. In 1859, when Bigelow compiled his *History of Mount Auburn Cemetery*, the trustees urged families to contact them if they needed trees or shrubbery removed, since the vistas were becoming obscured. They regarded the multiplication of trees as a "serious evil."

From Eddy's tomb we drove up to the George Washington Tower. Like something from a medieval castle, the single round tower stood atop the highest point in the cemetery. The "mount" is only 125 feet high, but the two balconies of the forty-foot tower give a panoramic view of Cambridge, Boston, and all the surrounding modern urban sprawl.

The tower graces much of Mount Auburn's promotional literature and was one of the major "improvements" with which early trustees sold the cemetery. The day we visited, the view was nice, if somewhat hazy. Jacob Bigelow, its designer, wrote that the tower served as a landmark "to which mourning hearts and eyes are daily turned, of those who would fain seek in its shadow for what remains on earth of their children and kindred." In other words, it served as an object toward which people in town could look whenever they missed their loved ones: keeping Mount Auburn forever in mind.

As we left the tower, a group of prepubescent boys took over, shouting to each other in voices rang from the gravestones. They chased each other around the lower balcony (thirty feet above the ground) with sticks, having an impromptu sword fight. We wondered where their parents were.

Below the tower lay the deep valley where the cemetery had been dedicated in 1831. A temporary amphitheater and a stage had been erected. Justice Joseph Story of the United States Supreme Court gave the main address. The ceremony drew 2,000, many of whom were unconvinced they wanted to bury their loved ones so far from town. While urban burial grounds weren't beautiful or conducive to visits, they were perceived as safe. Burke and Hare had been hanged in Scotland only two years earlier. Grave robbers were a real concern.

Despite that, the horticulturalists believed in the educational benefits of nature. Sloane points out that, at the time, "Americans closely identified domestic tranquility with agriculture and horticulture." Tom Weil agrees, noting that "funeral greenery symbolized an idealized afterlife as described by King Arthur in Tennyson's *Idylls of the King*."

As conceived and carried out at Mount Auburn, the cemetery provided a "didactic" landscape that taught visitors to respect the dead in addition to considering their own mortality. "The cemetery would be an island in the maelstrom of society," according to Sloane. A quote published in the *Christian Review* in 1848 said that a walk in Mount Auburn would "quench the fire of passion," restrain ambition, allay vanity and frivolity, and most importantly, "admonish the shortness of time and the reality and nearness of eternity." Why such a lovely place would be more effective at instilling a sense of *tempus fugit* than the Boston burying grounds with their grimacing deaths'-heads is unclear to me, unless the sentiment was similar to the Japanese reverence for cherry blossom time and the brevity of beauty.

Bigelow himself wrote, "It is desired that the place may become beautiful, attractive, consoling—not gloomy and repulsive." Edward Everett proclaimed in the 1832 edition of *Horticultural Proceedings*, "Trees, whose inexpressible beauty had been provided by the hand of the Creator as the great ornament of the earth, have rarely been planted about our graveyards." He saw Mount Auburn as a place whose "whole appearance as little calculated as possible to invite the visits of the seriously disposed, to tranquilize the feelings of surviving friends, and to gratify that disposition which would lead us to pay respect to their ashes."

As Mason and I turned away from dell and began to climb back up to the viewing tower and our rental car, a man appeared around a bend in the road. He walked toward us so quickly that we halted in surprise.

He said something in Japanese that I didn't understand. Mason turned to me. "Get out the map."

I don't like digging through my messenger bag when talking to a stranger. Nothing bad has happened to me yet, but I'm aware that is someone snatches the camera out of my bag, for instance, I am not going to be able to chase him down. Still, Mason speaks Japanese. I trusted him.

He and the stranger bent over the poster-sized map. I studied the Japanese man: a yellow tie, a blue windbreaker, leather loafers, crisply creased slacks. He looked like a Japanese tourist, not a robber. The man straightened from the map, nodded his thanks, and headed off toward the front of the cemetery.

"What did he want?" I asked.

"He said he'd been lost in here for hours," Mason reported. "He offered to buy your map, but after talking to him, I thought we might need it."

We consulted the map again. I wanted to see the grave of the poet Longfellow.

Of course, once we climbed back into our car, we found other monuments of interest along the way. Small statues, the size of dolls, topped each of a pair of gravestones. On the left, a child with long ringlets lay on his back with his arms around his bare torso. A swath of cloth wrapped his hips. His bare legs crossed at the ankles. A thoughtful angel knelt above him, her arms crossed over her chest like a corpse's.

The feet of the dead child pointed toward the feet of an older child. The second boy lay on his side, one arm folded loosely at his waist. The other arm reached over a dog or a lamb that served as his pillow. The weathered animal had lost its distinguishing features.

These were the sons of Henry Noll. I wondered what it would be like for the parents to visit the family gravesite and face such a striking image of what they'd lost. I know child mortality was shockingly high in the past. I know that families often did not have photographs of their children, since photographers were initially rare and the process expensive. But to keep the image of your children lying atop their graves for decades, centuries... Had anything, short of death, ever dulled that grief?

Another remarkable monument in Mount Auburn was the grave-faced sphinx outside the Bigelow Chapel. Its granite plinth said, "American Union Preserved, African Slavery Destroyed By the Uprising of a Great People, By the Blood of Fallen Heroes." Nearby stands a cenotaph to Robert Gould Shaw, who commanded the 54th Massachusetts Volunteer Infantry, the all-Black battalion that inspired the movie *Glory*. A Roman-style marble stele had been attached to a shadowy temple façade.

As we roamed the cemetery, I took dozens of photographs. The shadows grew long, but I had to keep photographing "one more thing." Surely, the guard would drive the miles of winding roadways and let everyone know to leave before he locked us in, right?

Eventually, we located the general area of Longfellow's grave. It didn't face the road at all. We parked the car and found the right path.

Henry Wadsworth Longfellow was the most popular and well-known poet of the 19th century. He taught modern languages at Harvard until 1854, when he resigned so he could spend all his time writing. We still remember him for his "Midnight Ride of Paul Revere." He received honorary degrees from Oxford and Cambridge universities, then became the first American to have a commemorative bust placed in Westminster Abbey.

His grave in Mount Auburn stands along the Indian Ridge Path. It's a simple granite sarcophagus on a raised patio paved with large square stones. The postcard from the receptionist showed it at the height of springtime, surrounded by flowering dogwood. It looks fitting as the resting place for a famous poet.

When I visited in late April, the surrounding trees were still bare. The late afternoon sun painted the granite with honeyed light. I snapped a quick photograph.

Along Longfellow's path hurried more people than we'd seen in the graveyard so far. They bubbled with excitement, so we trailed them.

A man pointed silently up into an old pine. There sat the biggest bird I have ever seen, easily as tall as a small child. Atop its chestnut brown body, its rusty brown head regarded us with yellow eyes. Its beak curved like a fishhook. In Mount Auburn, I saw my first Golden Eagle.

The Japanese tourist strode up. "Konnichiwa," he said to Mason, like they were old friends. He was still trying to find the way out.

The Franklin obelisk, the Granary Burying Ground, Boston

HERE RESTS THE DUST

King's Chapel, Granary, and Central Burying Grounds
Boston: April 16, 2002

WE PASSED THE MONUMENT TO THE IRISH FAMINE as we came up School Street from the subway station. One of the emaciated statues had a live pigeon perched on her head. She reached upward hopelessly. Mason suggested it might be disturbing if she suddenly came to life, snatched the bird, and gobbled it down.

A right turn at Tremont Street brought us to King's Chapel Burying Ground, the first graveyard in the Massachusetts Bay Colony. The colonists officially established the graveyard in 1630, mere months after they'd founded the city. A plaque said that the land probably belonged originally to Isaac Johnson. His will directed that he be buried on his own property—and here he lies. Once he was planted here, this developed into the community burying ground. Eventually, that meant thousands of settlers buried near him.

The initial colonists of Boston were such Puritans that they didn't even allow images engraved on their tombstones. Their markers that survive are thick, heavy stones recording only names and dates. William Paddy's stone, dated 1658, is one of the oldest remaining grave markers in New England. Nearby stands the marker for a Puritan with one of the strangest names I've ever come across: 24-year-old Hopestill Barns, who "deceased" in 1676.

In 1688, the British governor seized land from the older part of the graveyard to build King's Chapel. The burying ground takes its name from that church, if nothing else. The graveyard continued to be secular, unaffiliated with the adjacent Anglican church. That meant that no distinctions were made in the graveyard in terms of sect, or even of race. When people died, they needed to be buried. Until 1660, when the Granary Burying Ground opened nearby, everyone in Boston had ended up in King's Chapel Burying Ground.

Charles Bahne's *Complete Guide to Boston's Freedom Trail* points out that the Puritans must have spun in their graves when the chapel was built. Aside from the simple desecration, the Anglican Church had been the reason they'd fled to the New World in the first place.

Although the original Puritans forbade anything but text on their grave markers, later preachers differentiated between ornamentation inside churches and on gravestones. This led to the skull and crossbones that appear on so many of New England's earliest headstones.

The King's Chapel graveyard sported some spectacular death's-heads. One of the stones from 1690 had a leering skull shaped like a Dia de los Muertos sweet. The bony forehead had raised eyebrows, but only a pair of upended angles suggested his nose. His clenched teeth went straight across like pickets in a fence. The wings that stretched out behind him had row upon row of feathers. Where we see a macabre reminder that our ancestors were all too familiar with the skull beneath the skin, they saw a memento mori—a nudge, as if they needed it, that no one knew the hour of his inescapable demise and a reminder that everyone should be prepared to meet his or her Maker at any moment.

Of all the headstones in this graveyard, my favorites stood along the front walkway, watching modern Boston pass by outside their iron gate. Several gravestones depicted the struggle to snuff out life's candle: Father Time, a robed patriarch with a knee-length beard, faced off against a skeletal Death.

Primary among the famous people buried in King's Chapel Burying Ground is the first governor of the Massachusetts colony, John Winthrop. After his election as governor, Winthrop led 700 religious "Separatists" (what we'd call Puritans) to leave England and settle on a hilly peninsula they named after Boston in England's East Midlands. Winthrop proclaimed that this new Boston would be "a shining city on a hill," a beacon to all others who wanted to lead exemplary religious lives. By the time Winthrop came to the graveyard, Boston had swelled into a city of 2,000 people.

Since Winthrop died in 1649, I suspected the brick and granite table monument covering his grave must be a later addition. The style was wrong for a Puritan grave marker. The book *Preachers, Patriots, and Plain Folks* confirmed my suspicion, reporting that the new monument had been erected in 1920.

In the center of King's Chapel Burying Ground lies William

Dawes, the other man who rode to Lexington to announce the "British are coming!" He had the misfortune of being neglected by 19th-century poets, so Paul Revere's is the name we connect with the Midnight Ride. Revere lies down the street at the Granary Burying Ground, under a monument much grander that Dawes's. Someone had marked Dawes's stone with a small American flag in order to draw tourists over to it.

Not far from the church wall stands the headstone of Elizabeth Pain. Some books, including *The Smithsonian Guide to Historic America*, imply she inspired Hawthorne's Hester Prynne in *The Scarlet Letter*. Pain's marker gives no indication that she was seduced and impregnated by a churchman. Still, the possibility seemed significant on the day Mason and I visited in 2002, when the Pope had just summoned all the American cardinals to Rome to discuss the Catholic Church's ongoing sex abuse scandal.

By the 1740s, gravediggers at King's Chapel Burying Ground lamented that they were burying the dead four deep. In 1795, after the graveyard had surpassed full and headed toward critical mass, ground burials finally halted. Even so, the outer boundary of the cemetery, ringed with subterranean family tombs, continued to accept new residents until the 1970s. I like the idea of three centuries of a family lying together. I wonder if that's true anywhere else in the US: maybe in New Orleans? So many of the old graveyards have been destroyed or have fallen into disuse and decay...

Also in this graveyard, at the very southwestern corner, stood what looked like a well, surrounded by a rusting, ornate iron fence. In reality, it was an airshaft for the subway, America's first, built in 1898. I didn't think much about that at the time, but it became significant when we visited the Central Burying Ground in the afternoon.

Mason and I strolled a few short blocks up Tremont Street to a graveyard that boasts the final remains of a large number of Revolutionary War heroes. I was amazed to see the Granary Burying Ground guarded by a small Egyptian-style gate. Egyptian grave ornaments didn't come into fashion until after Napoleon's Egyptian campaign nearly two centuries *after* this cemetery was founded. The 19th-century attempt to beautify the shadowy little patch of ground between the high-rises boded ill for the historical accuracy of what we were about to see.

Established in 1660 in an attempt to alleviate the crowding at King's Chapel, the Granary Burying Ground takes its name from a grain storehouse that once stood nearby. More than 2,300—perhaps as many as 8,000—corpses lay inside this small patch of ground, which barely covers two acres. It's a shame that all that fertilizer has not helped it to grow grass. When we visited on a warm April day, many of the stones had been rendered illegible by mud spattered on their faces from the winter rains.

Most unfortunate of all, few of the grave markers actually mark graves any longer. Around the dawn of the 20th century, groundskeepers realigned the stones to make it easy to mow between them. In some sort of twisted logic, ease of upkeep became more desirable than marking the resting places of the dead.

In some cases, the footstones—which once marked the foot of a grave like a footboard on a bed frame—now lean against their headstones. At least they hadn't been lost altogether. Perhaps some day some well-meaning soul will set them back up the way they belong.

When Mason and I visited, an attempt to catalog the gravestones seemed underway. To my immense horror, some idiot stuck numbered Avery labels to the faces of every headstone. Often the labels covered engraved artwork. I prayed that the stickum did not eat into the fragile stone and that removing the labels did not pull any details away. After all, these stones are considered so delicate that visitors can no longer make rubbings of them. What damage might a chemical adhesive do?

Numerous other dangers continue to threaten these stones. During our visit, workers sandblasted one of the surrounding high-rises. Debris littered the graveyard, raining down around the ineffective tarp they'd laid out to catch it. It appeared to be a miracle that this little patch of history survived at all.

I suppose public sentiment had a lot to do with it. The Old Granary Burying Ground is the final home of many of Boston's Revolutionary War patriots, including James Otis ("Taxation without representation is tyranny."); Robert Treat Paine (signer of the Declaration of Independence and first Massachusetts Attorney General); and victims of the Boston Massacre, including Crispus Attucks.

In the center of the graveyard stood a granite obelisk labeled

Franklin in large, proud capitals. It marks the grave of Benjamin Franklin's parents, Josiah and Abiah. The original stone he'd chosen was replaced by this one in 1827, erected by local citizens who wanted to lay claim to the glory of their native son, despite the fact that he'd preferred to be buried in Philadelphia. One of my antique postcards incorrectly identifies the monument as Franklin's own, a misconception that was undoubtedly good for tourism.

While Mason and I explored the graveyard by keeping only to the paved paths, three different tour groups passed by us in the dirt between the stones. An actor in Revolutionary-era costume led one group. Two other groups seemed composed of Boy Scouts, including a troop in uniform. I wondered what the kids were doing out of school on a Tuesday morning. And why weren't their leaders keeping them to the paths?

Another behavior that puzzled me was the way adults lined up to be photographed beside the monuments of Paul Revere and Samuel Adams. The concept of a souvenir photograph at the grave of a famous patriot struck me as bizarre, a kind of staged vacation photo op. Mason reminded me that some people like to have pictures of themselves on vacation. We're lucky if we come home from our trips with pictures of either one of us. Usually, we're busy photographing architecture or sculpture or city views, trying all the while to photograph as few people as possible. Different strokes, I suppose.

I didn't see anyone standing beside the grave of Frank, servant to John Hancock "Esqr," who died in 1771. Frank's small stone stands at the foot of Hancock's towering white obelisk, which had been erected by the commonwealth of Massachusetts. Hancock's monument includes a bewigged portrait surrounded by a wreath of oak leaves. The fact that Frank has no recorded last name leads scholars to believe he was a slave. Probably his master, who donated space in the family plot, also purchased his stone. I found the juxtaposition of slave and master an interesting commentary on Hancock, the first signer of the Declaration of Independence and Boston's richest citizen before the Revolutionary War.

Another gravestone that attracts pilgrims is that of Mary Goose. Mary was the first wife of Isaac Goose, whose second wife Elizabeth may or may not have been the famous Mother Goose. Legend has it that Elizabeth's son-in-law collected her stories into *Songs for the Nursery, or Mother Goose's Melodies*, but scholars find it suspicious that no copy of the original book survives. Many of the Mother Goose tales actually date back to France in the late 1600s. Still, some old Boston guidebooks identify Mary as Mother Goose. She was, I guess, a mother, if not the Mother.

In the Granary Burying Ground, ornamentation on gravestones ranges from the early awkward death's-heads we saw in King's Chapel Burying Ground through anatomically correct skulls to cherubs with portrait-like faces. I particularly liked the cherubs with hair etched by a delicate tool. These "soul effigies" indicate a huge shift in Christian philosophy, from the Puritan belief that only the Elect will rise to Heaven to a general sense that all souls take flight upon the body's death and Heaven is available to all.

Some of the stones can be traced to particular carvers, which demonstrates an advance in how people valued graveyards. Once tombstones were acknowledged as works of art—instead of a necessary evil—artists wanted to claim their designs. Some carvers even autographed their stones. Henry Christian Geyer advertised his talents in the local papers. He was a fisherman who had studied birds well enough to put realistic wings on his cherubs.

Unlike the earlier headstones we'd seen, the Granary stones offered epitaphs that recorded how the survivors felt about their losses. These seemed to have come into fashion in the late 1700s. One that struck me ended with "Look on this Babe and learn to Die. Here you must lie as well as I." That remembered Polly Burk Mackay, a four-year-old who died in 1783, "Daugr. of Capt. Alexander and Mrs. Ruth Mackay."

A stone toward the back of the cemetery commemorated John Hurd with a large urn in low relief. A plaque nearby traced the urns on so many stones after 1830 to the discovery of Pompeii and the Roman use of urns to hold the ashes of their dead.

Hurd's epitaph said:

> To this sad shrine who 'ere thou art draw near
> Here lies the Friend most joy'd, the Son most dear
> Who ne'er knew joy, but Friendship might divide
> Or gave his father Grief, but when he died.

In 1879, the last body sank into the Granary Burying Ground. Now the land seems valuable to Bostonians only for the tourists it lures. It's a sad barren patch of dirt, out of tune with the patriotism that swept the country after September 11, 2001.

We visited a final graveyard in Boston by accident. Worn out by the humidity and the glare, Mason and I debated an excursion up to Boston's North End to see Copp's Hill Burying Ground, where Cotton Mather is buried and there's a view of the bay. Before we made the hike, I needed to absorb some caffeine.

We walked into the Common to enjoy our iced mochas and, by happy chance, discovered the Central Burying Ground. I looked over the green grass tucked in around the weathered stones. Unlike the Granary Burying Ground, where we struggled to keep out of the way of other visitors, Mason and I basked in our solitude in this graveyard.

The trees in the Common glowed bright green with new leaves, but the oaks inside the cemetery were still barren. So many acorns and twigs littered the ground that it was uncomfortable to sit on, but this graveyard still offered more grass than either of the other two we'd seen that day. In fact, we didn't need to stay on the paths in the Central Burying Ground, because there weren't any.

Although it suffered from not having any benches and way too much street noise, I found the graveyard extremely pleasant. Starlings and sparrows collected twigs for their nests, while the robins listened for worms. Squirrels acted especially squirrelly, rolling in the dust, springing backward in shock from acorn caps, wrestling with sticks. It felt good to see life in the graveyard.

Founded in 1756, the Central Burying Ground had more recent monuments than we'd seen elsewhere in town. In place of death's-heads or soul effigies, these stones bore urns and willows. They seemed not to be carved very deeply here, or perhaps decades of grave rubbings had worn their faces down.

Many of the headstones slanted drunkenly forward or back or listed to one side. Most were staggered in such a way that suggested they'd never been moved. One of them, near where I sat with my notebook, retained its footstone in place. The arrangement did, as the guidebooks said, make a cozy little bed.

The most notable thing about the cemetery was that its old vault tombs were still in place. They stood inside a raised tumulus surrounded by a deep ditch. Rusted iron doors punctuated the grassy mound. Some of the family tombs still had marble nameplates. An explanatory plaque we remembered from King's Chapel Burying Ground said that the wealthy had always preferred the vaults, because they owned them in perpetuity. Also, I suppose, there was less chance their graves would be mislabeled if the grounds crew tidied up.

Originally the Central Burying Ground reached all the way to Tremont Street and connected with the Granary Burying Ground, but hundreds of graves had been removed when the city cut Boylston Street through. The excavation of the original subway in the 1890s displaced more graves. Families moved some remains to Mount Auburn Cemetery, but others were reinterred in a mass grave marked by a large slate slab. Estimates range between 1,100 and 2,000 bodies of the 5,000 original burials were exhumed. In terms of the removal of cemeteries in Manhattan, Chicago, Denver, San Francisco, and elsewhere, it's remarkable that any of the Central Burying Ground remains standing. I took a moment to close my eyes against the bright sun to be grateful.

As in the Granary Burying Ground, many of these gravestones mourned specific dead and seemed to address the living directly. The first of these stood nearest the gate. Mrs. Susanna Brown, who passed in 1797, directed,

> Go home my frinds dry up your tea
> rs For I shall rest till Christ apea
> rs.

Both "tears" and "appears" wrapped to the lines below, because the stonecutter hadn't left enough room and the spelling of friends was the most creative I've ever seen.

The sentiment in this epitaph demonstrated another stage in the development of Christian philosophy. Rather than rotting in the ground with the Puritans or her soul winging away with the Anglicans buried under their soul effigies, Mrs. Brown was content to "rest" in her grave until Christ's resurrection summoned the dead to be judged and sent to their final rewards. This, of course, was eventually replaced by the Victorian belief that all our loved ones awaited us in Heaven.

In the Central Burying Ground lay a number of Masons. I found the first square and compass on a stone dated 1801. I hadn't realized the members had become less secretive about their society so early. The most ornate Masonic gravestone of all remembered Mr. Frederick Gilbert, who died "Octr 2d 1802." The monument was adorned with a compass and the phrase "He liv'd within compass," seven stars, a moon and a sun, a shovel and a pick, and a skeleton lying in a toe-pincher coffin. His epitaph read:

> Sure as yon Sun shall leave old Ocean's bed,
> And o'er the Earth its genial influence shed;
> Sure as chaste Cynthia wanders through the skie,
> Or stars with bright effulgences shine on high;
> So sure had Gilbert's spirit soar'd above,
> To the celestial Lodge in realms of love.

It was sweet that his survivors thought so highly of him. I wondered what his story had been. He doesn't seem to have left much mark on history beyond his gravestone.

The nearby stone of Nathaniel Tolman, dated 1809, said:

> An angel's arm can't raise me from the grave
> Legions of angels can't confine me here.

In the Central Burying Ground, the grief of parents spoke eloquently on the stones. I found one particularly chilling epitaph on a tombstone shared by a brother and sister. William (died 1804) and Jane (died 1808) Fessenden were survived by their grieving parents, who remembered them with:

> And though you moulder with the dust
> Thou'rt fairer than the rose.

Not all the epitaphs were gloomy, though. The stone of Mrs. Lydia Bennett, deceased in 1807, bore this surprising epitaph:

> Here rests the dust unconscious close confin'd
> But far far distant dwells the immortal mind.

She sounds like a woman I would've liked to meet. I considered adopting her epitaph as my motto.

The only "famous" person buried in the Central Burying Ground was the bipolar artist Gilbert Stuart, whose painting of George Washington in his black judicial robes hangs in the National Portrait Gallery. Stuart also painted the unfinished "Athenaeum Head"— Martha Washington's favorite portrait of her husband—which appears on our one dollar bill. Due to his illness and sharp tongue, Stuart died a pauper, replaced by painters with better social skills. Confusion remains about which tomb belonged to him. He had no marker until 1897, when the Boston Paint and Clay Club erected a cenotaph adorned with a palm frond threaded through the thumbhole of a painter's palette.

The lack of famous people allowed me to enjoy the markers of common folk. Even though I was amused by the kind of historical fandom that inspired tourists to have their photographs taken beside Paul Revere's square stone column, I'd photographed Revere's monument for my own collection of famous people's gravestones. In reality, I knew very little more about Paul Revere than I did about Mrs. Lydia Bennett. He was elevated by mentions in the history books, but the deeds he'd performed in life were more significant than his tombstone. It was just a rock with his name and dates engraved into it. An inanimate object couldn't testify to the man's worth. In the early years of the 21st century, however, this rock continued to be the goal of pilgrims, who wanted to touch something grander, more eternal than themselves. In the end, any positive experience people have in a graveyard is a good thing.

In my own case, my visit to the burying grounds of Old Boston gave me much food for thought. So many dead people I've visited in my travels, I marveled, so many grave sites, so many gravestones. While I usually went out of my way to record the monuments of the famous, the nearly anonymous often touched my heart. I suspected that would be true of the people I knew in life as well.

Death and the Sculptor, Forest Hills Cemetery, Boston

SCULPTURE GARDEN

Forest Hills Cemetery, Boston: April 17, 2001

THIS PARTICULAR ADVENTURE began in the Globe Corner Bookstore in Cambridge, Massachusetts. I was hoping to find a guide to the colonial-era graveyards of New England when I came across a lovely little book called *Garden of Memories*. Although the slim volume was unpriced, it seemed worth buying for its color photographs. I hoped it would add something beautiful to our trip.

In fact, Howie at Twisted Village, a record store in Cambridge we'd visited earlier in the day, had already recommended the graveyard in Jamaica Plain, whose name he couldn't remember. He said it had a lot of sculpture, which is one of the things I'm most interested in. If I'd had the book before we'd gone record shopping, I could've confirmed the necessity to visit Forest Hills Cemetery. Finding the book seemed like fate.

After driving through the rather depressed area of Roxbury, we turned into the lush expensive suburb of Jamaica Plain. In the 18th and 19th centuries, Boston's elite came out from the city to build summer homes and country estates beside Jamaica Pond. Now the area has two neighborhoods on the National Historic Register and incorporates part of Frederick Law Olmsted's Emerald Necklace as green space. As we drove through in our budget rental car, I felt almost as out of place in Jamaica Plain as I had in Roxbury.

The graveyard provided a welcome haven. Founded in 1848, seventeen years after Cambridge's Mount Auburn Cemetery, Forest Hills had been nondenominational from the start. Its original gateway had been Egyptian, styled after the ancient portico at Garsey, on the Upper Nile. However, the cemetery's 19th-century clientele rejected that architecture as too pagan. They wanted something solid that spoke of good Christian values. What they got was a grand tripartite Gothic archway, more beautiful to my eyes than the Old Granary Burying Ground's strange little Egyptian gate.

Forest Hills' entryway was Gothic in a completely over-the-top fashion: flowery granite capitals above the crumbling sandstone blocks. It promised, "He that keepeth thee will not slumber." A six-pointed star adorned the top of the gateway, but *Garden of Memories* suggested that it was not a Star of David, but was instead a Solomon's seal, signifying the union of soul and body. That seemed an odd symbol for a graveyard, since they usually signify the separation of what's eternal from what's mortal.

The sculpture I most wanted to see stood right inside the gate, which was disappointing. I'd hoped for a quest in which we'd see many beautiful things before finally locating it. Nevertheless, "Death and the Sculptor" by Daniel Chester French is probably the most magnificent work of art I've seen in a graveyard yet. The large bronze combined relief work and statuary. Death was a stern-faced matron dressed in Grecian robes and a large-cowled cloak. She reminded me very much of Walter Crane's Pre-Raphaelite Winter in "A Masque of the Four Seasons." In French's sculpture, Death had wings, but didn't carry a scythe or hourglass. She merely reached her shapely arm out to touch the sculptor's chisel. He carved a relief of the sphinx and pyramids, a reference to Martin Milmore, for whom this monument had been made. Milmore sculpted a sphinx at Mount Auburn, but was buried in Forest Hills. In French's memorial to his friend, the sculptor twisted to look over his shoulder, but his gaze was not directed at Death but beyond her. Into eternity, perhaps?

The cemetery guide I'd brought with me, *New England Cemeteries: A Collector's Guide,* acknowledges that Forest Hills is lesser known, probably from surviving in the shadow of Mount Auburn, but is "unquestionably worth a visit." My chief regret is that we hadn't left ourselves more time to spend there.

Well, that, and the April day was *so* hot. I didn't feel the heat while being drawn from one statue to the next, but whenever I stopped to take a photograph, the sun beat down on me. It felt hotter than the 80s they had predicted. Humidity made the air heavy in my lungs. Still, I couldn't stop myself from looking at "one more thing" before I could turn back to Mason, who'd settled under some pines with a book.

A fabulous bronze angel drew me across a sun-struck meadow. Her hair rolled back from her no-nonsense face, bound by a circlet across her brow. Powerful wings raised behind her. *Garden of Memories* said she was another of David Chester French's works, his "Angel of

Peace."

Beyond the graveyard, French had sculpted the monumental figure seated inside the Lincoln Memorial in Washington, DC. He also did the Minute Man who stands at North Bridge, Concord. *Garden of Memories* said that he had six sculptures at Forest Hills—and I would have liked to see them all, since the two I discovered were so spectacular—but I didn't know how to locate them. The book needed a special map. I suppose I could have asked at the office, but I didn't want to impinge on Mason's patience too long. Our plan had been to leave Boston early and drive on to Providence, Rhode Island, where we planned to visit another garden cemetery the next morning.

So I wandered from statue to statue, using my camera as my compass. I found a lot of treasures. I gravitated toward the graces: drapery clad women sculpted as permanent mourners. One of my favorites had her flowing hair wound in a partial bun, as if she'd been too distraught to fix it properly. She leaned against a plinth, the urn balanced atop it clasped lovingly in her arms. A number of stone women stood on tombs, a single hand pressed to their chests. One, whose direct gaze was seemingly unscarred by sorrow, hadn't noticed the strap of her dress slipping off her shoulder. Elsewhere, Faith turned blind eyes upward as she cupped an anchor chain in her hands. Her gown, caressing every curve, slid dangerously low on both shoulders. The same was true of the bare-shouldered maiden on the Clapp tomb, who placed a floral wreath before a tablet labeled "Life More Abundant." Joyce Carol Oates, in her introduction to David Robinson's *Saving Graces*, notes that these mourning statues behave "as if grief were a form of erotic surrender."

A more demurely dressed angel with short cherubic wings held a round tablet, almost like a platter, which read, "The spirit shall return to Him Who made it." I liked the sense of God as artist.

As I walked, I noticed bare dark gray shoulders of rock poking from beneath the topsoil. The cemetery had drifts of forsythia in bloom, masses of sunny yellow flowers lining the ridges. They were shaded by evergreens, but the flowering cherries and apples suffered in the heat, their petals rusting before they fell. At one point, I found myself standing beneath an incense cedar: camera forgotten, simply inhaling.

During our visit, Forest Hills hosted an exhibition of contemporary sculpture. At first I wasn't sure how I felt about finding modern artwork sprinkled amongst the muses and angels in the graveyard, but the pieces we saw seemed especially appropriate. The first stood along the drive when we came past the old receiving tomb, where corpses used to be stored in winter until the ground thawed and they could be buried. On a short slope above the main road rose three twisted white geometric towers. The sculptor meant them to reinterpret the standard graveyard obelisk and to suggest, in their undulations, the eternal flame. Artist Susan Ferrari-Rowley called them "Spirit Vessels."

To the left of the main meadow rose a towering blue wishbone with a gold capstone: Linda Foss Nichols's "Aeolian Conduit." I wished for enough wind to hear if the giant harp truly did sing. In its shape and coloring, the wishbone implied the raising of hearts or lifting of hopes. It was a beautiful piece, my favorite of the new works we saw.

Around the shores of the lake clustered several more sculptures. We didn't get out of the car to admire them, since there was no protection from the sun around the water. A cluster of fluttering aluminum birds, strung on a lyre, spun as the breeze caressed them. Sculptor George Sherwood called his "Flock of Birds" "a portal for indicating the evanescent flow of spiritual energy."

Farther around the water lay a series of stepping stones inscribed with spirals and other ancient symbols. Eric Lintala's "Shards" denoted a sacred space, like the ancient pictographs they echoed: a place where spirits might dwell.

In the end, I was thrilled to have taken a moment to stop at Forest Hills Cemetery. It wasn't as breathtakingly landscaped as Mount Auburn, but the graveyard's simplicity set its artwork off to better effect. I astonished myself by liking the modern works. I enjoyed the sense of surprise as we came upon new pieces placed among the serious, funereal sculpture of the past.

It felt good to see a cemetery working so hard to make itself appealing to its neighbors in Jamaica Plain. Not only did the contemporary sculpture change year by year (although some of it was for sale and could be purchased for use as grave monuments), Forest Hills Cemetery hosted musical concerts in its chapel, as well as performances of the works of e.e. cummings and Anne Sexton, both of whom are buried there. Unlike the visits by Christ or Montezuma at Forest Lawn in Hollywood Hills, the events scheduled at Forest

Hills seemed respectful, entertaining, and appropriate. I hoped they would help to sustain this beautiful place in the 21st century.

2017 update: Unfortunately, events are no longer hosted by the cemetery, which has decided to focus on preservation rather than outreach.

The Old Dutch Church and Burying Ground, Tarrytown, New York

MORNING IN SLEEPY HOLLOW

Old Dutch Burying Ground and Sleepy Hollow Cemetery, Tarrytown, New York: April 19, 2002

"The dominant spirit...that haunts this enchanted region and seems to be commander-in-chief of all the powers of the air is the apparition of a figure on horseback without a head." — Washington Irving, The Legend of Sleepy Hollow (as are all that follow)

I MUST HAVE READ THE STORY AS A CHILD, probably the summer that my mom paid me a dollar per book to read literature by the likes of Mark Twain and Jules Verne. Unfortunately, *The Legend of Sleepy Hollow* didn't leave as strong an impression as Disney's ridiculous beanpole Ichabod Crane and the jack-o'-lantern-pitching horseman. As a child, I didn't revere Irving as much as Poe.

My favorite image of Tim Burton's setting of the tale was the fog-wreathed graveyard. After a friend lent us the DVD, I lingered over that cemetery scene with the remote control. The gravestones are marvelously aged and covered in lichen: manufactured, modern props. I wished the movie set could be real.

When I began to plan our big cemetery adventure, I knew I had to see Mount Auburn and the King's Chapel Burying Ground in Boston, Soldiers' National Cemetery in Gettysburg, and Grant's Tomb in Manhattan. In the midst of my wish list, my old friend Jeff stopped me. "You should go to Sleepy Hollow," he said. "It's only an hour north of Manhattan. It's beautiful up there. Some of the epitaphs are Dutch. Ichabod Crane and Katrina Van Tassel really are buried there, along with other characters from the story. You should go. It won't be like anything else you see."

"A drowsy, dreamy influence seems to hang over the land and to pervade the very atmosphere. Some say that the place was bewitched by a high German doctor during the early days of the settlement; others, that an old Indian chief, the prophet or wizard of his tribe, held his powwows there before the country was discovered by Master

Hendrick Hudson. Certain it is, the place still continues under the sway of some witching power that holds a spell over the minds of good people, causing them to walk in a continual reverie."

The trickiest part of our excursion to Sleepy Hollow was finding a place to stay for the night. Mason passed up the big business-class hotels by the Tappan Zee Bridge, hoping for something with more personality. As we followed Route 9 into Tarrytown (which had engulfed the village of Sleepy Hollow sometime in the past), we expected to find a motel. The village celebrates the Horseman on patrol cars and banners on every lamppost; surely, a place with such a sense of its own quaintness would have a bed for two weary travelers.

After an hour, Mason and I gave up searching in order to have dinner in a restaurant called Horsefeathers on the main drag. The pillows of fresh mozzarella in my salad melted in my mouth. Mason's turkey burger appeared too big to lift. As we finished eating at our sidewalk table, the sun burned red behind the mountains across the Hudson River. It was all too easy to sink into the dreaminess from which the area takes its name.

"The sequestered situation of this church seems always to have made it a favorite haunt of troubled spirits. It stands on a knoll, surrounded by locust trees and lofty elms, from among which its decent whitewashed walls shine modestly forth, like Christian purity beaming through the shades of retirement."

After a good night's rest at the charming Peekskill Inn ten miles farther up the "highway," we turned the car back south toward Sleepy Hollow. By ten a.m., the thermometer passed eighty degrees. The heavy air barely moved, sluggish with humidity. All around us, the trees flared vivid green. Who would have guessed that April in New York would feel so much like summertime?

As Mason drove through the cemetery gate, a striped chipmunk scurried past and disappeared into a bank of grass. When we stepped out of the rental car, the repeated screech of a jay split the air. The Pocantico River chattered quietly to itself below the parking lot. Mason headed toward the old yellow church while I stopped to read the historic plaque.

Frederick Philipse, the first lord of the nearby manor of Philipsburg, built this little church for his tenants in 1685. The bricks had been shipped from Holland, since the American brickworks weren't yet up to the task. Writing in the 19th century, Irving called the building "The Old Dutch Church" and the name stuck. The burial ground, dating back to 1640, preceded its church by two generations.

First, the good news: the plaque described the place as "one of America's oldest cemeteries," containing Dutch tenant farmers and their *huisvrows* (housewives?—it was undefined on the sign), Revolutionary War soldiers, and the characters of Washington Irving's tale.

The bad news? The Friends of the Old Dutch Burying Ground of Sleepy Hollow offered guided tours on Sundays from May to October. We visited on a Friday in mid-April.

> *"Over a deep black part of the stream, not far from the church, was formerly thrown a wooden bridge; the road that led to it, and the bridge itself, were thickly shaded by overhanging trees, which cast a gloom about it, even in the daytime, but occasioned a fearful darkness at night. This was one of the favorite haunts of the headless horseman and the place where he was most frequently encountered."*

Many of the tombstones had been carved from rust-red sandstone instead of the gray slate we'd seen in the Massachusetts burying grounds. I lingered in front of the grave of James Barnerd. His epitaph indicated he'd been a sailor:

> The Boisterous Winds and Neptuns
> Waves have Tost me too and fro.
> By Gods decree you plainly See
> I am Harbour'd here Below.

I loved the carver's creative spelling. Barnerd "departed this life" in 1768 at the age of 48. Though discolored by exhaust from the traffic nearby, a cherub with sagging jowls brightened his sandstone marker. Above the cherub's head floated something like a lotus blossom, probably a crown of divine fire.

Some of the sandstone markers had flaked until their inscriptions vanished. I wondered if the deceaseds' next of kin would have seen that as appropriate: just as their loved ones dissolved into the ground, the stones that remembered them crumbled to dust. I don't think these markers had been expected to carry names three centuries into the future.

Many of the graves had little metal signs poked into their dirt. I expected those would mark the graves of Ichabod Crane and the others, but instead the signs had been placed by the Tarrytown DAR (Daughters of the American Revolution—descendants of Revolutionary soldiers) and the modern-day Friends of the Cemetery.

Only after the American centennial in 1876 was *any* soldier who'd served in the American Revolution lionized as a patriot worth remembering, even mere foot soldiers.

Mason laughed at me for lingering over the Revolution-era headstones. The Dutch settlers' tombstones hung around the skirts of the church. Those were truly old. Even though the words were Dutch, the epitaphs ran to familiar patterns: "Hier Leyt Begraven" or "Here lyes Buried."

We searched and searched the sandstone tablets. Mason found the Crane family graves, but none of them named Ichabod. Eventually, I located Catriena Van Tessel, who died November 10, 1706. Nothing seemed to connect her to Irving's story. Perhaps he'd simply borrowed her name?

"To look upon its grass-grown yard, where the sunbeams seem to sleep so quietly, one would think that there at least the dead might rest in peace."

The cemetery *was* incredibly peaceful. The traffic's quiet hiss on Route 9 underscored the singing birds. Although I couldn't see them from the churchyard, lilacs perfumed the air. I breathed deep, trying to absorb the scent of spring.

I saw no indication that the headless horseman writhed restlessly beneath the sod. In fact, life seemed to be in full force, from spiders winding strands across the ancient stones to squirrels chasing each other up and down the stolid elms. Violets flecked the grass, visited by humming bees. Somewhere near the Pocantico River, a woodpecker knocked on a tree.

"...the favorite specter of Sleepy Hollow, the headless horseman ... tethered his horse nightly among the graves in the churchyard."

The old burying ground metastasized over the centuries since the colony's foundation. Surrounding the old church lay the original Dutch farmers. Beside them rest the Revolutionary veterans. Beyond those, as the hill begins to climb, recline combatants of the War of 1812. Next come sailors who plied the Hudson River trade. I found it strange to see that the oldest sandstone markers were often in better shape than many of the younger marble monuments, which had been melted by decades of rain turned acid by the proximity of New York City.

I passed the invisible boundary into another cemetery, founded in 1840, The true Sleepy Hollow Cemetery was less a churchyard than a "rural" cemetery after the fashion of London's Highgate and Cambridge's Mount Auburn. Beyond the Victorian reaches of that cemetery lay a modern memorial park, a swooping slope of granite markers that remembers the 20th century's inhabitants of the area.

Just shy of the crest of the hill in the Sleepy Hollow Cemetery lies the author of the *Legend* responsible for Sleepy Hollow's renown. Washington Irving rests inside a simple iron fence emblazoned with his family name. A plain marble tablet, streaked green with lichen, marked his grave. According to a bronze plaque placed in 1972 by remaining members of the Irving family, the "graveplot" is now a national historic landmark. At some point recently, the American Legion placed a flag on Irving's grave to pick it out from all the others, which I appreciated, since the plot's gate was locked. Irving served in the New York Militia in the War of 1812, without seeing action. I photographed his gravestone from the gate, smiling at the bluebells that brightened the grass between the graves. I hoped it made him happy to be home. I wondered if he'd become one of the spirits he wrote about.

"Indeed, certain of the most authentic historians of those parts...allege that the body of the trooper, having been buried in the churchyard, the ghost rides forth to the scene of the battle in nightly quest of his head; and that the rushing speed with which he sometimes passes along the Hollow, like a midnight blast, is owing to his being belated, and in a hurry to get back to the churchyard before daybreak."

The Sleepy Hollow necropolis held the tenth, eleventh, and twelfth graveyards of our trip, practically the halfway point. I must confess that the modern monuments did not attract me like the oldest stones. In fact, the presence of the new graveyard underlined the difficulty one has in trying to visualize the isolation of the village in the 1600s. Tim Burton captured that well in his movie: the era when Sleepy Hollow lay a three-day journey out of the metropolis, rather than an hour's jaunt.

I wasn't really ready to abandon the sense of peace the old burial ground gave me, but we had miles to go before rush hour began. Our plan was to blast through New Jersey and spend the night in Pennsylvania Dutch country. From one settlers' community to another, from true Dutch to Deutsch, from the Headless Horseman to Hex Hollow in the space of the afternoon: it is *good* to live in the 21st century. There were no places I would rather explore, no company I would rather keep, no time of year so beautiful as spring. I felt truly blessed.

If we did not find the horseman's grave, no matter. I chose an epitaph for him from those offered. Irving himself might have done no better than this:

Hark From The Tomb
A Doulfull Voice
Thy Ear Atends the Cry
You Liven Men
Com View the Ground
Were You Must Shortly
Lie.

Soldiers' National Monument in the National Cemetery,
Gettysburg National Military Park, Pennsylvania

THESE HONORED DEAD

Soldiers' National Cemetery, Gettysburg National Military Park
Pennsylvania: April 20, 2002

AS A KID, I WENT TO GETTYSBURG on a road trip with my family. In those days, the four of us traveled in an over-the-cab camper attached to my dad's pickup truck. The camper contained a kitchenette and toilet and slept four in reasonable comfort, but the truck's cramped cab didn't allow the four of us to ride together. Dad always drove. Mom always navigated. My brother and I alternately slept and fought in the camper on the back.

The memories of my original visit to the Gettysburg National Military Park are discolored by the worst carsickness I've ever suffered, brought on by the miles of driving over the rolling hills of Pennsylvania. Of the National Park, I remember only a vast grassy meadow, repetitive gravestones in a little graveyard, and a driving tour of the battlefield that didn't calm my mutinous stomach.

My adult obsession with graveyards made it necessary to revisit the Soldiers' National Cemetery at Gettysburg.

The battle of Gettysburg represented the Confederate Army's high-water mark during the Civil War, but it also changed the way bodies of American servicemen were treated. Prior to 1863, governments took little responsibility for dead soldiers. Generally, camp followers or locals buried the dead in huge trenches on the battlefields where they fell. If graves were labeled at all, often the painted planks didn't survive their first winter. Soldiers' National Cemetery embodies the nation's first attempt to identify all the dead and mark their remains.

Our friends Timothy and Alison offered to guide us around the battlefield. Their comfortable home in southern Pennsylvania lay about an hour away from Gettysburg. On the drive over, Tim told ghost stories about wandering the wooded areas of the battlefield at night, snapping random photos to see what might appear on his film. To his surprise, some exposures revealed balls and streaks of light.

The Gettysburg battlefield is reputed to be one of the most haunted areas in the United States. The Travel Channel calls it one of the world's creepiest travel destinations and reports that ghosts have been recorded at Gettysburg for more than a century. That's not a surprise, really. Over the course of the first three days of July 1863, 51,000 men were wounded, killed, or went missing there. That's a lot of spiritual energy for the rocks and rolling meadows to absorb.

While the North seemed able to provide an inexhaustible amount of weaponry and clothing for its soldiers, three years into the conflict, the Southern Army desperately needed simple things like boots. General Lee had heard that shoes were being manufactured in Pennsylvania. After Lee led his troops north in search of supplies, the Battle of Gettysburg began on July 1, 1863.

In addition to resupplying his army, Lee's attack on Northern soil drew the Army of the Potomac away from the beleaguered Confederate capital at Richmond, Virginia. The South required an overwhelming success to inspire their allies in Europe to finally back their cause. For a while, it seemed they might get it.

By the end of July 1st, Lee's army routed the unprepared Union troops. The battle appeared as if it would be another victory for the South in a string that included Charleston and Bull Run.

Union soldiers fled through the streets of the little village of Gettysburg to the hill overlooking Evergreen Cemetery south of town. Rather than pursue, Lee's army camped for the night. They had suffered high casualties that day and the general did not know the size of the Union force.

Throughout the night, both sides received reinforcements. By July 3rd, the Union Army numbered 6,500 men against 15,000 Southerners. Confederate General Pickett directed his men in successive waves through an open field toward the Union line atop Cemetery Ridge. More than 6,000 boys in gray were wounded, killed or went missing, demolished by Union cannons atop the hill. Union troops took 1,500 casualties.

Pickett's folly became obvious to me when Timothy parked his van outside the gates of Evergreen Cemetery. Across the road rose Cemetery Ridge. The bare hillside provided no cover for either side.

My friend Jeff is a student of history. Later, when I told him about our visit, he summed up the American Civil War for me: "Military science had advanced to the point where they knew how to do the most damage possible to a human body, but military strategy hadn't begun to take that into account—and medical science had no idea how to cope." In other words, the Civil War was fought by two opposing lines of men armed with weapons that could shatter bone from a distance. Once wounded, a soldier had a very poor chance of survival, since both anesthesia and antiseptics were experimental. Hence, more than 7,000 dead in a three-day battle.

After losing thirty percent of his army, Lee withdrew on July 5th. General Meade, in charge of the Army of the Potomac, chose not to pursue. His men made attempts to bury their own dead, but the job was too immense. When the Union Army finally withdrew from the field, thousands of corpses lay where they'd fallen, rotting in the humid Pennsylvanian summer. Whenever townspeople came across a body, they threw dirt over it and left it in place. Our friend Tim reported that people could smell the battlefield as far away as York, thirty miles distant.

Women arrived from across the countryside to volunteer as nurses. Every public building in Gettysburg became a hospital. As men died, they were hastily buried in yards or gardens.

Throughout the summer, citizens of Gettysburg attempted to repair their homes, replant their crops, and deal with the devastation left behind by the battle. The groundskeeper of Evergreen Cemetery was off fighting in the 138th Pennsylvania Infantry, leaving behind his pregnant wife Elizabeth to struggle with burying the dead. She set aside a plot inside Evergreen for slain soldiers, but clearly there wouldn't be enough room unless she filled the cemetery. Scandal erupted when she buried two Confederate men in the cemetery's consecrated ground. Although their bodies remain to this day, their graves were never marked, for fear of vandalism.

The sad state of the thousands of corpses remaining unburied on the battlefield drew the attention of Pennsylvania Governor Andrew Curtin. He championed a movement to buy land from the village to provide a cemetery where all Northern soldiers could lie with their comrades. Eventually, money was raised to purchase a "boot-shaped" piece of ground alongside Evergreen Cemetery. Reburials began in

October 1863, four months after the war had moved on.

Those were the days before dog tags. Occasionally during the Civil War, when men suspected they were being ordered to their deaths, they'd write their names on scraps of paper and pin them inside their clothing. Without those little notes, corpses at Gettysburg could only be identified by company insignia or marks of rank on their uniforms, or by the contents of their pockets, so long as they hadn't been robbed after death. Superintendent of Exhumation Samuel Weaver insisted that all temporary graves be opened in his presence, so that he could personally identify the corpses. As much as he was able, Weaver recorded hair color and height of the decomposing dead, to be compared with the government service records on file for each man.

A ceremony to dedicate the new cemetery was planned for November 19, 1863. Sort of as an afterthought, David Wills, a lawyer whose house faced the town square, invited President Lincoln to speak at the dedication. Months after the battle, shallow graves still littered the surrounding countryside, but since the war itself had moved southward, Northerners could again travel safely. Over 50,000 people descended on the shell-shocked town to celebrate the creation of the first national military cemetery.

Lincoln traveled to the ceremony by train. Standing amongst new-made graves, he delivered the Gettysburg Address: "We have come to dedicate a portion of that field as a final resting place for those who here gave their lives that that nation might live.... But in a larger sense, we cannot dedicate, we cannot consecrate, we cannot hallow this ground. The brave men, living and dead, who struggled here, have consecrated it far above our poor power to add or detract."

For the first time, a battlefield in the United States was seen as holy ground, consecrated not by the power of God but by the blood of men slain there. Strangely enough, soldiers became holy not by their deeds in life but at the moment of their deaths. For the first time ever, bodies of common men were not treated as an inconvenient byproduct of war, but as its holy relics. It was a revolutionary concept. I'm fascinated by the beatification of simple soldiers and the sanctity of the ground in which they lie.

In the cemetery, corpses had been sorted not only by army (Confederate bodies were left where they lay) but also by the eighteen states from whence they came, so that each section is marked with the number of Michiganders and Minnesotans who died in the battle. Beyond that accounting, pains were taken to name as many men as possible. Even so, stone blocks labeled "Unknown" mark more than half of the graves inside Soldiers' National Cemetery. In the intervening years, historians have identified many of the 1,608 men labeled "unknown" by comparing descriptions made by Weaver to government records and survivors' memoirs.

Nearly a year passed before reburials ceased in Soldiers' National Cemetery. The 3,654 men interred there are a fraction of the 51,000 casualties. Some men lie in Evergreen Cemetery. Others were fetched home to their family graveyards. Confederate soldiers waited to be moved until 1872, when they were shipped to Richmond, Charleston, Savannah, and Raleigh, and reburied with equivalent respect. Even with the dispersal, hundreds of corpses were undoubtedly missed amongst the stands of trees punctuating the rolling Pennsylvania hills. Whether or not it is haunted, the battlefield remains a very creepy place.

The holy ground of the military cemetery became a place of pilgrimage from the start. These days, two million people visit the battlefield at Gettysburg each year, making it one of the most popular historical destinations in the United States.

Grant's Tomb, General Grant National Memorial, New York City

"LET US HAVE PEACE"

General Grant National Memorial and the World Trade Center site
New York City: April 23, 2002

AFTER WE CROSSED BROADWAY, Mason and I stumbled upon a memorial to the firefighters lost when the World Trade Center collapsed on 9/11. Bright chains of origami cranes decorated the fence around an old brown church. Beside them hung tattered missing person flyers. Amongst the ephemera fluttered faded navy blue T-shirts, each silk-screened with a different fire company emblem. My eyes stung, burned by the eloquence of those empty shirts.

Around the corner, we peered through the big iron fence into the churchyard. In the afternoon light, the grass glowed intensely green. Dense trees raised a verdant canopy above the old stones. I longed for the sense of peace inside, but a big padlock held the fence closed.

I wound my fingers through the bars and gazed at the old headstones. The graveyard seemed strangely familiar. Not until we came home and I looked through my files did I realize this was Saint Paul's Churchyard. A photograph clipped from the *Boston Herald* captured the tranquil cemetery snowed over with debris fallen from the World Trade Center's Twin Towers. Papers and torn insulation drifted against the old, irreplaceable monuments. A volunteer in a hazmat suit wheeled the junk out by the wheelbarrow load.

The Graveyard Shift: A Family Historian's Guide to New York City Cemeteries reports that Saint Paul's Churchyard historically had its own ghost. After Shakespearean actor George Frederick Cooke died destitute in 1812, his skull was allegedly sold to pay his bills. Rumor says that he appeared, posthumously, as Yorick in *Hamlet*. His ghost prowled amongst the stones in the churchyard, seeking his head.

Unable to enter the church or the cemetery, Mason and I moved on. Another block farther along, a huge destruction zone gaped. Dust stirred up by the earthmovers hung motionless in the air. Entirely by accident, we'd reached Ground Zero.

261

Mason huddled against a nearby skyscraper to look furtively into our guidebook. "The subway station should be *right* here," he insisted.

Should be, but was gone. Our guidebook had been published pre-9/11. The station we wanted had vanished into the crater of the World Trade Center.

Mason recovered sooner than I could. He led me up the shadowy canyon of a street between skyscrapers to another subway station. From there, we had an easy ride uptown.

Collapsed on the subway seat, I had the same sick feeling that came over me in the Peace Museum in Hiroshima. The realization that thousands of people had shrieked in the face of death—right where I'd stood—nearly reduced me to tears. I'd wanted to visit the World Trade Center site, pay my respects, but not like this. Not by chance.

Mason trained me to visit the thing I most want to see at the start of our trips. That way, everything else is gravy. If there's a transit strike or one of us gets sick or something else unforeseen happens, I've already accomplished my goal. In all of Manhattan, I'd most wanted to visit Grant's Tomb.

President Grant's mausoleum is an enormous edifice composed of 8,000 tons of white granite. It looms 150 feet high: a square box of a building, crowned with a cupola ringed with Doric columns. John Hemenway Duncan, the architect, meant for it to echo the tomb of Mausolus, one of the Seven Wonders of the Ancient World, as well as the Mausoleum of Hadrian in Rome, known more familiarly now as Castle Sant'Angelo. By referencing the splendors of the past, Duncan unleashed a new wave in Federal architecture. Before the completion of Grant's tomb, national memorials tended toward obelisks: think of the Washington Monument in DC. Grant's Tomb laid the foundation for the Lincoln Memorial. In addition to being a true tomb—because Grant's body lies within—the General Grant National Memorial is the largest mausoleum in North America. That alone put it on my must-see list.

Despite his service as the 18th president of the United States, Ulysses S. Grant was better loved for winning the Civil War. During his lifetime, many credited him with ending slavery. His feelings on racism were progressive: during the war, he favored arming "negro" soldiers. Unfortunately, scandal and corruption in his cabinet marred his presidency. After two terms, he retired to bankrupt his family with a series of bad investments. In 1884, he was diagnosed with cancer of the throat. Racing against time, he wrote his memoirs, published posthumously by his friend Mark Twain. Twain gave up most of the profits to support Grant's wife Julia for the rest of her days.

Nine days after he wrote the final word, Ulysses S. Grant succumbed to his cancer. He expected to be interred at West Point, but they refused Julia permission to be buried alongside him. Other cities such as Galena, Illinois and St. Louis, Missouri hoped to host his tomb.

When initially offered burial space by the mayor of New York City, Julia Dent Grant held out for something a little more centrally located, preferably in Central Park. After it became clear that the mausoleum would cost the family nothing—and she could be buried alongside her husband—she accepted the site just west of Harlem.

Grant's funeral occasioned a huge international outpouring of grief. Sixty thousand people marched in the seven-mile-long funeral parade, including President Grover Cleveland and former Presidents Chester Arthur and Rutherford Hayes. Over a million people lined the parade route. Officers of both the Grand Army of the Republic and the Army of Northern Virginia carried the coffin into a temporary tomb made of brick. For the first six months, Grant's body had a twenty-four-hour military guard, which was replaced—as time dragged on and the mausoleum languished unfinished—by New York City policemen.

Shortly after Grant's death, a Grant Monument Association had been established to collect money for the tomb. Richard Greener, the first African American graduate of Harvard University, served as secretary and personally secured many of the subscriptions. When the tomb was finally completed in 1897, 90,000 people had donated a total of $600,000.

The architect's original plan called for sculptures on the balcony and a grand staircase down to the Hudson River. Six hundred thousand dollars wasn't enough money for that. The staircase idea was scrapped and decorations on the tomb's pediment scaled back to reliefs of Federal eagles at each corner. Two muscular young ladies, representing Victory and Peace, sit with their backs to a plaque that reads "Let Us Have Peace." Those words closed Grant's memoirs.

When Mason and I visited, we had the whole National Memorial area nearly to ourselves. Two tiers of red, white, and blue bunting draped the front of the monument. Four large flags hung between the entrance columns. When visitors walked up the steps, the patriotic colors completely dwarfed them.

I put away my camera, wondering if I should have left my backpack back at the apartment where we were staying. I remembered how I'd gotten in trouble in the gift shop at Gettysburg for carrying it, three days earlier.

That day, as I browsed the shelf of cemetery books, one of the cashiers beckoned me. When I came over to her register to hear her better in the crowded gift shop, she asked, "Did you drive?"

Puzzled, I answered, "No."

"Did you come on a tour bus?"

I shook my head, unsure why she polled me—of all people—about my arrival.

Exasperated, the cashier demanded, "How did you get here?"

"Some friends brought me."

"Where are they now?"

"I don't know." People lined up behind me at the register. "In here somewhere."

"You need to find them. You'll have to put your backpack in their car. They do have a car, right? You can't bring a backpack in here. It's a national security measure. Didn't you see the signs when you came into the shop?"

"No," I said, quite honestly. "There were probably fifty people standing on the porch when I came in. It was raining."

"Oh." She realized why the shop had suddenly gotten so busy. "Well, it's against the rules for you to have a backpack or any kind of bag in here," the cashier declared officiously. She was a gray-haired lady with a cat-shaped pin on her sweater. "A terrorist might bring a bomb in here."

That seemed outrageously unlikely to me, but this was clearly not a woman with whom to argue.

"I'm sorry not to have known." I put a stack of books on the counter: *The Victorian Celebration of Death*, *Beyond the Gatehouse: Gettysburg's Evergreen Cemetery*, miscellaneous pamphlets about Civil

War-era graveyards. It was nearly a hundred dollars' worth of books. "I wanted to buy these. Can you reshelve them for me?"

"You can come back for them after you put your bag in the car."

"No. The van is too far away. I'll just order them on Amazon."

She looked at me in my pink T-shirt: my camouflage for cemetery jaunts. She looked at the pricey stack of books. With an avaricious gleam in her eye, she suggested, "Why don't you pay for them before you leave?"

My friend Alison appeared at the counter. "Did you see the books on Victorian mourning costumes?"

"I would like to, but I'm being thrown out of the bookstore." I took the credit card from my backpack and laid it atop the books on the counter.

"Why?" Alison asked.

"They're afraid I might have a bomb in my backpack."

Alison laughed loudly enough to turn heads across the gift shop.

"No, really," I protested. I signed my charge receipt and handed it back to the lady with the cat brooch. "Do you need to see my ID?"

"No, that's good enough."

Later, I found it peculiar that she trusted me enough to use a charge card, right after I'd all but been compared to the men who stole airplanes and used them as bombs against a national icon. At the time, I was ashamed of being punished for something I could never imagine doing.

The whole mortifying exchange replayed in my mind as I hefted my backpack. I wasn't about to travel all the way back down Manhattan to leave my camera at Jimmy's apartment. If I couldn't check the backpack with the rangers, maybe Mason could sit outside with it while I poked around Grant's Tomb. I wasn't sure how much there was to see inside anyway.

The architecture turned out to be the best part. The dome soared above our heads, airy and ornate, hinting at how busy the strong, simple façade might have been if Duncan had gotten his way. Four sculptural pendentives held allegorical figures representing stages in Grant's life, including "Civil Life" and "Military Life." Coffered archways held up a balcony ringed by columns. Above them, eagles spread their wings. It was Victorian and overblown in a way the outside had not been.

I marched over to the ranger station and asked, "Can I check my backpack with you?"

"I guess." The ranger didn't seem concerned about it.

I told him the Gettysburg story.

"Oh, they're twitchy over there," he said. "No one's going to blow up this place, but definitely no one is going to blow up a gift shop at the edge of a battlefield. I got in trouble there for wearing a fake period gun into the gift shop," he confessed. "It didn't even have a hole drilled in the barrel."

Despite his amusement, I could see how the Gettysburg gift shop clerks might be uncomfortable with weapons they could see, simulated or not. In 1998, a French tourist shot a re-enactor with a period rifle loaded with a real bullet. Still, this guy behind the desk was a Park Ranger, an authority figure who worked on the edge of Harlem every day. If he didn't see me as a potential danger, it was all good.

His relaxed perspective settled me down. At the time of our visit, New Yorkers had already lived with the threat of terrorism for more than six months. They believed what had happened on 9/11 was a fluke. I guess you had to feel that way or you would have already left town. I thanked him and excused myself, taking my backpack with me.

Mason and I explored the rotunda, reading historical panels that discussed Grant's military service, his presidency, the construction of his tomb. Rooms toward the back of the main floor displayed flags, battlefield maps, and other paraphernalia of the Civil War.

We saved the main draw for last. An opening yawned in the center of the floor. We leaned against the balcony to look down on the sarcophagi that are the grand final resting places of Ulysses Simpson and Julia Dent Grant. Made of red Wisconsin granite in imitation of Napoleon's sarcophagus at *Les Invalides* in Paris, the two stone boxes weighed eight and a half tons each.

I wondered if Julia had ever gave a second thought to her choice of location for her tomb. Until the 1930s, half a million people paid their respects each year at Grant's tomb. Then visitors tapered off. Fewer people survived who had participated in—or even remembered—the Civil War. The wars of the 20th century made war itself seem less grand and glamorous.

The Park Service assumed the monument's care in 1959. Now the

WISH YOU WERE HERE

site averages 100,000 visitors a year. I am glad Mason and I made the trip, even if we got lost in Harlem on the way back—once again looking for a subway station we couldn't locate.

As we retraced our steps back to the station nearer Grant's Tomb, I thought about the Tule Lake Relocation Center and Guantanamo Bay, about the *Arizona* Memorial and the Atomic Dome, about bigotry and fear of "the other," about a world where Muslim men could be swept off the street and held without charges by my country's government. Would we ever grow up and stop fearing each other because of the color of our skins, or the names we give to God?

I thought about Grant's wish, echoed in the slogan above his mausoleum: Let Us Have Peace. While fear swirled all around us, true and lasting peace seemed a long way off.

Jimmy, the friend of Mason's with whom we were staying, had gotten his job in Manhattan after the 9/11 attack, when Manhattanites left the city in droves and downtown apartments were relatively reasonably priced. He worked in the historic Woolworth Building, a neo-Gothic high rise that was the tallest building in the world until 1930.

The turn-of-the-century Woolworth Building used to stand in the shadow of the towering World Trade Center. After September 2001, it looked down into a pit. Jimmy offered to take us up to his office on visitor's passes.

Before we left Manhattan, it felt important for me to deal with the reality of the World Trade Center's obliteration. Jimmy warned us that the crater appeared to simply be a construction site, except that you can see four stories into the ground. He was right: the empty gravesite wasn't anything special to see.

In its place, I envisioned the cathedral skeleton of the World Trade Center's remaining wall. Looking down on the earthmovers and dump trucks, I was not nearly as touched as I had been by those empty T-shirts at Saint Paul's. The loss of a building meant nothing to me. The power lay in my empathy for the strangers who died there.

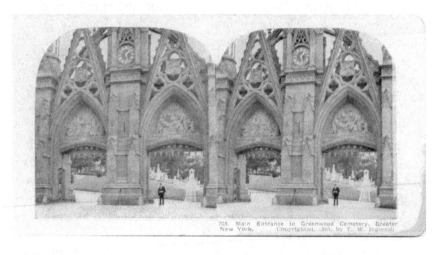

Vintage stereoview of the gateway to Green-Wood Cemetery, Brooklyn

A CEMETERY THAT ONCE RIVALED
NIAGARA FALLS

Green-Wood Cemetery, Brooklyn: April 24, 2002

AFTER TWO YEARS OF LANDSCAPING, Brooklyn's Green-Wood Cemetery hosted its first burial in 1840. Green-Wood followed the garden cemetery movement pioneered in the United States by Cambridge's Mount Auburn. That is, these cemeteries didn't belong to churches, but accepted wealthy people of all faiths. They used the beauty of their grounds to attract clientele.

The Graveyard Shift: A Family Historian's Guide to New York City Cemeteries explained, "Green-Wood's beauty ultimately inspired the contest to design Central Park." In the 19th century, sightseers took trains to Green-Wood merely to walk its paths. Grassy hillsides welcomed picnickers. In the 1860s, the graveyard pulled in half a million visitors a year: a tourist attraction rivaling Niagara Falls. I *so* looked forward to seeing it for myself.

Since Green-Wood was so lovely, a large variety of souvenirs pictured it in the 19th century. These were originally collected on sightseeing tours or as souvenirs from imaginary vacations. *Famous and Curious Cemeteries* reports that, by 1862, there were over a thousand stereoview cards of Green-Wood. Stereoviews were stiff cardboard cards with a pair of duplicate photographs mounted on them. You slipped the cards into a stereopticon viewer, peered inside, and the image magically became three-dimensional.

Alongside Brooklyn's Fifth Avenue rose the huge Gothic Revival archway I recognized from a stereoview in my collection. Pierced like lace, the breathtaking brownstone gate ascended in high arches. While I'm doing my best to collect all the stereoview cards of Green-Wood I can, I find that a photograph I've taken myself is still the best memento. Mason stopped at the side of Green-Wood's driveway so I could leap out of our rental car and take a picture.

When we pulled up to the gate, a guard stepped out of a little office. "Can I help you?"

"We just want to look around," I chirped. "Do you have a map?"

He returned to his office and brought out a large map marked with plot numbers, not names, which made it useless to me. I had no idea what plot numbers I wanted to see.

He saw my Pentax camera with its telephoto on my lap. "Photographs are forbidden."

"Really?"

"Absolutely."

Lush lawns stretched before us, shaded by stately old trees. Summer had come to Brooklyn in every shade of green. The cemetery looked magnificent.

Thoroughly disappointed, I asked, "Do I need to leave my camera with you?"

"Oh, no." He stepped away from the car. "Lock it in the trunk."

Mason pulled over beside the sales office so I could put the camera away. The car parked ahead of us had a sign in its window labeled, "Location scout." I snarked that photography must be no problem, when you paid for the privilege.

We passed the chapel, built in 1911 by Warren and Wetmore, the firm that designed Grand Central Station. The chapel stood on land that used to be Arbor Water, one of the famous ponds of Green-Wood. I have a lovely stereoview of Arbor Water, seen over the shoulders of marble angels. The pond was sacrificed to offer customers a place to hold funeral services at the cemetery. Green-Wood has long been a landscape in flux.

The ground facing the former pond rose in terraces lined with mausoleums. The architecture spanned Egyptian pyramids to columned Greek temples to the Romanesque receiving tomb. I was thrilled to finally see sites I'd adored through my stereopticon.

Green-Wood reportedly has twenty miles of drives, though I'd also read they'd torn up the least-used passages to provide more burial space. In addition to that, we were surprised to see new customers buried inside old plots. Raw dirt scarred the green grass. Still, I understand that new burials bring in money for maintenance. A cemetery of this age wasn't going to be able to expand its borders, so they needed to find space where they could plant paying customers.

Signs along the asphalt roadways urged us to drive slowly. The roads twisted and curved so that I would've thought it impossible to get up much speed. Finally we crested a hill and parked. We wandered from monument to monument, blithely crossing the road until a white car nearly ran Mason down. The car looped back and a security guard called us over: "Can I help you?"

Since he offered, I cheerfully assumed he could help us locate monuments I'd come to see. I've talked to groundskeepers from California to London; they always know the best stories, the prettiest graves. "I'd like to see Charlotte Canda's tomb," I said.

The guard snorted. "I don't know where anyone is buried. You have to ask at the office. Be careful crossing the road."

After he accelerated away, I turned to Mason. "Why did he ask to help us?"

"I suspect he was checking on us. It's good you put the camera in the trunk."

We discovered a memorial I would have liked to document: a marble cameo inside a verdigris frame. "Precious Georgie" had been one of the twin sons of an abolitionist preacher from Brooklyn. Engraved on his monument was a poem that made my skin crawl. It began, "He looked up at his mother and whispered, 'Does Jesus love me? What will he say when he sees me?'"

Atop the hill, Mason tried to grasp the lay of the land. Green-Wood contains 478 acres holding more than 560,000 souls. Until the 20th century, it was the largest landscaped cemetery in the world. "Should we head back to the office?" he asked. "They might have a map that's actually useful. Maybe you can buy a photo pass."

We drove at the same leisurely pace back toward the gate. On the way, we passed a tomb I would have photographed. Two seated angels in magnificent relief flanked the ornate cutwork door of the Stewart mausoleum. The angel on the right held a slender trumpet as tall as his shoulder. They reminded me of the exquisite William Morris tapestries in London's Victoria and Albert Museum. These angels had been designed by Augustus Saint-Gaudens, sculptor of the figure called *Grief* at Rock Creek Cemetery in Washington, DC. They had been controversial in their day, since they didn't depict death as gloomy.

I was in a rapture of beauty when the security guard's car raced round the corner and nearly rear-ended us. We edged over as much as we could to let him squeeze by.

He pulled alongside our car and stopped, rolling down his

window. "Can I help you?" he asked again.

"We're heading back to the office to get directions," Mason said.

"Keep going this way, then you're going to want to go left at the bottom of the hill."

"I'd figured that out," Mason said to me as the guard gunned his engine and left us in his dust.

The cemetery office bustled with people behind a high counter. Eventually a woman came to see what we wanted.

"I'm a member of the Association for Gravestone Studies," I said. "I write a monthly column about visiting cemeteries. I would like permission to take some photographs."

"Not for publication," the woman snapped.

"The guard at the gate said that photos aren't allowed at all," I reported.

"Not for publication," she repeated.

"Is there anyone I can talk to about taking a couple of photos for my column?" I asked. "I would be willing to pay for a photo pass."

"You could try to talk to the superintendent, but he's in a meeting,"

I'd forgotten how fast New Yorkers talk when they want to get rid of you. "Well, I've come from California to see Charlotte Canda's grave. Could you give us directions?"

She pulled out a poster-sized map and traced our route with a yellow highlighter. "But you can't photograph it for publication," she reminded.

"I understand."

As I turned away, Mason gestured toward the hardcover book standing up on the counter. It was Jeffrey I. Richman's *Brooklyn's Green-Wood Cemetery: New York's Buried Treasure*, a book I'd only ever seen on eBay. "Are those for sale?" I asked.

The woman who'd been speaking to me had already hustled off. The man whose eye I caught merely shrugged and went to find someone else to help me. Before we left the office, I had a copy of Richman's book and his two booklets of self-guided walking tours. I couldn't photograph their graveyard, but the staff at Green-Wood would take all the money I'd give them for souvenirs.

In my stereoviews, Charlotte Canda's memorial is a gothic fantasy enclosed by a lacy iron fence. A small chapel with twin spires houses a statue of the virgin, one hand over her bosom. Six granite steps lead down to the lawn. A pair of worshipful angels kneel at the edges of the plot. Canda's gravesite is the pinnacle of Victorian memorial art.

Charlotte Canda was the only child of a French émigré who'd fought in Napoleon's army before coming to New York to open a girls' school. A prodigy, Charlotte designed the ornate memorial for an aunt. After a party to celebrate Charlotte's seventeenth birthday, horses pulling her carriage bolted through a raging storm. Flung to the street, Charlotte died in her parents' arms.

During the 1850s, Charlotte Canda's gravesite was the most visited monument in the country. Richman reports, "On any given Sunday, a crowd gathered around it." A 1985 issue of *American Cemetery* magazine said that Canda's monument was "still one of the most popular of the cemetery's numerous attractions." More than the graves of Samuel Morse (inventor of the telegraph), Elias Howe (inventor of the sewing machine), or Lola Montez (a Gold Rush-era dancer of questionable talent who seduced Franz Liszt), I wanted to see Canda's monument.

Time hadn't been kind to the soft white marble. It sorely needed cleaning. Fingers had broken from the virgin's hand. The iron fence evaporated. (During World War II, many cemetery fences were collected up during iron drives. I'm not sure when this one disappeared.) Rather than a grand plot surrounded by trees, Canda's memorial looked cramped and forlorn. The disappointment I'd battled since the gatekeeper made me lock up my camera overwhelmed me.

A grounds crew's truck rushed past. Trash swirled in its wake. Cautiously, I stepped into the road to retrieve a plastic-swathed photograph of two children. I felt even more melancholy with the discarded picture in my hand.

It just wasn't fun to look at a graveyard I couldn't photograph. I've visited hundreds of cemeteries, recorded thousands of monuments. Without pictures to bolster my memory, all the cemeteries blur together: nuances of architecture, horticulture, and sculpture lost. I wanted to cry.

As discouraging as our trip to Green-Wood was, it put all the other cemeteries I've visited into perspective. From the caretaker in Florence who opened the English Cemetery to us—even though she had a lecture to give across town—to the guide in Rome who spent all day underground in the catacombs, from the Friends of Highgate Cemetery who bought their graveyard to save it from utter dissolution to the rangers in Black Diamond Mines Regional Preserve who repair headstones fragment by fragment, I've found people who love their graveyards and are committed to sharing them. They understand the only way for these relics of history to survive is if their beauty and fascination are transmitted to a curious public.

Green-Wood's management has the right idea when it hosts tour groups, book readings, and other performance events dealing with the personalities buried there. In addition, though, I felt they needed to allow journalists to record what touched them. Their refusal to allow photographs for publication negates both the reason the cemetery originally opened to the public and the justification for survivors to lavish so much money on its monuments. These works of art were intended to be viewed by as many people as possible. How else would the bereft be certain the world understood their grief? How else could Precious Georgie—who no longer exists in any living memory—survive? Green-Wood, more than any modern memorial park, was designed to be appreciated by the public. Without an audience, it is merely exorbitant real estate tarted up to go to sleep.

Update: Several months after this essay initially appeared on *Morbid Outlook*, I received a note from Rich Moylan, President of the Green-Wood Cemetery. While I gratefully accepted his corrections to factual errors in the piece—even when they contradicted published sources—I can't back down from the negative experience I had at Green-Wood. Never before or since have I been intimidated by the behavior of cemetery employees.

However, I'm willing to believe that cemeteries, like people, have bad days. I conceded that perhaps the man at the kiosk at the entry gate was just feeling unhelpful, which is why he told me I couldn't take photos in the cemetery and made me put my camera in the car trunk. Maybe the women in the office were stressed by having a movie location scout on the premises at the same time as my visit, which is why they didn't want me to ask about taking photos or discuss allowing me to buy a photo pass. Maybe the security guard has slowed down his driving and doesn't run people off the road any more.

Moylan countered, "Movie location scouts are routine here. *The Departed* and *No Reservations* are two fairly recent movies filmed here. Not a week goes by that we don't get at least one request. We do charge for requests that we approve and the funds go toward our preservation efforts."

He also wrote: "We have a very open photography policy, which is available for the asking." I'm glad this is true now, but apparently it wasn't the case when I visited in 2002, since I asked everyone I could get my hands on about taking pictures. When I wouldn't retract my experience, Moylan eventually spoke to the Chief of Security, who seemed to lump professional photographers with everyone else. Moylan told me he'd corrected the misconception. For the record: all Green-Wood asks is that photographers consult them before publishing a photo so that it can be properly credited.

The good news is that in 2006, the US Department of the Interior named Green-Wood Cemetery a National Historic Landmark. It is only the fourth cemetery in the nation to receive this designation.

Moylan takes pride in the cemetery's restoration program, which he says has "restored hundreds, if not thousands, of memorials over the past ten years." In 2009, they were raising funds to recreate an angel that disappeared over sixty years ago from pianist-composer Louis Moreau Gottschalk's monument. Green-Wood has also worked with the New York Restoration Project to plant nearly 500 new trees. Throughout the cemetery, over 7,500 trees have been tagged and catalogued.

In the future, Green-Wood would like to open a Visitor Center away from the cemetery's main office, so that tourists can be kept separate from mourners. Green-Wood provides 1,500 burials and 2,200 cremations per year, while welcoming 300,000 visitors. The Visitor Center will include museum space to display "original artworks by the nearly 300 artists of note resting here. The collection now exceeds 100 paintings by over 70 of those artists."

"In other words," Moylan says, "we are actively planning for that day when we are no longer an active burial place but rather an outdoor museum. We want to make certain that we are fiscally stable so that we do not become a ward of the state or a beautiful but neglected necropolis like Père Lachaise."

He invited me to come back to Green-Wood Cemetery. I look forward to having a different experience next time I see it.

Bethany Lutheran Indian Cemetery, St. Louis, Michigan

CRADLE TO GRAVE

Bethany Lutheran Indian Cemetery, St. Louis, Michigan: June 8, 2003

THE SKY TO THE NORTH LOOKED MENACING, stacked with piles of towering clouds, purple as a new bruise. Mom and I listened to the classical station out of Lansing, the Michigan state capital, as we drove off to visit yet another country graveyard.

The emergency alert system blared across the radio to announce a tornado watch for a handful of counties. Mom identified the areas as all south of us. She didn't seem worried. I tried not to be.

We continued west, before heading north. Mom promised that if the weather got scary, we'd turn back.

I'd come home, five months pregnant, for my baby shower. My doctor didn't want me to travel after I reached the six-month mark, since my high blood pressure and the history of heart disease in my family made my pregnancy risky. Once I reached Michigan, my daughter-to-be had started to move around strenuously. Her favorite trick seemed to be somersaults.

Mom noticed that cars coming toward us had their headlights on, though it was only early afternoon. The radio updated the tornado watch to include counties closer to our destination.

"Remind me again what a tornado watch is?" I asked.

"It's when conditions are right to a tornado to form," Mom answered. "A warning is when one's already been sighted."

The sky opened up and scattered hail the size of marbles all over the road. Visibility dropped to twenty feet beyond the burgundy nose of Mom's Buick. My heart sped up as Mom's foot came off the gas. The weight of the rain slowed the car immediately.

"There's an overpass ahead," Mom said. "If it's still bad when we reach it, we'll wait there until the storm lets up."

I remembered the Weather Channel video of the family bailing out of their van to hide beneath an overpass as a tornado bore down on them. Even though I'd left Michigan more than a decade before, my nightmares still featured tornadoes. I spent too many drills huddled in hallways as a schoolgirl, hands folded over the back of my neck to protect it from flying glass.

My daughter took that moment to drum her heels against me. I wondered if I was going to be sick. I asked Mom, "Do you have any peppermints in your purse?"

She did.

Unlike California traffic, which will blast forward into a blinding rain until someone hydroplanes into a guardrail, Michigan traffic slowed to fit the visibility. People used to driving in weather knew how to behave themselves.

When the overpass came into sight, we could see blue sky beyond it. The storm was sweeping past us.

Mom's hands relaxed on the steering wheel. "I'd rather go onward than go back into that storm," she said.

"How much farther is it?"

"Maybe half an hour."

We made the connection onto M46. Things began to look more suburban. Somehow that made me feel safer, as if anonymous ranch-style houses provided more protection from a tornado than the cornfields we'd been passing through.

A few more miles brought us into St. Louis, the "middle of the mitten," purported geographical center of Michigan's lower peninsula. Named for St. Louis, Missouri, the town had been founded in 1853. In 1869, salt miners discovered a cold-water spring that appeared to have healing powers. The town made itself over as a spa. In its heyday, St. Louis, Michigan boasted several opera houses, a widely known hotel with baths in its basement, and a huge Victorian house on Main Street referred to as the Castle. I only knew about St. Louis because my dad hauled cattle to the Michigan Livestock Association's auction there every Monday.

"What were you doing in St. Louis?" I asked my mom.

"We stopped there for dinner on our way back from Traverse City." Mom and Dad used to go up to that resort town on Lake Michigan every winter for a Farm Bureau convention. Well, Dad went to the convention; Mom usually went to museums.

She continued her story: "I thought we were stopping off so I could meet some of the people he sees every week at the auction. Instead, I found out he'd left the trailer here so that he could pick up animals on our way home. I had to drive myself back from here."

Typical. I changed the subject. "How did you find out about the cemetery?"

"From Doris."

"Was she your waitress?"

"She owns the café," Mom said. "She'd heard I was interested in cemeteries."

That made me laugh. Originally, Mom started traveling around the state to photograph unusual graveyards for me. The reality was that she likes to drive—and it's always more fun if you have a destination in mind. It amused me that she was being tarred with the same brush that considered me eccentric wherever I asked about historic graveyards.

I'd collected postcards of the Native American cemeteries in the Upper Peninsula, which showed little wooden houses over the graves. The St. Louis cemetery was very small, Mom warned me, but the fact that it held only "praying Indians"—Native Americans converted to Christianity—made it a first for me. I wasn't sure what we'd see. I hoped I'd brought enough film.

I don't remember being aware of Michigan's native peoples at all as a kid. Their presence lingered on in place names—Saginaw, Mackinac, Tittabawassee Menominee—but "Indians" seemed as extinct as the French trappers who'd named Detroit, Grand Blanc, and Sault Ste. Marie. Maybe I grew up with kids who had Native American ancestors, but the only ethnicities I noticed in my little hometown were the Poles and Germans at school and the lone Chinese family at my parents' church. In my admittedly limited small-town experience, Michigan in the 1970s was of European descent. I knew that African American families lived in Flint, but I didn't know any of them.

In the 21st century, twelve tribes—branches of Chippewa, Ojibwa, Ottawa, and Potawatomi—owned twenty-two casinos, which might be how most modern Michiganders come in contact with Native Americans these days.

Mom drove through the village of St. Louis, population 3,000. It had a pretty little downtown with big churches on the street corners and restored Victorian mansions dating back to the days of taking the waters. We passed the stockyard where the auction took place, then crossed an elbow of the Pine River.

The cemetery lay alongside a winding country road, across from a big house surrounded by cars: hosting a graduation party or a birthday, everything shimmering with fat droplets of water. I imagined everyone crowding into the house, dodging the hail.

The graveyard had been built long before the invention of cars, so of course it had no driveway. Mom pulled her Buick over as much as possible on the narrow shoulder. The lawn grew as thick and emerald as summer in Michigan could make it. It felt cushiony beneath my feet. My shoes were soon soaked as we climbed the embankment. I took my 60-something mother's elbow, trying to steady her, then she took my hand to help haul me up the last little bit. My daughter hiccuped with all the activity.

A white-painted wooden sign named the Bethany Lutheran Indian Cemetery in careful Old English calligraphy. An ornate ironwork fence stood beside that, with an age-darkened bronze plaque set into a stone plinth. The Lutherans of the Saginaw Valley placed the rededication tablet in 1931. It contained no historical information that might have explained what we had come to visit.

The graveyard occupied a tiny patch of flat ground, edged by trees on two sides, with a field of wheat waving beyond it. A tall whitewashed wooden cross took pride of place, surrounded by small white marble stones, a single marble footstone, and a couple of tablet stones: maybe 20 marked graves in all.

A heavy iron chain fenced the cemetery. From its links hung cast-iron medallions. As I stalked the perimeter, trying to frame a photograph, I wondered at the cemetery's survival all these years. Obviously, the land behind it had been logged, then cleared of brush and rocks. Few patches of primeval forest remained standing in Lower Michigan, but I could imagine how this must have looked when the missionaries came. The pines would have crowded so close together that sunlight barely reached the ground.

Lutheranism is the oldest Protestant strain of Christianity. That it survived when the Inquisition had stamped out earlier heresies was a testament to the evangelical zeal of its converts. Primary among Lutheran beliefs is that no human act can save a soul. In direct opposition to the Catholic rituals of confession and absolution, Martin Luther said that God alone chose whether to save or damn a person. God couldn't be bribed or bargained with. Good acts wouldn't earn favor or forgiveness. All human beings were forever damned because Adam and Eve trusted their own strength, wisdom, and knowledge. In other words, biting the apple—a direct challenge to God—could never be expiated.

In Luther's view, the only hope for humanity was faith. One needed to surrender to the belief that any god who would damn all his creatures because two made a mistake might also arbitrarily choose to save some. Therefore, it was necessary for those who had faith to testify to the heathens. Not because it did the preachers a bit of good, but because only by hearing the word of God did the heathens stand a chance of redemption.

The Bethany Lutheran Indian Cemetery stands as a monument to that evangelical spirit. In 1847, Edward R. Baeierlein arrived from Germany to preach to the Great Lakes Chippewa living in the dark heart of Michigan. When Baeierlein arrived in Frankenmuth—a German colony that continues to exist, albeit as a tourist destination—mid-Michigan was a nearly impenetrable forest. Baeierlein followed a French-Indian guide ten hours into the wilderness to where a band of thirty Chippewa lived in bark-covered "wigwams." He stayed with his flock for five and a half years, until the Lutheran Synod reassigned him to India. During that time, he built a log church, complete with a steeple and bell, translated the New Testament and some German hymns into Chippewa, and buried Pauline, a sixteen-year-old convert who'd died of tuberculosis. In order to inter the "churched" separately from the "heathen," Baeierlein himself cleared a "plot of ground on a little hill, built a fence around it, and erected a tall cross." With no coffin available, Pauline was buried in the native fashion, in a grave lined with tree bark so that no dirt would touch her.

Her marker still stands in the southwest corner of the graveyard. It called her the wife of Peter Naugassike. It surprised me to find the headstones had European names. Probably these were baptismal names, but it also made me sad with the hindsight of 21st century cultural sensitivity. Not only had the Indians had their culture supplanted, their land colonized out from under them, their livelihoods and ways of life dismantled, but they'd also (voluntarily?) given up their names.

I hoped it bought them a place in Heaven.

Several of the headstones bore no names at all, but said merely "Indian Child." I stopped in the wet grass and bent awkwardly to touch the marble. It struck me that whoever had gone to the trouble of burying the children, had ordered and paid for a grave marker, had not given the little ones a name or even a gender. The poor things remained in memory only in enforced anonymity.

As I mistakenly lamented people's callousness, I came across a tall marble stone on the western edge of the cemetery. It quoted a series of Bible verses before stating, "As the records of the Evangelical Lutheran Mission Church of the German Evangelical Lutheran synod of Missouri, Ohio, and other states were destroyed by the great Chicago conflagration of AD 1871, the names of most of the children could not be ascertained. Suffice it that the word of God says, The Lord knoweth them that are His."

I had to turn to the appendix of Baierlein's book *In the Wilderness with the Red Indians* for more history of the cemetery. The book's editor, Harold W. Moll, reports that simple pine boards originally marked the graves. Tradition holds that these were replaced with marble headstones in 1901 by Dr. G. Miessler (Baierlein's replacement at the Bethany Mission, who watched the Chippewa uprooted and sent to a reservation). Because the Chicago Fire destroyed the burial records, only partial information could be retrieved from the weathered forty-year-old headboards.

Moll goes on to say that the half-acre cemetery was given to Holy Cross Lutheran Church in Saginaw (thirty-some miles away) in 1931. When they cleared the brush away, parishioners found the marble markers in a pile. Only the marker on Miessler's first wife's grave was returned to its original position. The others were simply "reset in orderly fashion."

The cemetery has been rededicated a number of times. I suspect it was recently cleaned up again, when St. Louis celebrated its sesquicentennial in 2003.

For decades now, I've visited the graves of children. I'd never understood the guilt and grief that compelled parents to place lambs or cherubs or teddy bears—companions or guardians—on the graves of their offspring. Now, nearing forty and carrying my only child, I began to grasp the crushing erasure of dreams a parent might feel. My daughter would be the only thing I'd ever have in my life that would be completely and entirely irreplaceable.

I thought of my cousin Karen, whose grave started my whole quest to understand cemeteries, and thereby death and bereavement and survival. Karen's epitaph reads, "Say she is not dead, only sleeping." I thought of my aunt, a young mother who lost her firstborn and went on to have five more who lived, but who told me at my brother's funeral that she never, ever forgot that first loss.

For so many years—decades, centuries, millennia—women buried child after child after child. In some places in the world, they still do. I wondered if I would ever have the courage to let my daughter ride in a car or cross the street or go to school or leave my sight. Without faith that God watched over her—took care of her—how could I ever be able to trust that she'd be okay?

Because, I understood, faith had not protected all those other mothers' children. Prayers had not saved their lives. Belief in God did not hold off the inevitability of death. It only gave you hope that you had a place to meet again afterward.

As much as I love cemeteries and the sense of peace visiting them brings to me, the St. Louis graveyard was the last I would visit for a long time. After I returned to California, my pregnancy fulfilled the predictions of difficulty. At thirty-one weeks, my blood pressure skyrocketed to 200/110. I was hospitalized, only to be pumped full of chemicals to keep my baby and me alive. She was delivered seven and a half weeks early. She weighed less than a bag of sugar and was not as long as my forearm. Without the magic of modern medicine, I would have been another woman killed by childbirth. She and I would have shared yet another single grave.

Looking back on our excursion to St. Louis, I'm amused that my mother chose a graveyard as our destination on that day of terrifying weather. Still, despite the hail and morning sickness, we had a wonderful visit. I'm still awed by the crystalline shimmer of raindrops on the lush green grass as the sky cleared to cerulean and the white stones gleamed, washed clean.

Mom and I stopped for ice cream on the drive back to my parents' farm. I never felt closer to her, to my daughter-to-be, to the women who'd come before us and would follow after. I felt like a link in a chain that stretched all the way back to Eve, joined through my womb to the grave and the future.

I couldn't wait until my daughter was old enough to take an interest in cemeteries herself.

BIBLIOGRAPHY

Ariès, Philippe. *The Hour of Our Death*. Oxford University Press, 1991.

AZ London Street Atlas. Geographers' A-Z Map Co. Ltd., 1990.

Bahne, Charles. *The Complete Guide to Boston's Freedom Trail*. Newtowne Publishing, 1993.

Baierlein, E. R. *In the Wilderness With the Red Indians: German Missionary to the Michigan Indians 1847-1853*. Wayne State University Press, 1996.

Barton, Bruce. *Pictorial Forest Lawn*. Forest Lawn Memorial-Park Association, Inc., 1955.

Beck-Friis, Johan. *The Protestant Cemetery in Rome: A Guide for Visitors*. Allhems Forlag Publishing House, 1956.

Benesová, Miroslava and Chládková, Ludmila. *Národní Hrbitov v Terezíně*. Czech Republic, undated.

Bigelow, Jacob. *History of Mount Auburn*. Applewood Books, 1988.

Brock, Eric J. *New Orleans Cemeteries (Images of America)*. Arcadia Publishing, 1999.

Brooks, Chris. *Mortal Remains: The History and Present State of the Victorian and Edwardian Cemetery*. Wheaton, 1989.

Burd, Frank. *Gettysburg*. Americana Souvenirs and Gifts, 2000.

Cole, James M. and Frampton, Rev. Roy E. *Lincoln and the Human Interest Stories of the Gettysburg National Cemetery*. Sheridan Press, 1995.

Cooper, Michael. *Exploring Kamakura: A Guide for the Curious Traveler*. Weatherhill, Inc., 1993.

Cott, Jonathan. *Wandering Ghost: The Odyssey of Lafcadio Hearn*. Alfred A. Knopf, 1991.

Cross, David and Bent, Robert. *Dead Ends: An Irreverent Field Guide to the Graves of the*

Famous. Plume, 1991.

Culbertson, Judi and Randall, Tom. *Permanent Californians: An Illustrated Guide to the Cemeteries of California*. Chelsea Green Publishing Company, 1989.

Culbertson, Judi and Randall, Tom. *Permanent Italians: An Illustrated, Biographical Guide to the Cemeteries of Italy*. Walker Publishing Company, 1996.

Culbertson, Judi and Randall, Tom. *Permanent Londoners: An Illustrated, Biographical Guide to the Cemeteries of London*. Walker Publishing Company, 1996.

Culbertson, Judi and Randall, Tom. *Permanent Parisians: An Illustrated Guide to the Cemeteries of Paris*. Chelsea Green Publishing Company, 1986.

Curl, James Stevens. *The Victorian Celebration of Death*. Sutton Publishing, 2000.

Ditton, Richard P. and McHenry, Donald E. *Yosemite Road Guide*. Yosemite Association, 1989.

Ehl, Pertr, Părík, Arno, and Fieldler, Jirí. *Old Bohemian and Moravian Jewish Cemeteries*. Prague: Paseka, 1991.

Facaros, Dana and Pauls, Michael. *Italy: Three Cities—Rome, Venice, Florence*. Cadogan, 2000.

Farber, Jessie. "Boston's Granary Burying Ground Improvements are Completed." *AGS Quarterly*, volume 26: number 1. Association for Gravestone Studies, 2002.

Farmer, David Hugh. *The Oxford Dictionary of Saints*. Oxford University Press, 1997.

Farrant, David. *Beyond the Highgate Vampire: A True Case of Supernatural Occurrences and Vampirism That Centered Around London's Highgate Cemetery*. British Psychic & Occult Society, 1997.

Felsen, Gregg. *Tombstones: Seventy-Five Famous People and Their Final Resting Places*. Ten Speed Press, 1996.

Florence, Robert. *City of the Dead: A Journey Through St. Louis Cemetery #1*. Center for Louisiana Studies, University of Southwestern Louisiana, 1996.

Florence, Robert. *New Orleans Cemeteries: Life in the Cities of the Dead*. Batture Press, 1997.

Gandolfo, Henri A. *Metairie Cemetery, an Historical Memoir: Tales of its Statesmen, Soldiers, and Great Families*. Stewart Enterprises, Inc., 1998.

Gay, John and Barker, Felix. *Highgate Cemetery: Victorian Valhalla*. John Murray

Publishers, Ltd., 1988.

Gottlieb, Freema. *Mystical Stonescapes of Prague Jewish Town and Czech Countryside.* Prague: Tvorba, undated.

Guiley, Rosemary Ellen. *Vampires Among Us.* Pocket Books, 1991.

Guzzo, Pier Giovanni and d'Ambrosio, Antonio. *Pompeii.* L'Erma di Bretschneider, 1998.

Hancock, Ralph. *The Forest Lawn Story.* Academy Publishers, 1955.

Harvard Student Agencies, Inc. *Let's Go: The Budget Guide to Europe 1990.* St. Martin's Press, 1989.

Hearn, Lafcadio. *Kwaidan: Stories and Studies of Strange Things.* Tuttle Publishing, 2005.

Inskeep, Carolee. *The Graveyard Shift: A Family Historian's Guide to New York City Cemeteries.* Ancestry Publishing, 2000.

Irving, Washington. *The Legend of Sleepy Hollow.* David McKay Co., 1928.

Johnston, Hank and Lee, Martha. *Guide to the Yosemite Cemetery.* Yosemite Association, 1997.

Kadri, Sadakat. *Cadogan City Guides: Prague.* Cadogan Books, 1996.

Keister, Douglas. *Forever L.A.: A Field Guide to Los Angeles Area Cemeteries and Their Residents.* Gibbs Smith, 2010.

Keister, Douglas. *Going Out in Style: The Architecture of Eternity.* Facts on File, 1997.

Keister, Douglas. *Stories in Stone: A Field Guide to Cemetery Symbolism and Iconography.* Gibbs Smith, 2004.

Kennell, Brian A. *Beyond the Gatehouse: Gettysburg's Evergreen Cemetery.* Evergreen Cemetery Association, 2000.

Kull, Andrew. *New England Cemeteries: A Collector's Guide.* Stephen Greene Press, 1975.

Lamb, Brian and the C-SPAN Staff. *Who's Buried in Grant's Tomb? A Tour of Presidential Gravesites.* National Cable Satellite Corporation, 2000.

Linden-Ward, Blanche. *Silent City on a Hill: Landscapes of Memory and Boston's Mount Auburn Cemetery.* Ohio State University Press, 1989.

Manchester, Sean. *The Highgate Vampire: The Infernal World of the Undead Unearthed at London's Highgate Cemetery and Environs.* Gothic Press, 1991.

Marion, John Francis. *Famous and Curious Cemeteries: A Pictorial, Historical, and Anecdotal View of American and European Cemeteries and the Famous and Infamous People Who are Buried There.* Crown Publishers, Inc., 1977.

May, Antoinette. *Haunted Houses of California.* Wide World Publishing, 1990.

Melton, J. Gordon. *The Vampire Book: The Encyclopedia of the Dead.* Visible Ink Press, 1999.

Miller, Elizabeth. *Dracula: Sense and Nonsense.* Desert Island Books, 2006.

Murphy, Edwin. *After the Funeral: The Posthumous Adventures of Famous Corpses.* Citadel Press Book, 1995.

Nadeau, Remi. *Ghost Towns and Mining Camps of California: A History and Guide.* Crest Publishers, 1992.

Nicolai, Vincenzo Fiocchi, Bisconti, Fabrizio, and Mazzoleni, Danilo. *The Christian Catacombs of Rome: History, Decoration, Inscriptions.* Verlag Schnell & Steiner, 1999.

O'Reilly, James, Habegger, Larry, and O'Reilly, Sean. *Paris: True Stories of Life on the Road.* Travelers' Tales Guides, 1997.

Pateman, Jean and Gay, John. *In Highgate Cemetery.* Friends of Highgate Cemetery, 1992.

Pergola, Philippe. *Guide with Reconstructions of Roman Catacombs and the Vatican Necropolis.* Rome: Vision SRL, 1990.

Peters, James Edward. *Arlington National Cemetery: Shrine to America's Heroes.* Woodbine House, 1986.

Petruzzi, J. David. *The Complete Gettysburg Guide: Walking and Driving Tours of the Battlefield, Town, Cemeteries, Field Hospital Sites, and other Topics of Historical Interest.* Savas Beatie, 2009.

Portella, Ivana Della. *Subterranean Rome.* Arsenale Editrice, 2002.

Porter, Phil. "Mackinac Island's Post Cemetery." *Mackinac History: A Continuing Series of Illustrated Vignettes.* Mackinac State Historic Parks, 1999.

Powers-Douglas, Minda. *Translating Tombstones: Your Guide to Symbolism and Meaning in the Cemetery.* Epitaphs Magazine Publishing, 2008.

Reed, J. D. and Miller, Maddy. *Stairway to Heaven: The Final Resting Places of Rock's Legends*. Wenner Books, 2005.

Reinert, Eric A. *Grant's Tomb*. Eastern National, 1997.

Rhoads, Loren. *199 Cemeteries to See Before You Die*. Black Dog & Leventhal, 2017.

Rhoads, Loren, editor. *Death's Garden: Relationships with Cemeteries*. Automatism Press, 1995.

Richman, Jeffrey I. *Brooklyn's Green-Wood Cemetery: New York's Buried Treasure*. Green-Wood Cemetery, 1998.

Richman, Jeffrey I. *A Self-Guided Walk through Green-Wood Cemetery, Walk #1: Battle Hill and Back*. The Green-Wood Cemetery, 1999.

Richman, Jeffrey I. *A Self-Guided Walk through Green-Wood Cemetery, Walk #2: Valley and Sylvan Waters*. The Green-Wood Cemetery, 2001.

Robinson, David. *Saving Graces: Images of Women in European Cemeteries*. W. W. Norton & Company, 1995.

Rufus, Anneli. *Magnificent Corpses: Searching Through Europe for St. Peter's Head, St. Chiara's Heart, St. Stephen's Hand, and Other Saints' Relics*. Marlowe & Company, 1999.

Rufus, Anneli S. and Lawson, Kristan. *Europe Off the Wall: A Guide to Unusual Sights*. John Wiley & Sons, 1988.

Sadek, Vladimir and Sedinová, Jirina. *The Old Jewish Cemetery and the Klausen Synagogue*. The State Jewish Museum in Prague, 1989.

Santini, Pastore Luigi. *The Protestant Cemetery of Florence, called "The English Cemetery."* Administration of Cimitero degli Allori, 1981.

Schwartzman, Arnold. *Graven Images: Graphic Motifs of the Jewish Gravestone*. Harry N. Abrams, Inc., 1993.

Sloane, David Charles. *The Last Great Necessity: Cemeteries in American History*. The Johns Hopkins University Press, 1991.

Snow, Constance and Snow, Kenneth. *Access New Orleans*. Harper Perennial, 1997.

Soukup, Vladimír. *Eyewitness Travel Guides: Prague*. Dorling Kindersley, 1994.

Stanton, Scott. *The Tombstone Tourist: Musicians*. Pocket Books, 2003.

Steves, Rick. *Europe Through the Back Door*. JMP, 1993.

Stoker, Bram. *Dracula: The Definitive Edition*. Barnes & Noble Books, 1996.

Tucker, Carll. *The Bear Went Over the Mountain: Finding America, Finding Myself.* Mary Ann Liebert, Inc., 2008.

Vogel, Frederick G. "Green-Wood: Brooklyn's 'Garden City of the Dead'." *American Cemetery magazine*, January—April 1985.

Waugh, Evelyn. *The Loved One*. Dell Publishing Company, Inc., 1965.

Weil, Tom. *The Cemetery Book: Graveyards, Catacombs, and Other Travel Haunts Around the World*. Hippocrene Books, 1992.

Wells, Charles Chauncey and Wells, Suzanne Austin. *Preachers, Patriots, and Plain Folks: Boston's Burying Ground Guide to King's Chapel, Granary, and Central Cemeteries*. Chauncey Park Press, 2004.

Wiencek, Henry and Kennedy, Roger G.. *The Smithsonian Guide to Historic America: Southern New England*. Stewart Tabori & Chang, 1989.

Wilson Jr., Samuel and Huber, Leonard V. *The St. Louis Cemeteries of New Orleans*. St. Louis Cathedral, 1972.

Wilson, Susan. *Garden of Memories: A Guide to Historic Forest Hills*. Forest Hills Educational Trust, 1998.

Wurman, Richard Saul. *Access Paris*. Access Press, 1990.

Wurman, Richard Saul. *Access Boston*. Harper Perennial, 1999.

Wurman, Richard Saul. *Access Rome*. Harper Perennial, 1999.

Wurman, Richard Saul. *Access Florence & Venice: Plus Tuscany and the Veneto*. HarperCollins, 2001.

Yalom, Marilyn. *The American Resting Place: Four Hundred Years of History Through Our Cemeteries and Burial Grounds*. Houghton Mifflin Company, 2008.

ADDITIONAL RESOURCES

As I've discovered in my travels, cemetery hours change with the seasons or even simply at the whims of their caretakers. While that information rapidly goes out of date in a book, I try to keep it current at CemeteryTravel.com.

Each of the cemeteries mentioned in this book has been featured as a Cemetery of the Week on CemeteryTravel. Short encyclopedic entries on each cemetery include dates of use, number of graves, addresses, phone numbers, cemetery websites, and additional resources like online tours, blog posts, photographs, and videos. You can check out the whole list of Cemeteries of the Week at *https://cemeterytravel.com/cemeteries-of-the-week/*. I also review every cemetery guidebook I can get my hands on.

If you are interested in keeping notes on your own cemetery travels, I've made a *Cemetery Travels Notebook*. It features 80 lined pages, interspersed with 20 full-page color photographs of cemeteries from Paris to Tokyo. You can find out more about it at *https://cemeterytravel.com/cemetery-travel-notebook/*.

In addition, you might be interested in the Association for Gravestone Studies, an international group dedicated to the study and preservation of gravestones wherever they may stand. AGS publishes a monthly email newsletter, a quarterly magazine, and a yearly scholarly volume called *Markers*. Their annual convention draws cemetery aficionados from all over the world. They can be found online at gravestonestudies.org.

Individual grave sites can be researched at Findagrave.com, where volunteers are attempting to catalog every tombstone they can find, as well as providing brief biographical information about the people below.

Thanks for coming along on my adventures. I hope you've been inspired to have some of your own.

ABOUT THE AUTHOR

Loren Rhoads is the author of *199 Cemeteries to See Before You Die* and a memoir called *All You Need is Morbid*. She is the editor of *Death's Garden: Relationships with Cemeteries, The Haunted Mansion Project: Year Two*, and *Morbid Curiosity Cures the Blues: True Tales of the Unsavory, Unwise, Unorthodox, and Unusual.* She's written about cemeteries for two Travelers' Tales books, Mental Floss, Scoutie Girl, Morbid Outlook, SEARCH magazine, and more, and served as the cemetery columnist for Gothic.Net, Gothic Beauty, and Legacy.com. She's been consulted as a cemetery expert by ABC's Blueprint for Living on Australia's national radio, *Travel & Leisure*, the *Chicago Tribune*, *American Cemetery* magazine, WeatherChannel. com, Boston.com, and io9.com. She's been a member of the Association for Gravestone Studies since 1999. She blogs about graveyards as travel destinations at CemeteryTravel.com.

INDEX